The Uses of Decoration

Frontispiece *Colin Wilbourn and Karl Fisher*
Passing Through. *Sandstone, glass, cement, steel and aluminium, 1997, St Peter's Riverside, Sunderland (photo by Colin Wilbourn, reproduced by permission of the Artist's Agency)*

The Uses of Decoration

Essays in The Architectural Everyday

Malcolm Miles

John Wiley & Sons, Ltd
Chichester • New York • Weinheim • Brisbane • Singapore • Toronto

National 01243 779777. International (+44) 1243 779777

e-mail (for orders and customer service enquiries): cs-books@wiley.co.uk.

Visit our Home Page on http://www.wiley.co.uk or http://www.wiley.com

OTHER WILEY EDITORIAL OFFICES

John Wiley & Sons, Inc., 605 Third Avenue, New York, NY 10158-0012, USA

WILEY-VCH Verlag GmbH, Pappelallee 3, D-69469 Weinheim, Germany

Jacaranda Wiley Ltd, 33 Park Road, Milton, Queensland 4064, Australia

John Wiley & Sons (Asia) Pte Ltd, 2 Clementi Loop #02-01, Jin Xing Distripark, Singapore 129809

John Wiley & Sons (Canada) Ltd, 22 Worcester Road, Rexdale, Ontario M9W 1L1, Canada

LIBRARY OF CONGRESS CATALOGING-IN-PUBLICATION DATA

Miles, Malcolm.
The uses of decoration : essays in the architectural everyday / Malcolm Miles.
p. cm.
Includes bibliographical references and index.
ISBN 0-471-48962-X (cased) — ISBN 0-471-48963-8 (pbk)
1. Architecture and society. 2. City planning. I. Title.
NA2543.S6 M55 2000
720—dc21 99–058869

BRITISH LIBRARY CATALOGUING IN PUBLICATION DATA

A catalogue record for this book is available from the British Library

ISBN 0-471-48962-X (cased)
ISBN 0-471-48963-8 (paper)

Typeset in 9/12pt Caslon 224 from the author's disks by Mayhew Typesetting, Rhayader, Powys
Printed and bound in Great Britain by Bookcraft (Bath) Ltd, Midsomer Norton

This book is printed on acid-free paper responsibly manufactured from sustainable forestry, in which at least two trees are planted for each one used for paper production.

For my son Dominic

Contents

General Introduction

This book contributes to an emerging literature of the architectural everyday. It is also a book about the aesthetic and social dimensions of the built environment, and the role of dwellers in the determination of what constitutes a city. The aesthetic and the social are sometimes seen as separate, even opposed, aspects of architectural production, as of modern art and literature, yet the relation between them, as between the biological, social and cultural elements of the environment, is one of complex interaction. It is not so much that these categories are each defined in terms of what the other is not, but that the construction of, for instance, an aesthetic dimension is itself socially produced, its meaning historically specific. Similarly, social actions have their own aesthetics, are not only functional but also expressive of value, and sometimes playful. So, just as cities are sites of social diversity as well as arrangements of form, the aesthetics of form are socially derived, and patterns of sociation conditioned by the design of space. The built environment, then, has many dimensions: permeating that of its design are others of memory, association, desire and occupation, all of which are terrains of difference and spatial production. And whilst acts of occupation may be decorative or seen as disorderly, they are the realities of urban living at least as much as design, and are the material of a study of the architectural everyday.

This book, in keeping with its emphasis on the everyday, is not a guide to urban policy or a handbook on urban design, and makes no prediction for urban futures, at most stating aspirations for a renewal of conviviality. Critical rather than practical, it sees urban futures as mutable, contingent on political, economic, cultural and social factors, which may lead to states of crisis or be conducive to sustainability. By drawing attention to the everyday it argues for local rather than global perspectives and a role for dwellers in the shaping of such futures.

This introduction sets out a little about the architectural everyday as a category which emerged during the late 1990s within the discourse of cities, and outlines the book's critical framework and the field of publications in which it is situated. This is followed by a brief description of the book's structure in nine chapters.

The Architectural Everyday

So what is the architectural everyday? Can it be defined in opposition to a city of public monuments, broad avenues and public spaces, idealised facades and vistas? This monumental city, produced since the eighteenth century through grandiose planning and reconstruction, often frames the image of a city projected through heritage and tourism. Or is the architectural everyday, now, in opposition not to the monumental city but to the city of financial districts and affluent residential enclaves, of waterfront developments, which are elements of a single, global city of abundance, the parts of which are linked by information superhighways and homogenised design, rather than geography? This global city frequently co-opts the monumental city, using the veneer of culture to conceal its avarice. But if the monumental city, which proclaims civic pride and virtue, depends on planning and design as well as technology and power, and if the global city depends more specifically on the power of money in increasingly unregulated markets, and these overlapping entities constitute a dominant city of centres, is the architectural everyday a city of margins? Is it a realm of suburb and inner city terrace, of small shops and market stalls which make up a streetscape lacking the status and symbolism of public and corporate edifices, easily overlooked but familiar in the lives of urban publics? Or is the other of this dominant city found in the informal settlements of non-affluent countries?

This model of two kinds of city, centre and margin, or dominant and dominated, may seem serviceable for the sake of argument, so that the monumental city and its post-modern corporate successor represent the operations of power in society, and imply a lack of power in marginal zones such as domesticity. But the difficulty in adopting such a model is that it normalises, could legitimate, the gap between what are seen as centres and what are seen as margins, whilst for the dweller, home is a kind of centre and the city beyond, outside the window, a margin. It is helpful, then, to remember that there is nothing natural about a model of centres and margins, or any other binary opposition, and that margins exist only when centres are inscribed on the terrain. The clearing of a site to construct a zone of entrepreneurial development is a case of such inscription, which recodes one set of spaces in a positive way, as a centre, and others more negatively as margins. One possible consequence of such development is that the fragile economies of making do, which enable a stability in marginalised neighbourhoods, is put at risk as the means of its support deteriorate in face of sharper divisions and the downward spiral of dereliction. But because the centres of urban development have no underpinning legitimation in terms of democratic will or social justice, there is no reason to grant uncritical acceptance to their redefinition of the city. From this may follow a new understanding that cities can also be defined through the uses of space as much as by design, that spaces do not have only one function or meaning but can be reclaimed as sites of participation in diverse ways.

So the problem is more complex than a simple opposition between a city produced by top-down planning and one of street life. Firstly, the architectural everyday, as an occupation of spaces, filters through the city of monuments and office towers, quietly (or sometimes noisily) disrupting and diversifying how that dominant city appears and is experienced. And if cities are events, then a simple opposition of grand and humble architectures does not allow for the dynamics of urban experience, when the grand may be humbled by unpredicted use, or be simultaneously experienced in contrasting ways by different publics. Similarly, the everyday may take on a new significance through particular events, as when roadside shrines appeared in the streets of Bucharest during the struggles leading to and after the fall of Ceaucescu, or flowers in The Mall in London after the death of Princess Diana. Secondly, if the architectural everyday is a kind of vernacular given to endless local variation, common characteristics are difficult to define. What links the building of huts and home extensions, the addition of stone-cladding and Georgian-style doors to terraced houses, or the placing of gnomes around ponds in suburban gardens, to the construction of informal settlements around the cities of the non-affluent world? All these are other than the dominant city, though to call them simply the dominated denies the autonomy and difference they might express. And does the architectural everyday extend beyond the legal and the semi-legal, to direct action as well as graffiti, fly-posting, skate-boarding and squatting? Does it extend beyond the city to the erection of tree shelters by protesters at the sites of new bypasses and airport runways?

Perhaps what links all these acts of occupation and appropriation is that they are statements of identity. The architectural everyday can be seen, too, as a process of improvisation, using whatever comes to hand. If its characteristic forms include the hut and the kiosk, the shelter and the market stall, then these forms are found, in different ways, in cities of both the affluent and non-affluent worlds. But it is the manner of their production, and more widely the production of space, rather than their incidental forms (interesting though these are), which set up the architectural everyday as an alternative framework through which to consider the city as a whole. The architectural everyday, then, is the spatial practice of dwellers, and raises the idea that cities might be produced by those who inhabit them. The next question is whether dwellers might occupy the place in which the image of the city, too, is determined. Dwellers lack the power and are often seen as lacking the knowledge necessary to undertake this task. That they have at least one vital part of such knowledge, however, is an assumption underpinning the book. This assumption is that dwellers are experts on dwelling, and that this knowledge is of an importance and intricacy equal to that of planners on planning, architects on architecture, and designers on design. The book does not argue against the expertise of professionals, quite the contrary, but against the privileging of that expertise to the exclusion of other knowledges. This is because architectural design and urban planning are not mere technical exercises in which others should not intervene, but denote historically specific structures and operations of power and value. The judgements made in such professions are determined not by functional or aesthetic considerations alone, however important those might be, but in context of the economic and political factors which determine directions for social change (or stagnation). Currently, there is little indication that the cities produced according to the ideology of productivity are sustainable. Is it possible, then, that cities could be regenerated according to the needs of dwellers? In a period of consumerism, this implies a differentiation of needs from the wants manufactured by commerce and mass media, and promoted in dreams of lifestyle which are, according to their own logic of ever-expanding markets, unattainable. Yet is it entirely fanciful to imagine cities in which the guiding principle is not coercion or productivity, but joy?

Such an aspiration might seem odd, when much of the recent literature, since Marshall Berman's *All That Is Solid Melts Into Air* (1982) and Mike Davis's *City of Quartz* (1990), or Neil Smith's *The New Urban Frontier* (1996), consists of urban war stories, and when urban development is increasingly driven by the agenda of capital, evidence for which is the erosion of public space by corporate space in the new urban form of the mall. Yet in other cases, such as the construction of mass housing, or mass transport links, the planners and designers of the post-war era were well-intentioned, and their desire to engineer a new society through design was utopian. It is in architecture and urban planning more than art or literature that this progressive aspect of modernism is most evident. But the non-achievement of the new society relates to the same problem as denoted by the permeation of the dominant city by acts of use: the city does not consist of forms alone; the city as event is a site of occupation, and occupation transforms cities in ways which are not always predicted. The aims of progressive architects and planners were undermined in as much as they saw their task as one of spatial organisation rather than social empowerment, so that in privileging arrangements of form over their use they devalued the role of dwellers in the production of space. The outcomes of this strategy are seen in the image of dilapidation which characterises many post-war estates. One aim of this book is to suggest there might be other ways of approaching the problem, without recourse to anti-urban solutions such as the garden city or unrestricted suburban sprawl. The inclusion of cases from non-affluent countries implies that experiences there have much to offer those who address the agendas of urban futures in the affluent world.

Frameworks

The critical framework constructed by the book is multi-disciplinary; it links conventional methods of planning and design to a separation of subject from object in the foundations of modernity. These problems are investigated in the first part of the book; the framework which emerges is applied to cases such as house decoration in Egypt and building in mud brick. The framework is derived in part from the work of the Frankfurt School, and in part from Henri Lefebvre's work on the production of space; it is also linked to the case for conviviality as an alternative to the concept of productivity, as proposed by Ivan Illich (1990).

The field of urban futures is an academic and professional territory to which many disciplines contribute, and a territory in which those who occupy the built environment now claim a place. The confluence of perspectives around such questions as what will constitute the cities of the third millennium, and whether the city remains viable as the primary vehicle of human settlement, leads to an understanding of the limits within which any single discipline can approach these questions. Perhaps one insight gained from a multi-disciplinary perspective is that thinking in oppositional pairs, such as the aesthetic and the social, or form and process, is not helpful if it means these aspects are seen in isolation from each other rather than in a dynamic relation: processes have form and forms are produced through processes, and their separation is a matter only of intellectual convenience. The architectural everyday, too, has a relation to the dominant architecture of a society which is more than that of an alternative. The two realms are present in the same space and time when it is accepted that the reality of a city is both its form and the experience which modifies that form for diverse publics.

The above discussion indicates something of how the built environment is considered in this book. Its title references Richard Sennett's *The Uses of Disorder* (1970), in which Sennett argues that it is through experience of informality and unpredictability in urban space that people gain maturity, and that defence of rigid boundaries inhibits personal growth and psychological integration. Sennett proposes, in effect, both a psychological and a social history of cities. A history of cities in Europe and North America since the seventeenth century might see the extension of boundaries, for instance when non-productive and awkward elements within society, such as the vagrant and insane, are excluded from visibility and confined in institutions. This is part of a purification of the city which brings it into greater conformity with an idealised concept of the city as a formal representation of civilisation. The monument, the vista and facade are the signs of this dominant city, and are characteristically white. In acts of decoration, on the other hand, in all the things people do themselves to state identity, the dominant city is disordered. Decoration is not a process of purification but of accretion and deconstruction, in the terms of the dominant city a kind of pollution or dirt. Endlessly diverse and always contingent, decoration undermines the ideal.

Not that everything is bleak. Cities are war zones only sometimes and in some accounts. In the last three decades of the twentieth century, a space of dialogue between dwellers and design professionals has begun to open, through advocacy planning and action research, the deployment of urban development action teams, involvement of user groups in the design of buildings for the public sector and the advent of self-build housing schemes. It is also evident in the increasing attention given to alternative, sustainable models of settlement found in non-affluent countries and produced by groups who have dropped out of the dominant society. Problems remain, not least of divergence between the languages and frames of reference used by professionals and non-professionals. But there are now enough models of collaborative practices and user-led schemes for these to be seen as a foundation for an alternative approach to urban futures.

The Literature of the Architectural Everyday

Amongst recent titles in this field are *Architecture of the Everyday*, a collection of critical essays edited by Steven Harris and Deborah Berke (1997); an *Architectural Design* profile on 'The Everyday and Architecture' edited by Sarah Wigglesworth and Jeremy Till (1998); *Occupying Architecture*, a multi-author book edited by Jonathan Hill (1998); and Ann Cline's *A Hut of One's Own* (1997). The appearance of these titles suggests a new interest in those elements of cities which represent the production of space by dwellers. That there is now a literature will itself lead to further research. Not that the questions are entirely new. Books such as Hassan Fathy's *Architecture for the Poor* (1973), and *Architecture for People*, edited by Byron Mikellides (1980) remain highly relevant. So does the critique of urban development advanced by Murray Bookchin in works such as *Urbanization without Cities* (1992). There is also a widening contextual literature, from post-colonialism to environmentalism. Examples, from many, include Anthony King's *Urbanism, Colonialism and the World-Economy* (1990); Nabeel Hamdi's *Housing without Houses* (1995) and, with Reinhard Goethert, *Action Planning for Cities* (1996); Raff Carmen's *Autonomous Development* (1996); *Environmental Injustices, Political Struggles* edited by David Camacho (1998); and Jennifer Elliott's *Introduction to Sustainable Development* (1999). Amongst studies of power as a framework for urban development, Kim Dovey's *Framing Places* (1999) is exceptional in its clarity. These books together take the field of urban futures well outside the narrow focus of any single discipline, and allow a range and freedom of debate which may inform new models of urban process.

Structure

This book offers no prescription, but sees in acts of decoration and the making of identities a reclamation of the city that is likely to lead to a future less brittle than that of idealism, less contradictory than that of design. Each chapter elaborates the issues raised in this introduction through a range of arguments, cases and theories, referencing an appropriate literature. Whilst intended to be accessible to a range of readers, the book does not seek to mask the complexities of its subject. Neither does it propose a new theory of the urban, as such, being no more than a series of critical reflections.

The book is structured in nine chapters. The first three set out the notion of a dominant city, and relate this to a theoretical framework. The next three examine cases in the non-affluent and affluent worlds which exhibit alternative values and approaches to those of the orthodoxies of modernism in urban planning and architectural design. The final three chapters consider departures from modernist orthodoxy in the cases of community architecture and the literature of the architectural everyday, interventions by artists in the urban process in post-industrial cities, and the concept of conviviality as an alternative to productivity.

Chapter 1 is a critique of habitual ways of seeing and thinking about cities. It takes the commonplace images of postcard city views to indicate aspects of a dominant conceptualisation of the city, aligned to certain visual conventions.

Chapter 2 extends the critique in terms of the recent literature of urbanism. It contrasts the war stories which, in part, characterise men's writing on cities with more complex analyses in the work of women urbanists.

Chapter 3 theorises the production of urban space and the relation of its aesthetic and social dimensions, drawing on the work of Henri Lefebvre. The Cartesian split of an observing self from an objectified world is proposed as the basis for a dominance of concept over lived experience; however, it also enables the autonomy necessary for critical reflection.

Chapter 4 introduces material from anthropology to argue that practices seen conventionally as merely useful have an aesthetic dimension. It investigates the case of *hajj* painting in the villages of upper Egypt to show the limitations of conventional approaches to aesthetics.

Chapter 5 offers a critical reflection on the work of Egyptian architect Hassan Fathy. Extending the discussion of the previous chapter, it argues that the fusion of design and construction in mud-brick buildings opens new ways to consider the production of space.

Chapter 6 examines the Nine Mile Run Greenway project in Pittsburgh – an effort to reclaim a site of slag heaps as public space and a zone of biodiversity. It sets this in contexts of environmental arts projects through the 1980s and 1990s.

Chapter 7 returns to the literature of the field, interrogating that of community architecture, particularly in relation to its notion of community; and summarising issues in the emerging literature of the architectural everyday.

Chapter 8 investigates recent cases of intervention by artists, contextualised by discussion of the post-industrial city which is the site for these interventions. It sees artists developing new strategies for art in non-gallery settings, which work within the crevices of the dominant city.

Chapter 9 considers definitions of sustainability, the concept of conviviality as an alternative to productivity, how people make their own environments, and how this process might lead to sustainable cities.

The City of Tomorrow and its Reclamation

Why should all this matter now? Perhaps every society sees itself as being on a cusp, at the dawn of a new era, and calls this an exciting time. A millennium, though no more than an accident of the calendar (and only one of the several available) intensifies this feeling. Of course, there is always a cusp between the past and the future. From this, the only possible vantage point of the present, history spreads out backwards and forwards. Projections of what is lacking in the present tend to be applied to the past in the construction of lost golden ages. And the idea of history as a decline, or fall from Eden, is mirrored in the idea of progress towards a future which is better. At the same time, history is characterised by events and turning points. In the field of this book, a turning point has been reached as a majority of the six billion human inhabitants of the Earth now live in cities. The fastest rates of growth are in the cities of the non-affluent world, but the model of the city remains globally that of the industrialised countries of the affluent world. This city is no more sustainable than the economic model it serves, which is one of constantly expanding markets and increasing profits, of contradictions and the manufacture of unsatisfiable desires. What, then, can be done and thought which is conducive to the building of cities for joy?

CHAPTER 1
VIEWS FROM ELSEWHERE

INTRODUCTION

This chapter is illustrated by, and offers a critical commentary on, postcards of city views[1]. This is more than a convenience, saving the writer the effort of taking his own photographs. Postcards are a commonplace form of imagery, sold in newsagents, souvenir shops, museums, station bookstalls and airport kiosks. Because they are so ordinary, their production and reception is largely uncritical. They illustrate a conceptualisation of cities which is both taken for granted and dominant. They normalise particular views of cities, or points of view on cities, rendering as if natural a particular idea of what constitutes a city and its relation to a surrounding countryside.

But a view is never neutral, and the postcard view replicates the narratives of heritage, tourism and urban development. Postcards promote cities, selectively representing and familiarising elements of city form; what they omit is the diversity of acts which constitutes urban life; even cards of multiple scenes follow a common model of skylines, vistas and monuments. In cities claiming global status, skylines are formed by office towers of competing height, their lighting lending a dramatic quality to night scenes. In other cases, such as images of Oxford, it is dreaming spires and the incidental intimacy of a cobbled street which constitute a statement of heritage as manufactured as the skyline. Whilst postcards are sold by the thousand in the cities of the industrialised world, their images derive from layers of cultural mediation reflecting and informing social, economic and political structures and values. Rather than lacking significance, the postcard view, often a view from distance, signifies a history and an ideology, and just as a name in a certain size and typeface locates a city on a map, so the postcard view locates a city in culture. The postcard is, then, an appropriate point of departure for a critique of urban concepts and actualities, and the gap between them. This book is about how cities might be reclaimed by their inhabitants, and become sustainable; an interrogation of the dominant city revealed in this commonplace visual genre begins to ask to whom cities belong and to reveal the mechanisms of power which affect the urban imagery.

The chapter compares the postcard with another commonplace visual genre, the snapshot, and then discusses the viewpoint of distance generally privileged by the postcard. It analyses examples of postcards from Oxford and Birmingham, and argues that such views are not neutral depictions of popular sites, but ideologically loaded, affirming given concepts of the city. The frame of reference is broadened through cases from Melbourne, Pittsburgh and Sheffield. The chapter contextualises these representations with reference to the work of Doreen Massey and Michel De Certeau, and current debates on urban futures and planning; it asks how the diversity of urban living which the postcard for the most part denies might be reintroduced into familiar urban imageries.

IMAGES OF THE FAMILIAR

The postcard and the snapshot in a family album have certain things in common: each is an everyday visual form; each is photographic; each is inexpensive; and each acts to preserve a visual (and perhaps other) memory of place. They differ in that the snapshot is taken by an individual, and is as likely to be a close-up as a distanced view. Like a postcard, it will be either kept as a souvenir or sent to a friend or family member, and its appearance may be less important than its role in opening a conversation. In saying 'do you remember when we were there . . .', it is the act of conversation which matters more than the topic, renewing a communion; but something is needed to begin. For this reason, the ineptness of figures cut off by the frame, red eyes in flash photography, and other technical imperfections of a snapshot, even lapses of memory whereby details cannot be identified, matter little, because the snapshot's purpose is social rather than descriptive. The postcard, too, has a social function associated with the cliché 'Wish you were here . . .', but, unlike the snapshot, is part of a wider visual culture the forms of which are determined by its producers not its consumers. The images of tourist posters, or the promotional literature of developers[2], are not dissimilar from the city views seen stacked in racks at a kiosk.

Whilst the snapshot uses a visual medium to regain memories of personal experience, the postcard emphasises city form over the practices and encounters of city life. It also generalises city form, unifying the elements of an urban fabric through devices such as the distant viewpoint, or by focusing on a monument which comes to characterise a city according to a specific history. This is necessarily one of many possible landmarks, but usually part of a dominant narrative. Hence New York becomes as if it were the twin towers of the World Trade Center and Paris the Eiffel Tower[3], Newcastle would be the Tyne bridges, Cairo the pyramids and Washington the Mall. The model breaks down when the covered market is taken as the sign for Ouagadougou, since this, although the city's most prominent landmark, retains its function as the place where a large part of the city's ordinary trade is carried out, and the vultures usually seen perched on its roof add another kind of quality to its image. The diversity of urban living seen in signs of occupation is denied, however, as cityscapes conforming to a narrow range of types in the postcards of the affluent world become almost interchangeable from one city to the next.

The urban postcard, then, is an everyday item by which dominant and generalised ideas of a city permeate contemporary urban consciousness. Postcard views privilege the visual sense, perhaps inevitably unless producers see a market in the tactile, tasty or smelly card, or a card which sings a song (a technology used in some birthday cards). And although an artist's sketch might do – as newspapers employed sketch artists in the nineteenth century, before the technology of photographic reproduction on newsprint became available – it is the photographic image which is omnipresent. Photography is also the technical means most appropriate to the distant viewpoint. But what kind of city is defined through the distance of a lens?

City Views – The Vantage Point

Distance – a city seen from its ramparts, through a viewfinder or through the windscreen of a car – makes possible the separation of the visual from the other senses; visuality then constructs its objects as dematerialised signs. The view from a high or distant vantage point is a frequent postcard type, popular perhaps because the consumer cannot so easily stand on a roof or high ledge or out in the water – photographers presumably make special arrangements. The view from such a point enables the spectator to see the city's skyline as a unified whole, and gives a feeling of power and possession by yielding to knowledge the city in its completeness[4], or perhaps, more accurately, a selective completeness, since sprawling suburbs or outlying industrial estates are outside the frame. Telescopes mounted on vantage points overlooking a city or surrounding landscape allow the spectator, on payment of a small fee, to take in the view a bit at a time, identifying each site. By moving the telescope through its arc, the whole view can be, as it were, collected. Sometimes such sites are given the name *belvedere*[5] and are marked on tourist maps as a point with radiating spokes, like a sunburst or a magic eye, and in the nineteenth century many European cities saw the construction of panoramic promenades for the enjoyment of middle-class publics – the Piazzale Michelangiolo in Florence, for instance[6]. The availability of such views today from high buildings[7] is a democratisation of the power to see from the position of the eye of god, extended by the aerial photograph and view from the economy cabin of an aeroplane. The view from above, before the twentieth century, belonged to a privileged class and remained partly conceptual.

That class included the holders of power and office who, from the eighteenth century, set out cities according to a rationale made visible in plans; and those able to afford houses, in cities such as Bath and Bristol, built on high vantage points. The first measured plans of a city were made by Alberti using a device to chart distance from a circuit of walls. The ability to describe, based on this view, precedes and perhaps engenders a desire to imagine a city through the act of drawing. From this, given power, wealth and appropriate technologies, comes the making of new cities, such as Washington and Karlsruhe[8]; and new districts in old cities, including the New Town in Edinburgh, Dublin's eighteenth-century squares, and the crescents of

Bath. From the steep, wooded slopes of Clifton in Bristol, the owners of eighteenth-century stone houses in sites such as The Paragon looked down on the Avon Gorge with a feeling of superiority. Another kind of totality was, from the beginning of the nineteenth century, provided by public admission to panoramas and dioramas[9]. With the rapid expansion of cities in the industrial period, accompanied by the construction of urban parks, some on high ground, and the building of iron bridges over rivers, observation from distance became more widely available. Painters depicted this subject-matter from the Impressionist period onwards: Camille Pissarro made several versions of a view looking down on the Pont Boïeldieu in Rouen in 1896; many of his scenes of Paris, such as the rue St Honoré (1897 and 1898), rue St Lazare (1893 and 1897) and Place du Havre (1893), amongst others, also use a high vantage point[10], and may have been influenced by photography and early forms of the postcard[11]. This enables him to depict the teeming mass of people and carriages which flows over the bridges and through the boulevards signifying a new metropolitan prosperity. What it does not allow is the depiction of the experiences of members of the crowd; in particular, a differentiation of the experiences of the rising middle class, for whom the boulevards were constructed as sites of dwelling and display, from those of a working class ejected from them except in a secondary capacity. Eduard Munch makes the vantage point explicit in *Rue Lafayette* (1891)[12], including a top-hatted figure on a balcony, looking down on the throng below, whilst Pissarro's distance from the street sits awkwardly with his anarchist sympathies[13]. His choice of the new boulevards as subject-matter must have been in the knowledge that Haussmann's redrawing of the plan of Paris, cutting wide streets through the old working-class quarters, was designed to provide ease of troop movements and to gentrify the city[14].

Today, postcards are sometimes composed with a degree of manipulation not much less than that of Impressionist art. A card of Melbourne, for example, shows the city ranged as a skyline of towers in the top half of the space, against a pale orange sky (Figure 1.1). Before it are sailing boats, a pier and bright water, blue flecked with orange like gold. The verticals of yacht masts interlock with those of buildings. The card is captioned 'Sailing boats surrounding St Kilda's Pier on Port Phillip Bay, with the Melbourne city skyline in the background'. One boat has red sails (in the sunset). Of course, the boats and the buildings are where they are, though the crescendo of the skyline is neatly framed in the rectangle; but what is conveyed is no longer a description but a concept of Melbourne, and by implication the global city as a type, a site of leisure and affluence. Wealth is created by the corporate city of skyscrapers, whilst the yachts represent consumption. The distancing of the built city lends the creation of wealth a mystique, as if, as in television soaps, life is all play and no one goes to work. So no worries there.

A similar conjunction of river sports and the corporate cityscape occurs in the promotional imagery of London's Docklands in the 1980s. Jon Bird writes on the estate agents' brochures which parade the delights of a riverside lifestyle, and on the distant viewpoint of this and the developers' materials:

Figure 1.1 *Postcard, Melbourne: Sailing boats surrounding St Kilda Pier (photo by Steve Parish Publishing Pty Ltd)*

> These panoramic representations of the city characteristically adopt an elevated perspective that distances the viewer and creates an image of totality. We look from a distance across, or down upon, the river and adjacent buildings, each scene suffused with a gentle light which plays upon the towers and the water. Nothing is unharmonious or out of place – these are viewpoints that allow us to possess the city in imagination. Similarly, the estate agents' advertisement stress the desirability of a riverside lifestyle: windsurfing, cocktails in St Katherine's Yacht club, a plethora of marinas . . . and round-the-clock security systems. (Bird, 1993: 126)

The built form of Docklands is complex, but its complexities are mediated by such descriptions, which project on to it a concept of an idealised or utopian city. In the cases of cities such as Melbourne, London and New York, in which much recent development has taken the form of corporate enclaves, the city is identified at a conceptual level with affluence.

City Views – Dreaming Spires and Central Business Districts

Spires, narrow alleys and half-timbered buildings in Oxford, York or Norwich act as foils to an architecture of brash commercialism in shopping centres which could be anywhere. Postcards do not depict the grid-locked traffic and long bus queues which are a prominent aspect of Oxford on any working day, or the chain-store outlets of its arcades; neither do they show the homeless people who occupy its streets in significant numbers, or joy-riders and burnt-out cars in its peripheral council estates. Oxford is represented as a city of dreaming spires. 'Dawn over the dreaming spires' (Figure 1.2) shows a view from a high angle, on a golden dawn with soft clouds forming a mock horizon, the golden buildings of colleges leading up to a skyline of spires, domes and turrets. Of course, Oxford does look like that, from that viewpoint, but the card frames the city, both literally by excluding its murkier suburbs and outer estates, and including several trees in the foreground to give a semi-rural feeling; and metaphorically through the predominant gold of the buildings. This is the Oxford of a gentle sublimity which Matthew Arnold described in terms of dreaming spires, though not the only Oxford, even in the nineteenth century; it is also the city in which Thomas Huxley and Bishop Wilberforce contended over Darwin's *Origin of Species* at a meeting of the British Association in 1860. And it is the Oxford, or Christminster, of Jude Fawley, which presents a face as fictional as Arnold's but which punctures the idyll.

Hardy writes of Oxford, as of rural Wessex, as it might have been a few decades before the time of writing (from 1887). His image is not so much of dreaming spires, as of a dream of the dreaming spires which seems at first unattainable, then becomes hollow and finally brutally rejecting. In the novel, the city is introduced as a distant view obscured by mist. A young Jude, at the top of a ladder, looks across the tiled roof of a barn awaiting an answer to his prayer that the mist will lift:

Figure 1.2 *Postcard, Oxford: Dawn over the dreaming spires (photo by Chris Donaghue, by permission of Oxford Photo Library)*

Figure 1.3 *Four images of Oxford combined as a postcard, Sofia Fotinos, 1999 (by permission of Sofia Fotinos)*

> Some way within the limits of the stretch of landscape, points of light like the topaz gleamed. The air increased in transparency with the lapse of minutes, till the topaz points showed themselves to be the vanes, windows, wet roof slates, and other shining spots upon the spires, domes, freestone-work, and varied outlines that were faintly revealed. It was Christminster, unquestionably, either directly seen, or miraged in the peculiar atmosphere. (Hardy, 1998:21)

Christminster is a fantasy coloured by (the golden) New Jerusalem[15], but its magic eludes Jude the outsider. The novel's plot parallels Hardy's loss of religious feeling[16], and, more overtly, charts the systematic destruction of a self-taught person in an elite world. Later, having returned by train to Christminster, and after waiting in the rain to hear traces of a ceremony inside one of the colleges (to which, that is, he does not have access), an older Jude seems to understand his predicament: 'I'll never care any more about the infernal cursed place . . .' (Hardy, 1998:329). But too late. The next day, as the story turns nasty, the children hang themselves in the closet.

Today, the contradictions of Hardy's Oxford have not gone away and the gap between town and gown is as wide as ever, but the most frequently seen postcard image is a version of the dreaming spires in a golden light. It is as if the mythification of the city which Hardy deconstructs through something approaching social realism is reinstated in these romanticising images; but then Hardy lived in Wessex, not Oxford. Other cards selectively extract buildings and frame them as if in a pleasant countryside, a device possible through the shape of the city which, following the flood plain of the river, is long and thin, so that green areas are at certain points close to the centre. Some green sites, particularly the university's meadows but also the local authority's allotments, have been preserved against development, and, from some places, the city's industrial areas and suburbs actually are invisible. A card of 'Summer View Over Christ Church Meadow' sets the cathedral-like cluster of buildings beyond leafy trees and a field of yellow flowers under a soft, blue sky. Its caption relates Matthew Arnold's description of the meadow as 'one of the last enchantments of the Middle Ages', adding: 'a unique area for recreation just minutes from the busy city centre. Old English Longhorn cattle . . . can be seen grazing throughout the year'. The meadow clearly plays a valuable role in preserving biodiversity and public space in the city's environs. But the card shows the meadow as a (non-peopled) countryside within which to represent the city. It would be futile to argue that postcard producers should abandon attractive imagery, to show the mediocre architecture of a shopping centre, a skip for rubble, a burnt-out car or a drunk lying in the street; such images (Figure 1.3) would never sell.

The postcard Oxford seems, in its golden stone and green spaces, to refer to a content of anti-urbanism in English culture and society, affirmed by currents in town and country planning which produce the leafy suburb and the garden city. Elizabeth Wilson, a supporter of a renewed and vibrant urbanism, argues that town planning in the UK after 1945, in context of a policy for state intervention in urban development and a need for post-war reconstruction, adopted a utopian stance influenced by earlier model towns and villages. She cites Bourneville (1879) and Port Sunlight (1888), each founded by industrial philanthropists adjacent to their factories – the Cadbury family at Bourneville and William Lever at Port Sunlight – and notes that these were intended for the upper sector of the working class[17]. Wilson cites the post-war influence of Patrick Geddes and his support for Ebenezer Howard's ideal of the garden city. Howard was prominent in the foundation of the Garden City Association, which aimed to extend discussion of the ideas proposed in his book *Tomorrow! A Peaceful Path To Real Reform* (1898). In many ways, Howard stood for radical social and political ideas; amongst those who influenced him was Kropotkin, whose theory of mutual aid – that humans survive through collaboration rather than competition, and live best in a community – is a founding text of social anarchism[18].

Peter Hall and Colin Ward, calling for a reappraisal of Howard's ideas, draw attention to the conditions in which the garden city was proposed: after two decades of agricultural depression and a drift of people to towns in which large areas of housing had been demolished to provide space for railways, shipyards and docks, the living conditions of both the rural and urban poor were deplorable. From this, Howard arrived at a diagram of three magnets, seeking to clarify why people (the needles) were attracted to towns. Between the city's economic and social opportunities, but overcrowded and unhealthy conditions, and the countryside's fresh air but lack of employment or social mixing, Howard located the town–country as a focus of the good points of both. Hall and Ward cite Howard:

> Town and country *must be married*, and out of this joyous union will spring a new hope, a new life, a new civilisation. (Howard, 1898:10, cited in Hall and Ward, 1998:19)

The means to this was the creation of new towns within the countryside, a policy later effected in a revised form in Milton Keynes. Low land prices, Howard argued, would enable up to 32 000 people to occupy 1000 acres surrounded by a permanent green belt five times the size of the city. Howard's proposal was highly detailed, specifying occupations and amenities including a concert hall, museum and art gallery; and a central park about the size of Kensington Gardens surrounded by a glass arcade in which people could promenade during wet weather and do their shopping. It is one of the earliest proposals for what, with a certain irony given Howard's radical sympathies, has become a shopping mall[19]. The concept of a garden city, dispersed in endless suburban variations and inner city parks, and extant in the empty green spaces around 1960s tower blocks, is validated by, and continues to inform, an English sensibility for the countryside. This is the same sensibility that requires urban images to be framed by trees and meadows, and if it is utopian, its ideal is a retreat from many of the conditions of metropolitan life – the teeming mix of people in streets, the overlap of social classes in the occupation of space and a presence of diversity which makes any static conceptualisation of the city difficult to maintain. Wilson emphasises the sexist aspect of Howard's (and Geddes') suburban vision, and sees a partial alternative in Jane Jacobs' *The Death and Life of Great American Cities*, with its support for high density, bustling street life[20], in which women participated rather than being confined to well-designed kitchens.

Another text from the nineteenth century – Canon Barnett's *The Ideal City* – offers a different, more urban Utopia:

> The country may still be best for some people . . . but the movement of men [sic] is obviously from country to city; we must . . . fashion our cities after the highest pattern. We must make them good for the health and the wealth of citizens. (Barnett, c.1893-4, in Meller, 1979:55)

Barnett's ideal city, based on Bristol, entails social mixing, an equalisation of wealth and provision of museums for public betterment; histories are written in the accumulation of buildings over time, but the city's spirit is new and the streets lit by electricity. Yet the city is in sight of hills[21]. The difference between Barnett's sight of hills and a postcard view is the viewpoint: Barnett looks out of the city to hills which are a source of dreaming. The postcard looks into the city, framed by hills and meadows which recode it as a dream. This strategy is close to that used frequently in the heritage industry, to reframe the past as an evenly textured field of acceptability. By utilising facets of history, such as the timber-frame house and thatched cottage of Shakespeare's England, replete with roses round the door and honeysuckle in the garden, a sense of inevitability is lent to a history which is usually conservative, culturally and politically[22].

A different set of impressions, embracing modernity but not Barnett's egalitarianism, is created by cards of Birmingham. It is portrayed as a city of culture and renewal, with its new Hyatt Hotel, Convention Centre, and public art in Centenary Square (Figure 1.4). Although there are nineteenth-century civic buildings within a short distance, and an early twentieth-century memorial on the site, nothing in the card denotes a past, the oldest building being the 1970s repertory theatre. From the late 1980s, Birmingham City Council invested considerably in a remodelling of the city centre, commissioning several major pieces of public art as well as pedestrianising New Street and Victoria Square. Towpaths were renovated and public space recreated along the canal network, part of which forms the far boundary of the Convention Centre site. This is – the views make clear – a metropolitan city which requires no framing by surrounding hills. Centenary Square, the open space in the centre of the city, is mainly paved, with only incidental beds of flowers. But what does the new centre represent?

The question around which discussion revolves is whether the centre is a cultural district or, on the Burgess ring model[23], a central business district disguised as a cultural district. Public art, according to the evidence of postcards available at New

Figure 1.4 *Postcard, Birmingham: Hyatt Hotel, ICC, and Repertory Theatre (photo Van Greaves, by permission of the photographer)*

Street station, plays a significant role in determining the cultural coding of the site and its legitimation as public space. The card in Figure 1.4 shows three commissions: the co-ordinated scheme for brick paving and street furniture by Tess Jaray and Tom Lomax, a fountain by Tom Lomax (in the foreground) and Raymond Mason's resin statue *Forward* (1991), in the distance between the hotel and Convention Centre. These monuments are the subject-matter of cards produced by at least three companies[24], all of whom use Mason's statue, which is included also in multiple views. Public art is part of the tourist trail in Birmingham, and is becoming collectively the city's sign, but recent studies by Patrick Loftman and Brendan Nevin, researchers at Birmingham's two universities, conclude that although the intention behind the redesign of the city centre was to attract inward investment, this has produced an economy which has few benefits for some local publics[25]. The Convention Centre and associated business services are commercially successful, but questions remain as to whose city is thus reconfigured, who has access to it and to what extent public expenditure has produced private gain. Following a change of administration in 1993, the city's priorities moved from architectural schemes to support for the infrastructures of housing, social services and education. Loftman and Nevin reiterate the claim that resources put into prestige projects were diverted from programmes more responsive to the needs of disadvantaged neighbourhoods. They conclude by asking if current differentials between rich and poor will widen, what that will do for Birmingham's image and how the city authorities will recoup their previous under-investment in basic services.

Meanwhile, the story told by postcards of Birmingham is increasingly one of public monuments. Victoria Square becomes, following its pedestrianisation, provision with a grand flight of steps and a fountain and the commissioning of stone and bronze sculptures, a kind of post-modern Baroque piazza (Figure 1.5). Seen from below, the monuments are arrayed against the backdrop of the Council House, the wings of which gather the site into a coherent whole. Seen from above, standing in front of the Council House, on the other hand (a view not found in postcards) there is an awkwardly vacant space before the circuit of stone balls which mark the top of the steps; the scene falls away in a fragmented set of glimpses, more like a Mannerist painting. Dhruva Mistry's sculpture in the centre of the fountain, like a Baroque river goddess, called by the artist *The River* (1993), has been adopted in local parlance as the 'Fluzi in the Jacuzzi' (Figure 1.6)[26]. The epithet is not original but was used in the late 1980s for a modern, bronze sculpture of the River Liffey in O'Connell Street, Dublin. What is clear from the range of cards available is that Birmingham presents itself, eager for new investment, as a global city, adding a layer of late modernist art, architecture and public space to its Victorian heritage. Its investment, a sprat to catch a mackerel, is not so much in building new places, though it includes that, as in building a new image, or symbolic economy.

Global cities contain the enclaves which are collectively the global city of financial districts in Frankfurt, Tokyo, New York, London and elsewhere, held

Figure 1.5 *Postcard, Birmingham: The Sphinx, Victoria Square (by permission of the Salmon Studio)*

Figure 1.6 *Postcard, Birmingham: Fluzi in the Jacuzzi (photo Harold Higgs, by permission of the photographer)*

together by electronic highways. The characteristic imagery of the global city is seen in the publicity material for Canary Wharf (noted above), and in the hype around the Millennium Dome in Greenwich. For the most part, the global city does not rely on, or even require, popular support. More, it uses high-technology surveillance to ensure that people who use its pseudo-public spaces are suitably behaved. But the Millennium Dome, whilst linked to the global city, is different in being a site for the de-politicisation of politics, for the public consumption of Cool Britannia ruled by the new one-nation party. Politics is a forum for the expression of difference, just as the traditional city street is open space, but the Dome is a publicly-funded, privatised space to which entry is by (quite costly) ticket. A card of the Dome[27] echoes the rhetorical imagery of Docklands, using the same combination of lilac-pink skies, a bright river and gleaming architecture. London is trailed across the horizon, only the tower of Canary Wharf standing high enough to cross the cloud barrier into the pink zone. Formally, the Dome and Canary Wharf are inter-linked: the tower forms a vertical at one end of the Dome site, the masts of which are aligned with the top of the lower layer of cloud, as the tower and the Dome are the only recognisable structures, the rest being merged in a twilight and electric-light shadow world. To the far left, three laser beams play over the sky. Form without content, the Dome epitomises top-down solutions just as its image stands for the construction of a city as a fiction independent of everyday life. Much is made of the Dome's scale, and the partnership of public and private funding it represents (a partnership of commercial and political influence); yet it is the postcard which gives the clearest view, though the reader is asked to imagine it: the Dome is an annex of the global city.

A high proportion of prestige urban development uses waterfront sites. As well as Docklands and Greenwich, examples include Cardiff Bay and Battery Park City, and these are discussed in Chapter 8 as cases of post-industrial cities in which the city's image is reframed by waterfronts and cultural districts. Melbourne's first Crown Casino, opened on a waterfront site in 1994, is part of a programme of urban development which, like the Dome, involves public subsidy and private gain, and has become in turn a major source of tax revenue[28]. Amongst other attractions are a Formula One racetrack (on the site of a city park) and an electronic toll road to the airport. A second casino opened in 1997 on a previously public site. Kim Dovey notes that the most important spaces, the gaming floors, were outside the architects' control, designed to maximise income from gamblers of all classes; and that all entrances are through malls. The interface between the development and the waterfront is a territory of consumption spectacularly marked by pyrotechnics (or a territory of the spectacle accessed by consumption):

> The eruptions of joy marketed on the logo now erupt in an hourly spectacle of huge gas fireballs from a series of towers lining the riverfront. This is essentially advertising masquerading as a fireworks display, public land turned into the world's longest billboard. (Dovey, 1999:163)

A card of the Crown Southbank Complex illustrates the fireball promenade, with two other waterside vistas (Figure 1.7). The photographic images are electronically enhanced; bright, almost fluorescent, colours and crystalline reflections in the river take the place of the lilac, pink and grey of the Dome postcard. No need for subtlety here – the statement is of spectacle, designed to sell the city's future, which is that of the global city – the city of late capitalism. In such a great place, how could you fail to have a great time? Each view in the three sections of the card has a central perspective and long recession; and the pavement (in the view on the right, under the fireballs) seems to be wet to echo the river. This is the imagery of idealism, denoting a stately progress, a vista, which is a site for the display of power through which the spectator is awed, translated into the language of consumerism[29]. The coldness which Richard Sennett ascribes to the modern city, following a protestant need for inwardness which requires the environment to be drab (Sennett, 1990:46), is inverted in these highly coloured scenes; yet the impersonality and alienation remain. Anyone, it might be said, can walk along the fiery promenade, and anyone with money can play in the casino until their money runs out; but not all kinds of spatial practice, or occupation, are likely to be welcomed. In the card, the vistas are depopulated, and somewhere, it is certain, surveillance cameras will be hidden, producing endless photographic images of the site. But the world of the city postcard is not that of experience, was never inhabited, only imagined.

OTHER CITIES

The postcard's representation of the here in 'Wish you were here' is a kind of there, an elsewhere remote from the everyday life which takes place in urban streets. Doreen Massey argues that the public realm constituted by metropolitan (or cosmopolitan) streets is highly gendered and public space a masculine realm, and that modern culture, which is largely urban, privileges the visual sense and links this to '. . . the point of view of an authoritative, privileged and male, position'[30]. As other senses are diminished in value, life is impoverished by its dematerialisation, its reduction to the view which is most distant, most remote from bodily senses – things can be seen in the distance or through a car wind-screen, without being approached; but they cannot be touched, smelled or tasted in the same way, and sight tends to have a longer range, too, than hearing. Massey reasons that the visual is privileged exactly because it has this possibility for detachment: 'the sense which allows most mastery' (Massey, 1994:224), which is also a possibility for objectification. In some cities, such as Los Angeles, or some neighbourhoods, such as the Bronx, the view through a car windscreen (with the doors locked) is also a retreat to safety.

The gaze enabled by distance and height is problematised by De Certeau following his narrative of the view from the World Trade Centre. He admits to an

Figure 1.7 *Postcard, Melbourne: Crown Southbank Complex (by permission of Scancolour)*

almost erotic enjoyment of being 'lifted out of the city's grasp' and writes: 'An Icarus flying above these waters . . . His elevation transfigures him into a voyeur' (De Certeau, 1984:92)[31]. He notes that a wish to see the city from above came before a means to do so was invented, that linear perspective predates the planned city, but he asks what practices can be identified in the everyday life which the distant viewpoint homogenises or makes invisible. He sees the conceptualised city as 'decaying' in face of a breakdown of its systems; this draws attention and value back to the encounters of everyday life through which space is produced by occupation:

> one can analyze the microbe-like, singular and plural practices which an urbanistic system was supposed to administer or suppress, but which have outlived its decay; one can follow the swarming activity of these procedures that, far from being regulated or eliminated by panoptic administration, have reinforced themselves . . . (De Certeau, 1984:96)

From this he arrives at the idea that walking is to an urban system what speech is to language: an appropriation, an acting-out of place, and a negotiation of possibilities (De Certeau, 1984:98). The process of the city epitomised for De Certeau by walking breaks up any imposed sense of place and fragments the city into an endless number of contiguous cities, each constantly remade by new acts of negotiation and sociation.

De Certeau's model (or non-model) of mutation is subversive of any dominant narrative of the city, of mythification through monumental architecture and ordering through surveillance. It also relates to an aspect of recent feminist writing on the city in which Elizabeth Wilson and Doreen Massey both begin books by relating personal experiences of urban journeys, which will be considered further in the next chapter. The point, here, is that reading a personal narrative leads to realisation that such narratives allow difference; no single, authoritative conceptualisation of a city can be produced through such stories, though they do not preclude areas of commonality. The postcard view, in contrast, normalises specific concepts, tells a single, predetermined story and privileges the concept over actuality. This parallels the privileging of the visual over other senses, the viewpoint of distance over that of immediacy or intimacy; whilst in the visual medium of architectural design, city form is brought into conformity with the dominant conceptualisation of the city. But to speak of the city as having a concept distinct from its built form is to make an artificial separation. A more useful comparison, which can be derived from the work of De Certeau, Wilson, Massey and others, is between city form and its occupation. Or, in Henri Lefebvre's terms (discussed in Chapter 3) of conceived space and lived space.

The city of lived space never disappears. It re-emerges in urban graffiti, suburban barbecues and street parties, as well as in political demonstrations. Perhaps also in the delight of watching sites of demolition, the literal fragmentation of the urban text. Stephen Barber, in the short texts which make up *Fragments of the European City* (Barber, 1995) plucks and elaborates an idea from the mesh of impressions produced by his travels in cities such as Belgrade and Berlin. There is no attempt to unify the narrative. Whilst postcards unify each city according to a set of prototypical scenarios, Barber's texts seek a more open identity. He begins:

> The European city is a hallucination made flesh and concrete, criss-crossed by marks of negation: graffiti, bullet-holes, neon. (1995:7)

and writes of demolition sites:

> Demolition of the city's elements strengthens what remains, and also strengthens the sense of a vital damaging through which the city takes its respiration. . . . The visual arena of the city must move through concurrent acts of construction and obliteration, extrusion and intrusion, incorporation and expulsion. (1995:29)

Barber's city and that of the postcard are both products of culture, mediated, distanced from the everyday. Yet for Barber, distance offers criticality related back to the immediacy of experience.

But could widely reproduced images, of which the postcard is one type and the poster another, contribute to the conditions for radical social change? Can postcards, for instances, celebrate difference, or the sites if not the acts of everyday life? Firstly, there are a few cases of postcards which show ordinary street scenes; a card of Sheffield (Figure 1.8) depicts a residential street, a taxi moving up the hill between terraced houses and parked cars. The city centre's towers are framed by this, though remain below the horizon; the caption reads: 'A classic view of Sheffield looking out from one of the numerous hills . . .'[32]. More exotic, and perhaps exoticising for the white tourist's eye, is a series of cards of Egypt by photographer Maurice Subervie. One shows a barrow piled with vegetables in a Cairo street, a mix of people in traditional and westernised dress, and the fronts of two small shops. Over the entrance of one are faded political posters. Secondly, it is possible to find cards which depict difference within one frame. This may still be in the form of landmarks reflecting different urban cultures rather than the processes of urban dwelling, as in a card from Pittsburgh which shows the golden dome of the city's Ukrainian Church, which is on the south side – a bohemian and transitional neighbourhood – between two signature buildings in the downtown area (Figure 1.9). The three buildings form a kind of set, the cross on the dome touching the top of the frame, but what remains in the mind is the difference between the cultures represented – of global affluence and local belief.

Finally, a question remains unanswered: if, as Massey argues, the visual sense is identified with a masculine sense of power, can visual media be effective in contributing to a transformation of urban consciousness? Can visual means enable, for instance, women to take back their right to the city? The possibility is suggested by the work of artists, including Barbara Kruger and Cindy Sherman, who play

Figure 1.8 *Postcard, Sheffield: City view from above Hunter's Bar (by permission of Hedgerow Publishing Ltd)*

Figure 1.9 *Postcard, Pittsburgh: The domes of St John the Baptist Ukrainian Church (1895) on Pittsburgh's South Side blend in with the city's skyscrapers (photo Joel B Levinson, Pittsburghscape, by permission of J B Jeffers Ltd)*

Figure 1.10 *Rotterdam: poster (photo M Miles)*

with signification, adapting the languages of mass media to alternative purposes. Perhaps, too, imagery can be used to draw attention to absences in normalised vocabularies. Luce Irigaray (1994) writes of the gendering of language as an aspect of patriarchy the undoing of which is a long process. More immediate, she claims, would be a visual display which reasserted the feminine:

> To anyone who cares about social justice today, I suggest putting up posters in all public places with beautiful pictures representing the mother-daughter couple . . . Such representations are missing from all civil and religious sites. This is a cultural injustice that is easy to remedy. There will be no wars, no dead, no wounded. This can be done before any reform of language . . . . (1994:9)

Irigaray is writing polemically, drawing attention to the lack of such images in western culture, not giving a practical tip for a new society; her proposal is a trope through which to suggest the construction of a new narrative through which people, especially but not only women, might picture ahead and value a new role and place in society. Whilst Irigaray writes of a positive imagery denoting a feminine imaginary, there is also a possibility for an imagery which doubts (or negates) the dominant narrative, such as a billboard poster seen in May 1999 in a street in Rotterdam: on the left is a photographic image of a woman, presumably of one of the city's inhabitants, at her desk; on the other the text (in English, the language of international culture and trade) 'Melly Shum hates her job' (Figure 1.10)[33]. Billboard images are part of a sophisticated visual culture, which sometimes takes more creative risks than public art; this constructs a dialogue between spectator and image, into which such a non-consumerist message can intervene. Perhaps an alternative genre of city postcards could operate in a similar way. If the narrative written by monuments, public art, most postcards and tourist posters, like that of the conventional city plan, is one the urban dweller is required to accept, it is also open to subversion by adaptations of its forms.

Notes

1. This chapter revises and extends an essay for *Urban Visions* (edited by Stephen Spier, University of Liverpool Press, 1999), in turn derived from a lecture to the Oxford Photography Society at the Museum of Modern Art, Oxford, 26 November 1998.
2. See, for instance Jon Bird's comparison of the promotional image and actuality of London's Docklands development (Bird, 1993:126–7). Bird writes: 'The publicity material produced by the LDDC and Olympia & York presents an image of harmony and coherence, a unity of places and functions not brutally differentiated into the respective spheres of work, home and leisure, but woven together by the meandering course of the river into a spectacular architectural myth of liberal *civitas*.' (1993:126)
3. Marina Warner writes on the Statue of Liberty and Eiffel Tower as signs for cities: 'Stripped of use and service, they resist obsolescence. They are in the first place expressions of identity: Paris's sign has become the Eiffel Tower . . .' (Warner, 1987:6). It could be added that whilst monuments erected in public spaces take on a generalised

role as landmarks, the way many dwellers and visitors navigate the streets of a city is through co-option of everyday elements of streetscape as personal landmarks – the importance of a particular deli in New York or pissoir in Paris might in this sense be equated with the Statue of Liberty or the Arc de Triomph.

4. For discussion of the relation of a desire for totality to the development of the idea of curiosity, as in the cabinets of curiosity in which post-Enlightenment scholars and patrons displayed their collections of medals, natural forms and exotica, see Pomian, 1990:45–64. Pomian writes: 'Curiosity is therefore a desire and a passion: a desire to see, learn or possess rare, new, secret or remarkable things . . . which have a special relationship with totality . . .' (1990:58–9).
5. The word 'belvedere' was first used, according to the *Shorter Oxford English Dictionary*, in 1596. It is defined as a turret on the top of a house, or a summer house erected where it commands a fine view.
6. The *Blue Guide* describes Piazzale Michelangiolo as 'one of the most celebrated viewpoints in the world'. Nearby are walls designed by Michelangelo, linking the Forte dei Belvedere to the Porta Romana and Porta San Niccolò. (*Blue Guide to Northern Italy*, 7th edn, London, Black, 1978:474–5). The Piazzale is part of a circuit of scenic roads – the Viale dei Colli (Avenue of the Hills) constructed from 1865; the reproduction of Michelangelo's *David* (and other work) which makes up his monument dates from 1875.
7. An example is the World Trade Center, New York. The spectacle of distance from its 110th floor is described by Michel de Certeau: 'Beneath the haze stirred up by the winds, the urban island, a sea in the middle of the sea, lifts up the skyscrapers over Wall Street, sinks down at Greenwich, then rushes again to the crests of Midtown . . .' (De Certeau, 1984:91). Another would be the Hancock Tower in Chicago.
8. See Sennett (1994:265–70) for discussion of the planned cities of the Enlightenment, including Washington and Karlsruhe. Sennett links the planned city to a tendency to urban purification and identification of health with circulation and respiration.
9. The terms are used from 1796 and 1823 onwards, respectively.
10. For illustrations of the works noted, see Brettell and Pissarro (1992), plates 1, 2 and 3; 59, 60 and 61; 35, 36 and 37; 38, respectively.
11. Richard Brettell writes of the Rouen scenes: 'His vantage point is unrelated to the scene itself . . . and, for that reason, the viewer has no sense of participation in the urban spectacle before him [sic]. (Brettell and Pissarro, 1992:xvi). On Pissarro's Parisian images he argues that the viewpoint is conditioned by the artist's choice of hotel room or apartment, though this in turn was selected for its view. Pissarro's adoption of a viewpoint above the street was affirmed by his experience of the Caillebotte retrospective at Durand-Ruel in March 1984. Caillebotte's *Rue Halévy seen from the Sixth Floor* (1878) serves as a model in this respect (illustrated in Brettell and Pissarro, 1992:xxvi, fig. 13).
12. In the Nasjonalgalleriet, Oslo. Illustrated in Brettell and Pissarro (1992:xvii, fig. 6).
13. These sympathies are demonstrated by Pissarro's series of drawings *Les Turpitude Sociales* (1890).
14. For an account of Haussmann's work for Napoleon III, see Sennett (1994:329–32).
15. One card, produced by Oxford Picture Library, depicts the skyline in an orange glow, a few pieces of roof glinting. At the side of the image, under the heading Oxford, is the text: '"That sweet city with her dreaming spires" (Matthew Arnold 1822–1888) remains the most popular catch-phrase to describe Oxford, and it is still appropriate. Seen from any high point, the city appears as a cluster of towers and spires; this image, combined with the University's fame as a seat of intellectual excellence, gives the place its unique character.' (Oxford Picture Library, card G156.)

16. Dennis Taylor, in the notes to a paperback edition, elaborates on the reference to New Jerusalem: 'Hardy made several markings [in Revelation] and appended in his Bible the dates, 1863 . . . when Hardy still retained his religious visionary imagination, and 1870, when he had lost it.' (Hardy, 1998:414).
17. Wilson notes that rents were high, and cites Phillip Henslowe's description in a work published by the Bourneville Village Trust of the intended tenants: 'a superior class of quiet and respectable tenant' (Henslowe, 1984:4, in Wilson, 1991:101). Such developments, it seems from this, are efforts at social engineering, transforming a supposedly unruly working class into a quiet lower middle class.
18. Kropotkin lived in exile in Brighton whilst Howard was formulating his ideas. Hall and Ward state: '. . . [Howard] must have read the articles which Peter Kropotkin . . . contributed to *The Nineteenth Century* between 1888 and 1890, which a decade later were collected in the book *Fields, Factories and Workshops*.' (Hall and Ward, 1998:12). Later, Letchworth, a prototype of Howard's model of development, linked to new towns at Stevenage, Hatfield and Welwyn, became a 'haven for radicals and bohemians' (Wilson, 1991:102). Kropotkin's ideas were known also by Seurat and, as noted above, Pissarro. They are noted again in Chapter 9 in relation to the concept of conviviality proposed by Ivan Illich.
19. Hall and Ward suggest the inspiration of Howard's 'Crystal Palace' was the arcades of cities such as London and Leeds; also the concept of a 'Winter Garden' beginning to be seen in seaside resorts (Hall and Ward, 1998:21).
20. Wilson continues: 'She believed that large cities were "just too big and too complex to be comprehended in detail from any vantage point". For this reason, individuals should be left alone, cities would spontaneously create themselves.' (Wilson, 1991:151). Wilson argues against such *laissez-faire* tactics, and against Richard Sennett's case for an anarchic city in which conflict forces participation (Sennett, 1996), seeing a need for responsible planning whilst redefining the elements and allegiances of that responsibility.
21. 'The citizens who have hills in their neighbourhood are drawn to think of the other side, and to dream of things which they make into pictures as did men of the Italian cities.' (Barnett, c.1893–94, in Meller, 1979:56).
22. An interesting story-line developed in BBC radio 4's rural soap The Archers during May 1999 (whilst this book was in its first stages of drafting): a builder from Birmingham, with a reputation for starting new jobs whilst leaving existing ones unfinished, in the course of modernising Honeysuckle Cottage – originally Walter Gabriel's home – uprooted the eponymous honeysuckle, leaving it in a heap on the lawn. Perhaps this is a coded narrative of the attack of urban misrule, with its fragmented value structure, on the timeless aesthetic of the countryside.
23. See E W Burgess (1925) 'The Growth of the City: An Introduction to a Research Project', in LeGates and Stout (eds), 1996:89–97. The diagram on p 93 shows Burgess's concept of a city, based on Chicago, as having a central business district (the loop) surrounded by shifting zones of settlement. The more affluent zones are in the outer ring, areas of highest conflict, such as the ghetto, in the ring around the loop. Burgess based his model on biology (also Geddes' first discipline); as the city grows, industry invades the intermediate circles, and residents who can afford it move further out. Burgess proposed the model as a theoretical type which could be projected on to any city, omitting specific geographies of waterfront or ravine. See also Savage and Warde, 1993:9–11, and Miles, 1997:35–6.
24. On several visits to Birmingham during 1998–99, the author bought cards showing public art in Centenary Square at the newsagents in New Street station. The companies involved are J Salmon Ltd, E T W Dennis & Sons, and Regatta Studios. The first two are

national postcard producers. In a series first appearing on the racks in 1999, Regatta Studios include at least five single images of public art from Centenary Square and Victoria Square: Raymond Mason's *Forward*; an earlier statue, *The Three Wise Men* (sculptor not credited) portraying Matthew Boulton, James Watt and William Murdoch; Antony Gormley's *The Iron Man*; and Dhruva Mistry's *The River* (in two versions, one centred on the fountain-sculpture, the other a view of the surrounding architecture from within the pool, showing Mistry's pair of stone sphinx sculptures).

25. Patrick Loftman and Brendan Nevin, 'Pro-growth Local Economic Development Strategies: Civic Promotion and Local Needs in Britain's Second City' in Hall and Hubbard, 1998:129–48.
26. Another card, by Regatta Studios, shows the same sculpture, but states, in the caption on the reverse, the original title, artist's name and date, adding '(otherwise known as the Floozie [sic] in the Jacuzzi)'.
27. Reproduction was not allowed, and the card is no longer in circulation.
28. See Dovey (1999:161): '. . . the state becomes a quasi-shareholder with a growing dependence on its share of the profits.' This fits with adoption of the casino and its logo on city road signs. Dovey continues: '. . . the incorporation into the same frame as the street sign operates to frame the city as a casino-town. The signs become signifiers for "government says gamble"; those who navigate the city become subject to regular reminders to gamble.' (1999:162).
29. See also Dovey's commentary on the vistas of fascist architecture (Dovey, 1999:55–70), under the heading architecture to 'Take your breath away'. Dovey emphasises the question of grandeur and vista; the Nazi use of torchlight processions as an emotive campaigning device may also be a relevant comparison.
30. Massey, 1994:232. Massey cites three sources for her theory: Luce Irigaray interviewed in M F Hans and G Lapouge (eds), *Les Femmes, la Pornographie, l'Erotisme* (1978); Craig Owens, 'The discourse of others: feminists and postmodernism' in H Foster (ed), *The Anti-Aesthetic* (Bay Press: Seattle, 1985); and Griselda Pollock, *Vision and Difference* (Routledge: London, 1988).
31. De Certeau adds that the world seen from above is turned into a text – 'It allows one to read it, to be a solar Eye, looking down like a god. The exaltation of a scopic and gnostic drive: the fiction of knowledge is related to this lust to be a viewpoint and nothing more.' (De Certeau, 1984:92)
32. The card is published by Hedgerow Publishing Ltd, a local firm. Another of their cards shows the members of the city's rugby team posing naked, holding rugby balls in front of their genitals.
33. The site is Witte de Withstraat, a street in which there are several galleries of contemporary art.

Chapter 2
Urban Narratives

Introduction

Chapter 1 examined the viewpoint of distance in city postcards. This chapter considers contrasts in the multi-disciplinary literature of urbanism from the 1970s to the 1990s, contextualised by a more general ambivalence towards the qualities of metropolitan life in modernist writing on cities[1]. Within the literature of urbanism, approaches range across disciplinary boundaries and professional fields, and whilst the texts cited adopt critical positions towards the dominant city, the ways in which they do this vary from dystopian depictions of urban violence and desolation, to arguments for a reclamation of cities for women and marginalised publics, and proposals for the engagement of dwellers in the processes which determine the forms and social patterns of cities. The chapter asks to what extent such approaches are products of a distant viewpoint or of engagement, and whether it is possible to combine the distance of a critical position with the immediacy of struggle and the need to give form to visions of alternative futures.

Why should this matter? If, as some writers claim, cities at the end of the twentieth century are urban wastelands, they are also, at the opening of the twenty-first, home to a majority of the human population of the Earth. The fastest rates of growth are in the cities of the southern hemisphere, from São Paolo to Manila[2]. Conditions of habitation in both northern and southern hemisphere cities range between extremes of affluence and destitution; but amongst urban dwellers are a majority of the world's poor, and, amongst these, women outnumber men and have less control over the little they earn (Beall, 1997:39). Any call to abandon the city as the primary form of human settlement, however, would seem unrealistic without a massive depletion of the population. The city, besides, affords an anonymity, a freedom from observation by neighbours, and a concentration of cultural resources; large cities are sites of diversity and improvisation within high densities of habitation, from which the quality of metropolitan experience derives. That diversity includes difference in the construction, decoration and use of domestic environments as well as public space, so that acts of habitation and occupation become statements of identity. The image of the city as an urban wilderness, then, says little about how people go about their daily lives, despite prevailing conditions, or how fragile economies and fragile ecologies survive locally in harsh climates. But if there is a contradiction between received images of the city and its actualities, so, too, there is an ambivalence running through representations of the city in modern culture, and in the academic literature of modernity,

Figure 2.1 *Battery Park City: poetry set in railings, designed by Siah Armajani in collaboration with Scott Burton and Cesar Pelli (photo M Miles)*

whereby the city (which is the site of modernity, and of most cultural production, mediation and reception) is a place of excitement but also threat, a site of celebration or retreat. The chapter reviews this ambivalence, before contrasting the war stories found in some men's writing on cities with more searching analyses in the work of some writing by women.

Writing on Cities – Ambiguous Modernities

Set in the railings of North Cove at Battery Park City are lines by Walt Whitman, together with those of another American poet writing a century later, Frank O'Hara (Figure 2.1)[3]. Whitman reveres New York as the 'City of the World' and O'Hara as a place so complete one need never leave it (Beardsley, 1989:150–5). For Whitman, the city's extravagant diversity – all human life is there – is a totality composed of contraries. In a similar juxtaposition of difference and togetherness, Allen Ginsberg in *Howl*, characterises the city, in Richard Sennett's reading of the poem, as a site of 'frenzied erotic bonding and ritual among strangers in the slums and shadows of the city' (Sennett, 1990:237). These responses, and others in the literatures of urban modernity, proclaim a distinctive and engaging aspect to city life, especially that of a metropolitan city such as New York, Los Angeles, London or Berlin: the city is a site of diversity and transition, producing new feelings and patterns of sociation.

This new, and distinctly modern, reality of a metropolitan environment is identified by Georg Simmel in his essay 'The Metropolis and Mental Life' (1903). Simmel introduces the concept of over-stimulation, arguing that the city is a site of constantly shifting visual stimuli and rapid economic transactions. He links metropolitan cities to the growth of a money economy and dominance of intellectual concepts over bodily experience; and sees in city populations a blasé attitude produced through over-exposure to shifting actualities amidst which the dweller strives nervously to retain a grounded sense of self. This 'intensification of nervous stimulation' produces an inability to respond to sensations energetically, which 'constitutes the blasé attitude' (Simmel, 1997:175–8)[4].

For the sociologists of the Chicago School, such as Robert Park and Louis Wirth in the 1920s and 1930s, influenced by Simmel, the metropolitan city is a site of transition and continuous growth producing new kinds of opportunity[5]. But this optimism is a kind of opportunism, and differs from Whitman's. Whitman celebrates the city because it accommodates difference (including his own) at a personal level. Other writers, notably T S Eliot, depict a fragmented city in which difference produces a loss of coherence rather than a freedom of action. In *The Wasteland* (1922), Eliot likens a crowd teeming over London Bridge to the shades of the dead (Eliot, 1954:52, lines 60–65); and although he uses montage to introduce voices other than his own (and other than his own class), he still has no taste for the mass society this represents, retreating instead to an idealised, pseudo-Elizabethan past. The two worlds – modern and mythical – are juxtaposed in consecutive passages from Part III of *The Wasteland*, each depicting a journey eastwards. The first is an image of sluggish movement constructed through key words such as 'sweats', 'drift', and 'heavy', suggesting a contemporary industrial landscape around the Isle of Dogs. In the next passage, the colours become bright and the river's movement brisk, flowing rather than drifting; the barge is inhabited by two historical (and mythicised) characters, and the scene is unified by a swell which ripples both shores. Here, Elizabeth and Leicester inhabit a gilded shell, and other key words include the colours 'red' and 'gold', and 'brisk swell' as the couple are carried towards a white tower and peal of bells (Eliot, 1954:61, lines 266–291). Eliot's construction of a purified past casts the present by implication as impure, yet that past is irretrievably lost, which may be its attraction[6]. For Eliot, England was a place of voluntary exile, within which he finds in history and Anglicanism a meta-exile within the wider society, though perhaps a fictional place no more authentic than the Tudorbethan style in suburban architecture and furniture which became established in English taste, as a retreat from Modernism, during the 1930s. *The Wasteland* seems Eliot's last effort to grapple with a world of diversity, and hence of a sense of impurity which becomes, for him, too high a price for its fascination and promises of desire – these he sets beyond his grasp.

Ambivalence is found, too, in academic texts on cities. Marshall Berman protests against the destruction by urban development, in particular the building of the South Bronx Expressway, of part of New York's social fabric. But Berman does not depict a landscape of desolation; his protest is founded in identification with the city, a feeling which he grants, even, to Robert Moses, whose master plans brought about the destruction. Berman, like Whitman, celebrates the city, referencing landmarks such as the Brooklyn Bridge as signs for freedom of movement; he sees in Moses' work a progressive and well-intentioned modernism, aiming to overcome natural forces through the car. In his old age, Moses, who designed New York's riverside boulevards as landscapes of a modern sublime, was driven up and down Long Island in a limousine, fantasising a hundred-mile ocean drive and a bridge to join Long Island with Rhode Island. Berman grants Moses historical stature in his ability to persuade people 'that he was the vehicle of impersonal world-historical forces, the moving spirit of modernity . . .' (Berman, 1983:294); yet in Moses' remarks in response to objectors to the South Bronx Expressway – '"When you operate in an overbuilt metropolis, you have to hack your way with a meat ax"' and '"there's very little hardship in the thing. There's a little discomfort and even that is exaggerated"' (Moses cited in Berman, 1983:293–4) – suggests an analogy with Moloch, the destructive force in Ginsberg's *Howl*. Berman's *All That Is Solid Melts Into Air* , first published in 1982, then, is a story of both decline and affirmation. His framework, as indicated by the title, is a Marxist view of modern culture and the conditions of its production, and he employs a Marxist strategy of beginning from the exposure of discomforting social realities. Marx draws attention to the need under capitalism for continuous production of ideas, products and markets, for constant revolutions in the relations of production, and with them the relations of society (Berman, 1983:21). This produces the expansive but unsettling cultural and economic conditions described by Simmel[7], and, more recently, conventional patterns of urban development based on the needs of capital. Berman later recalls his own participation in protest against the Expressway which derived from Moses' reconstruction of the city, and seeing his neighbourhood destroyed for 10 years. He writes of the dismay of Jews that a fellow-Jew could do this to them, of disillusionment when the government which made the New Deal failed to stop the blasting through of a road which displaced 60 000 working-class and lower middle-class Jews, Italians, Irish and Blacks from their homes; and of secondary destruction when the noise and dirt generated by the completed road caused a second outflow of population. But all this is an attitude of engagement founded in a commitment to the city.

If Berman's position is equivalent, very loosely, to Whitman's, then perhaps Richard Sennett's is between Whitman's and Eliot's. Sennett, too, is a willing city dweller, living in Greenwich Village; yet his narratives of urban wandering, in *The Conscience of the Eye* (1990), convey a sense of disengagement. Whilst Eliot retreats to a mythicised past, Sennett cites the Paris of Baudelaire, but sees the world in which Baudelaire strolled as replaced today by a less demanding environment[8]. This remains, however, a mediation of a mainly literary past, even if its use is to proclaim difference. Sennett argues, in *The Uses of Disorder*, first published in 1970, that it is difference willingly experienced, and a deeper understanding of aggression, which creates urban stability. He advocates diversity, citing Jane Jacobs's case that cities decline as difference is eradicated[9], and writes that affluence leads to a move to suburbs enabling a strengthening of spatial boundaries[10]. Increased wealth leads to a retreat from sharing, so that households no longer share the diversity experienced unavoidably by people who regularly borrow from each other[11]. In the decline of social interaction as cities are fragmented into discrete zones, a notion of community appears which requires increasing enforcement because it lacks any authentic basis:

> Abundance . . . increases the power to create isolation in communal contacts at the same time that it opens up an avenue by which men [sic] can easily conceive of their social relatedness in terms of their similarity rather than their need for each other. (Sennett, 1996:49)

From this comes a false sense of community supported by exclusion. Hence white, suburban communities promote a myth of family life contradicted by the realities of child abuse, domestic violence, tax evasion and adultery, and yet demonise outsiders as threats to this wholesomeness[12]. Sennett sees this attitude as a prolonged adolescent mentality, in which the suburban neighbourhood stands for a model of a family in which conflict is denied (Sennett, 1996:66–7)[13].

Yet Sennett, in *Conscience of the Eye*, is, like Eliot, a detached narrator, walking through the city, receiving its nuances through his eyes, creating a personal taxonomy of city life. He notes 'the great, teeming chaos of cities', and that both fascination and terror 'come from the diversity within the city's borders'. He sees neighbourhoods spill into each other and enjoys the fluidity of the city's internal edges: 'Anyone walking through this diversity . . . feels an enormous vibrancy in the overlap of so many kinds of life' (Sennett, 1996:46–7). These edges, reflected in changing urban form, are differentiated not by people's rural or urban origins, as they would have been for Simmel, Park and Wirth, but by class, ethnicity and sub-culture. Sennett likens the procession of images on Fourteenth Street to the vistas of a Baroque city, though Fourteenth Street is not a product of design and its occupants are 'bent on survival' whilst 'its exchanges, curbs, and negotiations occur without much reflection' (Sennett, 1990:167). Perhaps reflection is an act Sennett reserves to himself as a *flâneur*, distanced by a literary eye from the patterns of street use through which he walks, patterns '. . . not too disturbing, if I also keep moving' (Sennett, 1990:124). The inference is justified by his references to Baudelaire, though Sennett claims that in Baudelaire's Paris affluence and deprivation were experienced more directly and together in the street: 'These disorders stimulated his muse' (Sennett, 1990:124). In 1980s Manhattan, in contrast: 'There is nothing sublime in this solitude; it seems to enhance the ordinary' (Sennett, 1990:125).

In narrating a walk of about three miles from his home to the French restaurants of midtown, a route perpendicular to Fourteenth Street, he tells of passing cocaine dealers, then a district of retired, mainly single, professionals (where half lettuces are sold in Korean shops), and an area of equestrian shops frequented by horse-riders and 'more delicate connoisseurs' of leather goods (Sennett, 1990:125). After that are spice shops, Murray Hill, a declining, conservative district around the Morgan Library, and finally the restaurants. This is another linear narrative of difference, and, to Simmel, Sennett attributes the perception that difference is not just allowed but concentrated by city dwelling[14]. With difference comes a chameleon self: ' a city's thick impasto . . . should break down the boundaries of the self' (Sennett, 1990:127), but in his experience this is not a deconstruction of boundaries so much as disengagement:

> New York should be the ideal city of exposure . . . It grasps the imagination because it is a city of difference par excellence . . . collecting its population from all over the world . . . By walking in New York one is immersed in the differences of this most diverse of cities, but precisely because the scenes are disengaged they seem unlikely to offer themselves as significant encounters . . . The leather fetishist and the spice merchant are protected by disengagement . . . social classes, who mix but do not socialize. (Sennett, 1990:128)

Yet it is precisely this urban condition which allows Sennett to be an urban wanderer lingering on the city's internal boundaries, enjoying a man's freedom to transgress neighbourhoods and ponder the shop-window displays of everyday items in the lives of strangers. His account is dated in its assumption of a masculine public realm, and uncritical of the gendering of spaces patrolled by Baudelaire and himself but closed to women other than in marginalised capacities – as Janet Wolff argues in her essay 'The Invisible *Flâneuse*: Women and the literature of modernity' (Wolff, 1989).

The question raised by Sennett's work, in particular by the shift of emphasis between *The Uses of Disorder* and *The Conscience of the Eye*, is whether his observations are those of a detached *flâneur*, or whether his use of a narrative based on his own walks through the city lends his work a quality of engagement. Or is his disengagement a product of an urban gaze which is a development of Simmel's idea of the blasé? The same question could be asked of Walter Benjamin, though here the response might differ, in that Benjamin, by applying a meta-level of criticism to his own critique of urban experience, makes transparent his position. Benjamin's Paris of arcades[15] is a labyrinth through which he moves in necessarily meandering ways rather than along Sennett's perpendicular routes. The labyrinth is a means of access, a quasi-ritual initiation, to the world represented by the metaphorical core of the city. Heinz Paetzold offers three explanations for Benjamin's conceptualisation: the labyrinth as a form of the market, in which varieties of commodity are displayed and where the *flâneur* writer is aware of the commodity value of writing; the labyrinth as an episodic construction of a self which has no given core, but is a sequence of instances or moments, its recollection the reconstruction of a biography[16]; and the labyrinth as a sign for human society under capitalism, from which to seek an awakening[17]. For Benjamin, then, personal memory, an investigation of public space and its intricacies of consumption and commodification, and historical memory reproduced in architecture, overlap in the same site.

Benjamin is the spectator watching the city but also himself watching, thinking, as revealed in the passage 'Polyclinic' from *One Way Street*:

> The author lays his ideas on the marble table of the café. Lengthy meditation . . . Then, deliberately, he unpacks his instruments: fountain pens, pencil, and pipe. The numerous clientele, arranged as in an amphitheatre, make up his clinical audience. Coffee . . . puts the idea under chloroform. What this idea may be has no more connection with the matter at hand than the dream of an anaesthetized patient with the surgical intervention . . . . (Benjamin, 1997b:89)

There are also in this text[18] descriptions, which Benjamin invests with a heightened sensibility, of incidental and everyday spaces; these include a betting office and a beer hall used by sailors. And of non-places, such as 'This Space for Rent', which act as grounds for the inscription of a critique of bourgeois society. Siegfried Kracauer, using the vehicle of another non-space, the hotel lobby, sees aestheticisation as a way to redeem urban consciousness from a lack of meaning[19]. Sennett, meanwhile, never says what (or if) he eats in the French restaurant; Benjamin tells the reader he drinks coffee.

Writing on Cities – War Stories

If writing on cities by men has tended, at least until recently, to assume a masculine public domain of strolling, by what other aspects is it characterised? Are, for instance, narratives of the city as a battle-ground or post-modern wasteland littered with the tatters of grand narratives, parts of a masculine genre? Is the view from the watch-tower like that from the bridge or the belvedere? The tendency to war stories is illustrated here by three cases: Mike Davis writes of the 'armed response' signs on the neatly trimmed lawns of suburban Los Angeles (Davis, 1990:223); Lebbeus Woods writes that 'architecture is war', and that this 'is no mere metaphor' (Woods, 1995:47,50); and Neil Smith adopts the frontier myth as a motif of gentrification (Smith, 1996). The imagery, in writing which is often visually evocative, relates to that of films such as *Clockwork Orange*, *Blade Runner* and *Strange Days*; it represents the city as the site of a dissolution of value structures, where power is subverted by negation, in graffiti, squatting and burning, rather than by mediation. But are these writers captivated, or captured, by the urban wars they report? Do they become part of the conditions they criticise?

In *City of Quartz*, which includes his essay 'Fortress L.A.', Davis begins with the scale of urban sprawl denoted by a phantom landscape of intersections around Llano del Rio: hundreds of square miles of open desert near Edwards Airforce Base are sectioned into rectangular plots ready for building. Llano, with a certain irony, was founded by a group of young socialists; it took them a whole day to drive there from Los Angeles, through fields and walnut groves. Today, developers 'regard the desert as simply another abstraction of dirt and dollar signs', as the region's natural wonder, a species of yucca called the Joshua tree, is eradicated like a weed – 'large, noxious weeds unsuited to the illusion of verdant homesteads' (Davis, 1990:4). These distant suburbs without boundaries are for those for whom other, more established and often gated neighbourhoods are too expensive. Enclaves, whether corporate or residential, are the urban form complementary to the suburb, concentrations rather than distributions of space. Davis writes of one of them:

> The carefully manicured lawns of . . . Westside sprout forests of ominous little signs warning: 'Armed Response!' Even richer neighbourhoods in the canyons and hillsides isolate themselves behind walls guarded by gun-toting private police and state-of-the-art electronic surveillance. Downtown, a publicly-subsidized 'urban renaissance' has raised the nation's largest corporate citadel . . . (Davis, 1990:223)

This is Sennett's urban edge turned into a literal barrier, maintained against the poor by armed guards. For Davis, it provides the image of a fortress city in a narrative of a second civil war which began, he argues, after the Watts rebellion of 1965, and is now institutionalised in the production of urban space. Later in the book, Davis captions a photograph of a bullet-holed police car 'Vietnam in the streets' (Davis, 1990:269).

Figure 2.2 *New York: Sony Plaza (photo M Miles)*

Central to this process of institutionalisation is the encroachment of privatised space on the public realm. Davis notes the negative connotations of the street in the term 'street person' (Davis, 1990:226), and sees the city as undergoing a process of double inversion as the malls which recently marked a periphery are reintroduced to the centre, where they stand in a denuded, sterile streetscape reached by car from other sterile, inward-facing enclaves. Davis sees a radical shift away from the liberal policies of Roosevelt and New York mayor La Guardia in the inter-war years, as from the earlier strategies of Olmsted in New York. Olmsted, he recalls, designed public landscapes as places for controlled social mixing, as safety valves following the New York Draft Riot of 1863. But efforts to stabilise society through the provision of outdoor recreation and attractive public space have been abandoned in favour of free market economics – and burning clears low-cost real estate for development. Davis writes that reformist approaches to public space are '. . . as obsolete as Keynsian nostrums of full employment' (Davis, 1990:227). Also defunct is space hospitable to the poor, because street people are upsetting to developers' clients, so that facilities which might be useful to them are minimised. Davis gives the example of a new design of street furniture, the bus bench with a curved seat to make sleeping impossible (illustrated, Davis, 1990: 235). Sprinkler systems, too, are employed in Los Angeles to randomly drench anyone sleeping in open space. Davis uses the military metaphor 'Eastern Front' to describe the dearth of public lavatories and drinking fountains in the downtown area, a measure directly aimed at the poor and homeless, since more affluent users are able to avail themselves of facilities in restaurants, hotels, corporate lobbies and art galleries.

The provision of restrooms in art galleries is a minor detail of the urban fabric, yet, as Sharon Zukin also argues, the provision of galleries themselves is part of a symbolic economy through which certain districts, and the city as a whole, take on a new identity. The symbolic economy fuels growth by recoding neighbourhoods through cultural association, and by recoding the city as a cultural (by implication, affluent) site (Zukin, 1996:45)[20]. The symbolic economy is indispensable to cities claiming a global status, as illustrated by the art which decorates sites such as Battery Park City or the south bank of the Thames[21]. An example of the kind of space produced is Sony Plaza in Manhattan (Figure 2.2), where all the retail outlets sell Sony products (Zukin, 1995:259-62). Banners hung outside Sony Plaza carry the legend 'Public Space', no irony being intended. Davis, too, links art to a privatised city, looking at the rival claims of Bunker Hill and the Westside as cultural centres in Los Angeles. He notes the importance of Rayner Banham's book *Los Angeles: The Architecture of the Four Ecologies* (1971) in consolidating a rejection of classical notions of a city centre, and charts the redevelopment of downtown Los Angeles since the 1980s as a zone of affluence signified by the Museum of Contemporary Art, the Bella Lewitzky Dance Gallery and Frank Gehry's Disney Concert Hall (Davis, 1990:74). Davis, like Zukin, notes the use of culture to property development when senior executives in development companies are patrons or board members of arts bodies, and that public art is used as an emblem of the corporatisation of the public realm[22].

Lebbeus Woods uses the context of war in the Balkans to provide the trope 'architecture as war'[23]. He cites Berman's account of Moses' development:

> The wrecking machines that levelled houses and urban blocks were no less destructive to culture than if they had been the tanks and artillery of an attacking army. The finished highways and parks . . . were actually monuments to the victory of autocratic authority over the fragile lives of mere people. (Woods, 1995:50)

But he goes beyond specific cases to argue that all development is war, that everyday reality conceals violence in the domestic sphere, and that protocols and manners which have been normalised (within the dominant city) are masks for a lack of relatedness amongst urban publics and individuals. Architects are engaged not in creating beauty but in the conquest of space (Woods, 1995:52). Woods is neither for nor against development as such, though his essay is critical of certain forms of urban clearance; but his aim is to create a transparency in the argument so that architects might be aware of the implications of their actions and act responsibly, making choices 'consciously, honestly . . . accepting personal responsibility for what they do', something he sees, today, as seldom the case – 'If it were, the likelihood is that more well-intentioned architects would not choose to build what they do' (Woods, 1995:53). In reaching this position Woods makes two points: that architects make superficial and misleading responses to ecological concerns[24], and that the benefits of building are relative to social and cultural positions[25].

Tropes like 'architecture is war' open interesting polemics but polarise discussion. Another trope – the yuppie as pioneer – is used by Neil Smith in his investigation of squatting and its repression in New York's lower east side. Smith, whose sympathies are with the squatters, sees an inversion of the pioneer myth in the recoding of inner city neighbourhoods as residual edges of savagery:

> Hostile landscapes are regenerated, cleansed, reinfused with middle-class sensibility; real estate values soar; . . . As with the Old West, the frontier is idyllic yet also dangerous, romantic but also ruthless . . . there is an entire cinematic genre that makes of urban life a cowboy fable replete with dangerous environment, hostile natives and self-discovery at the margins of civilization. In taming the urban wilderness, the cowboy gets the girl but also finds and tames his inner self . . . . (Smith, 1996:13)

Smith's analysis describes how a mythicised old west is used as a cover for the operations of capital. He links the gentrification of inner city areas with ideologically-rooted fashions for Tex-Mex food and cowboy boots, and the sale of commodities produced by native Americans in stores such as Zona on Greene Street; through the manufacture of such myths social conflict is displaced, Smith argues, and class-specific and race-specific social norms affirmed so that the impact of development becomes naturalised (Smith, 1996:17). He illustrates this with a poster proclaiming 'the taming of the wild wild west' to advertise the Armory Building on 42nd Street (Smith, 1996:13–14). The frontier myth, then, is an effective marketing device allied to a cultural recoding of districts such as SoHo but applied to less overtly attractive areas[26]. Neither decorative nor innocent, but ideologically weighted, it defines the poor as 'savages and communists' (Smith, 1996:17). But such images belong to the 1980s, and Smith concludes that, following the financial collapse of 1987, the new urban reality is a revanchist city produced by a vicious reaction by owners of gentrified properties in areas returning to pre-gentrification status against minorities including 'the working class, homeless people, the unemployed, women, gays and lesbians, immigrants . . .' (Smith, 1996:211). He notes Peter Marcuse's comment that an end of gentrification may be welcome (Smith, 1996:228), but suggests any hope that the city authorities will buy up for low-income housing some of the properties left in limbo by degentrification is unrealistic. A second wave of gentrification followed, anyway, in the early 1990s, accompanied by a camouflage of history in press reports likening Tompkins Square Park, scene of a long-term squat discussed by Smith at the outset, to Central Park in the 1930s.

Smith says less of gender than of gentrification, confirming received views that gentrification is in part accelerated by an increasing demand for housing from women professionals, though he points out that 'correlation is not causation' and that changes in the labour market are wide-ranging (Smith, 1996:100). He also notes the upward drift of neighbourhoods identified as zones of gay habitation. In the end, he argues for a retaking of the urban frontier, or, citing Peter Marcuse again, a democratisation of housing (Smith, 1996:231). He makes several references to Custer and the Sioux, and reveals a normally obscured aspect of the narrative: that most of the pioneers were squatters taking land for themselves, on which to make a living, who organised clubs to defend themselves against speculators and set up welfare circles for mutual aid. The Homesteading Act of 1862, which produced the situation to which Custer sought to apply a final solution, was a pragmatic acceptance by the state of a difficult situation. Smith concludes by saying:

> If we are truly to embrace the city as the new frontier today, then the first and most patriotic act in pioneering . . . will be squatting. It is just possible that in a future world we may also come to recognize today's squatters as the ones with a more enlightened vision about the urban frontier. That the city is become a new Wild West may be regrettable . . . what kind of Wild West is precisely what is being fought out. (Smith, 1996:232)

But any Wild West is a war zone, and there is an ambiguity as to whether moral force is on the side of the pioneers or the native Americans they displaced (who have not all gone away[27]). A question which might be asked of Smith, and Davis, is whether they are drawn into such metaphors through desire or critique.

Writing on Cities – A Right to the City

Recent writing on cities by women, in contrast, offers complexities and perspectives other than that of a game of cowboys (in which women would, if present, be the Indians). Four examples show this: Elizabeth Wilson, in *The Sphinx in the City*, notes the use of negative terms like 'disorientation, meaninglessness and fragmentation' for the post-modern city, adding that '. . . the city becomes a labyrinth or a dream. Its chaos and senselessness mirror a loss of meaning in the world' (Wilson, 1991:135–6). She argues that women in the city are seen (by men) as representing disorder, suggesting an urban realm of sexual licence and chaos (Wilson, 1991:157). Leonie Sandercock, in *Towards Cosmopolis*, recalls how, in the early phase of feminist discussion of the city 'We swapped "war stories" and gave each other support', but then introduces the voices of other women excluded from the professional or academic 'we' – the women of colour who cook and mind children for the white, professional women who construct critiques of cities. Their voices call for social justice as 'inseparable from a respect for and an engagement with the politics of identity and difference' (Sandercock, 1998b:18–20). Doreen Massey, in *Space, Place and Gender*, like Janet Wolff, draws attention to the depiction of a masculinised public domain in the literature of modernism: 'replete with descriptions of boulevards and cafés, of fleeting, passing glances and of the cherished anonymity of the crowd' (Massey, 1994:233). She writes that in face of works such as Manet's *Olympia*, there is no possibility of a woman spectator. Similarly, Marsha Meskimmon, in *Engendering the City*, writing about contemporary women photographers, notes the impact of commodity capitalism in the arcade: 'If the spectacular city is a desirable woman and "woman" is the object of the look, then the subject doing the looking is masculine by definition' (Meskimmon, 1997:15). In the work of women photographers she sees, in contrast, 'an interactive encounter between the body and the city' (Meskimmon, 1997:22).

Although to frame men's and women's texts on cities in a binary opposition replicates an oppositional thinking which itself contributes to men's war games, and both men and women have sought alternative modes of writing, Wilson's critique of aestheticisation, as dream or wasteland, could apply to the texts by Davis, Woods and Smith cited above. Wilson is the most critical of the mythicisation of the city, seeing such images as reducing the city to a site for the projection of pre-figured narratives. She notes John Thackara's cautionary approach to stories which constitute citizens as victims of modernity, adding that 'The post-modern view of the contemporary world as caught in an imploding catastrophe is nonetheless widely popular' and that current debate perpetuates an ingrained suspicion of the city. Perhaps, she asks, some observers obtain 'a perverse pleasure from the horrors of the post-modern kitsch-scape' (Wilson, 1991:136).

Two aspects of post-feminist writing on cities are the use of personal narratives (since the personal is political)[28], and a willingness to unpick complexities which go beyond an easy characterisation of the problem. Jane Rendell's account of living in a south London house in *Occupying Architecture* (Hill, 1998), is a case of the former (Rendell, 1998), and Sandercock's essay 'The Death of Modernist Planning: Radical Praxis for a Postmodern Age' (Sandercock, 1998b) of the latter, though the categories are merely convenient and by no means definitive. It should be added that a use of the first person is not exclusive to women writing on the city – Berman and Sennett do this, too. Perhaps where women's writing differs is in the kind of experience described rather than the form of description, though Massey argues that in late nineteenth-century French art, for instance, there is a distinct women's subject-matter of domestic interiors (Massey, 1994:234).

Rendell uses a conceit rather than a trope, deconstructing the conventions of architecture she was taught through a story of physically taking apart a house[29]. Part of her text is a step-by-step dismantling of architectural education, and part an investigation of what remains when the accumulated baggage of architecture is cleared away. Primary to that baggage is modernism's purity, its whiteness, subverted when Rendell visits Melnikov's house in Moscow and sees the ornaments with which Mrs Melnikov has cluttered the bedroom, making a (perhaps usefully decorative) mess of it. This leads into a critique of architecture's professional methodology and the privileging of form over occupation – Mrs Melnikov was, after all, only inhabiting a private space. It also leads to a realisation that not only architects make buildings; builders do it, too, as do dwellers adapting spaces to their needs and fancies. Hence, the production of a building to completion constitutes a small part of architectural time, compared to the 'use, reuse, destruction and decay of spaces and building components' in which social value replaces exchange value, and the occupation of space 'reinforces who we think we are and who we would like to be' (Rendell, 1998:232). Acts of decoration, then, like Mrs Melnikov's, are statements of identity, and the aesthetics of occupation entails a deeper meaning than allowed by consumerism[30].

Sandercock begins with an image of twilight in Los Angeles. Smoke rises as the city burns and 52 people are killed, thousands arrested. Is this another war story?[31] Not quite, more a discussion of what were described as the first multicultural riots, or 'the nation's first "multi-ethnic rebellion"' (Sandercock, 1998b: 163). Sandercock's argument is that the multi-ethnic character of cities and regions, at the beginning of the twenty-first century, requires a restructuring of urban theories and practices of planning. Sandercock, like Wilson, Massey and Rendell, begins with a first-person narrative, recalling her experience of living in inner-city Melbourne in the 1970s, seeing then an influx of Greek families (and restaurants), and, on revisiting the area recently, a second influx displacing the first, of Vietnamese. This pattern of repeated waves, as one generation of immigrants moves to more affluent districts and another, poorer and newer, less accustomed, generation moves in, is an element of Burgess' concentric ring model of city growth. As such, with its biological underpinning, it normalises conflict; but Sandercock takes this experience to define spaces of contended, or insurgent, citizenship[32], where immigration meets resistance. Whilst Burgess sees zones of conflict as inevitable, Sandercock sees them as a challenge to planning conventions; if the historic role of planning is the control of space, it needs, now, to reject complicity in the dominant culture and accept a new and complex diversity. Sandercock sketches six models of planning practice: the rationally planned city translated into the urban master plan; advocacy planning in the 1960s; radical political economy (seeing planning as in service to capital); equity planning in the 1970s; social learning and communicative action; and radical planning. Social learning and communicative action – a concept informed by Habermas's continuation of the critical project of the Frankfurt School – mark a potential new equilibrium in which the knowledge of dwellers begins to achieve a status comparable to that of professionals in a process of mutual learning. Sandercock cites the work of John Forester[33], which uses qualitative rather than quantitative evaluation, seeking to gain insights into the conditions of specific localities rather than project on to them the geometric models of past urban theory. Communicative action, then, reconstructs the Enlightenment project of a world which is better by opening up communication and dismantling distortions which act as barriers to discourse:

> The emphasis is less on what planners know and more on how they use and distribute their knowledge; less on their ability to solve problems and more on opening up debate about them. In this model, planning is about talk, argument, shaping attention. (Sandercock, 1998b:175)

But the agent of this remains the state-employed, professional planner. Sandercock sees communicative action as limited in how far it can go towards a counter-hegemonic outlook. To answer this, she proposes a model of radical planning which begins from awareness of inequality and an assumption that empowerment can operate effectively only outside bureaucracy[34]. Some implications of this are taken up in discussion of sustainability and development in the non-affluent world, in Chapter 9.

Sandercock argues that the notion of community is no less affected by reification than anything else, questioning assumptions about the rights of one supposed or defined community in relation to those of other equally supposed or defined communities, and to those of individuals. What rights, it might be added in the light of Smith's frontier stories, did settlers have in relation to native Americans (and native Americans in relation to anyone else)? The community, if such an entity has validity today[35], may not be infallibly right, and difference is an aspect of post-modernity which, Sandercock suggests, negates the idea of just and harmonious solutions. She recalls federal intervention to support civil rights, often against state power, and argues that the tension between the transformative and repressive powers of planning is not likely to be resolved, so must be accepted by planners, just as local power is not always transformative and can be repressive when protecting what are regarded as local rights or heritage. Here, in accepting certain ambivalences, Sandercock sees Friedman's concept of critical distance as helpful, allowing involvement without blindness. Massey, too, discussing the distancing of visual perceptions, notes that detachment need not always be disinterest (Massey, 1994:232). For Sandercock, this distance of reflection is not incompatible with listening to the voices of people and groups who have long histories of repression and displacement, whose culture is based in 'the state of living on/in the borderlands, living in between, on the margins' (Sandercock, 1998b:181). This gives rise to ways of being and ways of knowing which challenge the dominant culture by questioning how knowledge (including the knowledge used in making planning decisions) is produced:

> They argue that there are different ways of 'doing theory' . . . that theory is always embodied. They celebrate the value of experiential and other alternative ways of knowing, learning, discovering, including traditional ethnic or culturally specific modes: from talk to story telling, the blues to rap, poetry and song. This is what I call an epistemology of multiplicity. (Sandercock, 1998b:181)

Sandercock ends her text with reference to the struggle for land rights of the Wik people of Cape York Peninsula, Australia, where competing agricultural and native titles and different methods of stating ownership deny the possibility of certainties. Instead, law and planning need, she argues, to respond to local histories and circumstances, using both advocacy and negotiation[36].

Distant Views and Close-up Places

Marc Augé, in an anthropology of the non-places of post-modernity, cites Chateaubriand, travelling the world to visit the ruins of civilisations, writing descriptions from vantage points and seeing worlds unseen for thousands of years. Elsewhere, towards the close of *Postmodern Geographies*, Edward Soja looks down upon Los Angeles from City Hall (Soja, 1989:236–7). Augé comments that the ideal vantage point, combining movement and distance, is the deck of a ship. To what extent are the male writers noted above looking at the city from the perspective of a stroller always departing the scenes observed, like a passenger at the stern of a liner leaving port? Is the perspective from above always a view from the position of power, or do overviews serve other needs? Massey argues that, specifically, a privileging of the visual sense '. . . impoverishes us through deprivation of other forms of sensory perception'; she cites Luce Irigaray as saying that this impoverishment produces a dematerialisation of the body, and states that 'the reason for the privileging of vision is precisely its supposed detachment . . . necessarily . . . from a particular point of view' (Massey, 1994:232). The eye objectifies, gazes, then, as the visual sense offers a mastery affirmed by distance. Is an interrogation of cities which relies on a distant or disembodied viewpoint as much a part of the problem as of the solution? Is the construction of solutions anyway a position of power?

From the above comparison of texts by men and women writers on cities, however staged, two difficulties in conventional urbanism can be discerned: that conceptualisations of the city – as wasteland or Utopia – are abstractions, and as such desensualising and depopulating; and that the more widely the city's image is of terminal decline, the more likely it is that either the adrenalin of destruction becomes addictive, or that other, more evasive myths will be invoked, such as the rural idyll. The latter has a long history, in poetry as well as in the literature of town and country planning; its continuing attraction is demonstrated by renewed interest in the legacy of Ebenezer Howard (Hall and Ward, 1998). But exile is found, too, within the post-modern city. The city as war zone makes the urbanist a lonely frontiersman, a role more often adopted by the modern artist. Sandercock, rejecting such masculine roles, argues for an adaptation of planning to new kinds of knowledge derived from the complexities and actualities of city life; and Wilson for the metropolis as a place of liberation for women, for their 'right to the carnival, intensity and even the risks of the city' (Wilson, 1991:10). Planning remains, for these two writers, necessary to regulate market forces, but needs to move away from the colonialism and paternalism of the city of order and surveillance, towards a 'deep ambivalence' which might also be creative (Wilson, 1991:157). Sandercock adds: 'I don't want a city where everything stays the same and everyone is afraid of change', dreaming of a city 'where I have a right to my surroundings', and of a '. . . carnival of the multicultural city' (Sandercock, 1998a:218). This could become a mythicised future, as much a culturally mediated image as that of a war-torn past; the difference, apart from the embrace of difference and hence of mutability which the image entails, is that Sandercock offers a new methodology for urban processes, rather than fixing the characterisation of the city as an aestheticised form.

Notes

1. This chapter is a revised version of a paper given to the conference on Cities and the Millennium, organised by the University of East London and held at the Royal Institute of British Architects (RIBA), December 1998.
2. For an analysis of increases in metropolitan populations, up to c.1990, see Angotti (1993). Angotti lists 20 metropolitan cities in order of size, and shows their percentage increase since c.1875. Of the 20 cities, six are in Europe (including Russia) and north America; four are in Latin America and seven in Asia. The highest rates of growth are Los Angeles (261.5%), Jakarta (210.7%) and São Paolo (93.9%) (Agnotti, 1993:27).
3. This is part of a collaborative design for public space, by architect Caesar Pelli and artist Siah Armajani. Seating in North Cove is by Scott Burton. At the other end of a walkway by the Hudson is South Cove, designed by landscape architects Stanton Ekstut and Susan Child with artist Mary Miss (Beardsley, 1989:150–156).
4. Over-stimulation continues, particularly in shopping malls, theme parks and entertainment complexes. In Disney World, stimulation is provided by the non-contiguity of

adjacent elements; in the super-mall at Edmonton, Canada, 5.2 million square feet of consumption space, includes fake streets from Paris and New Orleans, a Spanish galleon, and hotel rooms themed after Rome, Hollywood or Polynesia. Margaret Crawford writes: 'While enclosed shopping malls suspended space, time and weather, Disneyland went one step further and suspended reality. Any geographic, cultural, or mythical location . . . could be reconfigured as a setting for entertainment.' (Crawford, 1992:16). Disney co-opts almost any cultural phenomenon, as demonstrated by its use in Disney World of a graffiti-covered subway car to represent New York (Cresswell, 1996:37).

5. For discussion of the Chicago School, see Savage and Warde, 1993:9–18, and, on Wirth (1993:97–119). Although influenced by Simmel's link of the city to the money economy, the Chicago School, in explaining urban growth through naturalised (that is, biological) models leads to an uncritical acceptance of development.
6. For discussion of *The Wasteland* in relation to Eliot's early life, see Gordon, 1977:86–119.
7. In this environment, static forms disintegrate, and, as Marx writes: 'All that is solid melts into air, all that is holy is profaned, and men [sic] at last are forced to face . . . the real conditions of their lives . . .' (Marx cited in Berman, 1983:21). The reference is to pp 475–6 in *The Marx-Engels Reader*, Tucker (ed.) (1978), New York, Norton.
8. Sennett does not compare himself with Baudelaire, and, in his work on the relation of city form to social attitudes to the body, *Flesh and Stone* (1994), makes only passing reference to Baudelaire (Sennett, 1994:314–5 and 338). He makes little more reference to Benjamin, noting only his epithet for Paris as capital of the nineteenth century, and, briefly and for another purpose, his arcades project (Sennett, 1994:322–3 and 332).
9. See Jacobs, 1961:29–73 for discussion of the street as an urban social form enabling mixing whilst offering safety.
10. For investigation of the relation between mass culture and an increasing rigidity of spatial boundaries, see Sibley, 1995:49–71.
11. Shared experience is still found in some southern European villages in which the village baker's oven is used for baking other foods by many villagers. An attempt to reinvent this communality is found in some alternative settlements, such as the co-housing scheme at North Street, Davis, California (Schwartz and Schwartz, 1998:29–35).
12. Sennett cites studies of suburbia by John Seeley and Herbert Gans (Sennett, 1996:71).
13. This text was first published in 1970; it describes that reality against which, during the late 1960s, a generation had rebelled by dropping out, finding in the sub-culture of dropping out a path to liberation. Whilst Sennett constructs a case for a more anarchic city without reference to the world of Bob Dylan, The Doors, The Grateful Dead and Timothy Leary, or student protests against the American war in Vietnam, Herbert Marcuse, in *An Essay on Liberation*, sees student protest as the way to an aesthetic society (Marcuse, 1969).
14. Sennett cites Simmel's 'Metropolis and Mental Life' as 'The Great City and Mental Life' and describes it as a lecture delivered in 1909 (Sennett, 1990:126). But Simmel's text was first published in the *Jarbuch der Gehe-Stiftung*, vol. 9, 1903, pp 185–206 (reference from Frisby and Featherstone, 1997:298).
15. For a critical commentary on Benjamin's Arcades project, see Buck-Morss, 1995. For Benjamin's writing on Baudelaire's Paris, see Benjamin, [1973] 1997a.
16. Paetzold cites Sigrid Weigel as the source of this reading (Weigel, 1996 cited in Paetzold, 1998a:22).
17. Paetzold writes: 'Here, of course, we find Marx's idea that the *capitalist mode of sociality* has created a second nature, by which human beings are determined in

reverse. Dreams and images brought forward by culture are necessary in order to keep open the process of social change' (Paetzold, 1998a:22).

18. The text begins: 'This street is named Asja Lacis Street, after her who as an engineer cut it through the author'. The reference is to the Latvian communist theatre director Asja Lacis, with whom Benjamin had an intricate relation during his days in Moscow and elsewhere – see Smith, 1986.
19. Kracauer writes: '. . . consciousness of existence and of the authentic conditions dwindles away . . .clouded sense becomes lost in the labyrinth of distorted events whose distortion it no longer perceives.'; to which the aesthetic rendering of 'a life that has lost the power of self-observation' might 'restore to it a sort of language . . .' (Kracauer, 1995:173).
20. Zukin has written extensively on this, from the gentrification of SoHo in New York as artists began to rent lofts in redundant industrial buildings (Zukin, 1989), to a critique of the issues of ownership and access when the presence of art galleries, or temporary exhibition of art in shop-fronts, is used to increase real estate values (Zukin, 1995; Zukin, 1996). She first published her research on SoHo in 1982 (republished as Zukin, 1989), the same year the Davis text was published in the USA.
21. Zukin writes: 'The ambiguity of urban forms is a source of the city's tension as well as a struggle for interpretation. To ask "Whose city?" suggests more than a politics of occupation; it also asks who has a right to inhabit the dominant image of the city. This often relates to real geographical strategies as different social groups battle over access to the centre of the city and over symbolic representations of the city' (Zukin, 1996:43).
22. 'The political clout of developers . . . ensures that municipal cultural policy maximally favors big Downtown or Westside projects, where on-site public art or adjacent museums inflate property values. The Community Development Agency's vaunted "culture tax" of one per cent on new development . . . has largely functioned as a sleight-of-hand subsidy to Downtown developers, whose expenditure on monumental kinetic forms, sullen pastel plinths, and fascist steel cubes, are partially recompensed by reduced landleases or advantageous density transfers' (Davis, 1990:77–8).
23. The essay cited here is a reworking of ideas initially published by Woods in a pamphlet in 1993 (Woods, 1993)
24. 'Architects speak of ecological concerns today in a rather thoughtless way . . . They are speaking in relative terms, of course, not only because the act of building and its consequences still create waste and pollution . . . but also because they introduce new forms of entropy into the existing environment' (Woods, 1995:49).
25. 'A building will only be beautiful and useful for those who benefit directly and tangibly from its existence. As for others, blind to its benefits because they occur at the expense of those that might have been their own, the building is little more than an instrument of denial' (Woods, 1995:50).
26. Smith writes that '. . . the integration of cultural and capital-centred explanations is vital', citing Zukin (1987) (Smith, 1996:42).
27. For reference to work drawing attention to the original ownership of Manhattan, by native American artist Edgar Heap of Birds, see Lacy, 1995:235.
28. Both Wilson and Massey begin their accounts with childhood memories of travel in the city, Wilson in London and Massey in Manchester (Wilson, 1991:1; Massey, 1994:185).
29. For example: '. . . in my home, walls were removed rather than built. This was not to enable the free flow of pure space as in the modernist open plan, but rather to intensify the occupation of space by overlaying one kind of living over another . . .' (Rendell, 1998:240).
30. A different but related point is made, in another context, by Sarah Buie in an essay on the contrast of markets with mass retail outlets: 'Aesthetics . . . is not actually about the

surface appearance of things, but about how the true nature of an undertaking . . . is embodied . . . the direct visceral way we understand what something means, what it is' (Buie, 1998:231).

31. Sandercock notes the over-use of Los Angeles to illustrate a post-modern condition, citing Soja (1989); Davis (1990); and Jameson (1984), (Sandercock, 1998b:163).
32. Sandercock cites Holston, 1995:44: 'Citizenship changes as new members emerge to advance their claims, expanding its realm, and as new forms of segregation and violence counter these advances, eroding it. The sites of insurgent citizenship are found at the intersections of these processes of expansion and erosion.' (Holston cited in Sandercock, 1998b:166)
33. See Forester, 1989.
34. Sandercock differentiates the approaches of John Friedman (for whom the planner maintains a critical distance from everyday struggles) and Allan Heskin and Jacqueline Leavitt (whose practice is to enter a community, giving generous time to unplanned communication). (Sandercock, 1998b:176–8). Sandercock cites Heskin (1980) and Leavitt (1994); also Hooks (1990).
35. The question of how communities, or publics, are constituted is also noted in Chapter 8, in the course of discussion of post-industrial cities and global lines of communication.
36. See also Jacobs (1996) for accounts of development on sites claimed by native peoples in Australia.

CHAPTER 3
THE PRODUCTION OF SPACE

INTRODUCTION

The production of space is more than the building of walls. These, dividing nothing from nothing, as it were[1], stand in space, or delineate a site, but space flows round and through them; yet already the idea of a site (or the desire to remain in it[2]) validates its physical construction, just as the act of building engenders concepts of spatial measurement. The relation of idea and act is mutual, but the understanding of space changes in history, and in post-Enlightenment society its conceptual form, in plans and designs, becomes dominant, whilst the spaces of the body, or of memory and association, are ascribed a secondary role. Chapter 1 considered representations of cities in postcards as evidence of the dominant space of the distant view; Chapter 2 contrasted urban war stories with more complex analyses by women in the recent literature of urbanism, indicating survivals of the associative spaces of everyday life. It is evident that the meanings people attach to space are not given, or always the same, but are derived from specific histories, so that it is possible to say that space is produced, just as time is produced, and may be experienced as cyclic or linear (at the same time). Consideration of a society's spatial practices offers insights, as French Marxist philosopher Henri Lefebvre argues, into its ideologies, from which it is possible to ask how and for whom a society's spatial practices are determined. This chapter begins with a specific case, the Thamesmead housing project in south-east London. Edward Robbins perceives an emphasis here on form over process, and professional expertise over spontaneous spatial organisation, which he sees as the root of the scheme's social failure. The chapter extends this critique at a theoretical level through a selective reading of Lefebvre, which underpins much of what follows in the book's other chapters, in particular discussion of the architectural everyday in Chapter 7 and conviviality in Chapter 9.

THE FAILURE OF UTOPIA: THAMESMEAD

Thamesmead was seen by those responsible for it, including the Greater London Council (GLC), as a means to a new, more socially just society in which decent housing would be provided for the poor. The GLC, up to its abolition by the Thatcher government, was noted for policies for access to culture, public transport subsidy and innovative provision of mass public housing, all of which suggest social

Figure 3.1 *Thamesmead: the tower blocks (photo M Miles)*

Figure 3.2 *Thamesmead: low-rise housing and concrete walkways (photo M Miles)*

progress. One of its last achievements was to put in place planning controls ensuring that development of the Coin Street site on the south bank of the Thames would include a major element of social housing, and, at Coin Street, tenants in a housing association eventually drove the development to the extent of appointing the developer. Yet Thamesmead survives from a time when the possibilities for such tenant-centred urban regeneration were not considered, and was an attempt at utopian social engineering based on a belief in a better world achieved through design, good design being seen then as determined by professional experts, just as decent housing was allocated to, rather than made by, its occupants. Whilst the benefits of prosperity were more evenly distributed by a new welfare state, the development, in the late 1960s, though well-intentioned, remained dependent on paternalistic assumptions that it is the built environment which shapes the behaviour of its inhabitants, not those inhabitants who shape the built environment. Today it is a landscape of concrete in which deprivation is not extreme but the feeling of a new society seems fanciful. Thamesmead is a helpful case to consider, then, because it combines the progressive thinking of the time with a contradiction between the implications of its intention that the poor should share in a new society, and the means employed to deliver this intention, which ensure that the poor do not make the new society themselves.

Thamesmead occupies a four-mile stretch of Thames shoreline in outer south-east London. A group of towers mark the edge of the 1600 acre site, along a main road (Figure 3.1), and act as wind- and noise-breakers for high-density low-rise housing over the rest of the site. Part of the site was previously occupied by an arsenal, and much of it was marshland; to meet planning requirements for marshy areas, habitation is above ground level, with garages and stores at the base of each block – a practice since abandoned in social housing schemes due to a high incidence of vandalism in spaces which cannot be directly observed by residents (Coleman, 1985:43). Thamesmead was seen as a complete environment, almost a new town, initially for 60 000 people, articulated as a series of discrete neighbourhoods (each of around 1500 dwellings) in which pedestrians are separated from cars by walkways, and the site as a whole articulated by differences of level and a plan which gives a variety of views from the blocks. It is not a completely arid environment – there are trees and open spaces, and an element of social concern is indicated by the provision of low-rise housing and the mix of housing with amenities such as schools, play and leisure areas, cycling paths, shops and community centres; but it has an overwhelming presence of concrete and prefabrication (Figure 3.2). The architecture is evidently functional and the only traces of decoration are those supplied by tenants in the form of garden trellises and plants, and the odd community mural or mosaic, but Thamesmead was not a cheap scheme, and although the level of costs was constrained, Robbins suggests that 'today such a level of investment in social housing would be considered generous' (Robbins, 1996:287). Why, then, did Thamesmead not produce the desired solution of a convivial city within the city?

There are at least three related factors: the remoteness of the site from centres of activity; the zoning of the site according to single functions of space; and the ideology underpinning the scheme's planning and design, which embodies a particular attitude towards the poor. These factors, more than deficiency in design or construction, combine to ensure that Thamesmead remains a site of marginality. Robbins is concerned with single-function zoning and ideology, but geographical separation from the cultural and economic hubs of London seems also of importance, and indicative of a pattern of development which moves increasingly towards the definition of a city of affluence within a less visible city of deprivation. The site is still, 30 years on, remote in terms of public transport, beyond the reach of the London Underground and the Docklands Light Railway (DLR), and beyond, too, the more recent projects of the Thames Barrier at Woolwich, London City Airport at Silvertown and the Millennium Dome at north Greenwich[3]. These projects mark a corridor of largely corporate development eastward along the river, of which the tower at Canary Wharf is the most prominent landmark, seen from all directions[4]. But whilst the Dome is linked to central London by an extension of the Jubilee Line, and high-income housing along the north bank across the river from the Dome is accessible by the DLR, Thamesmead, on the south bank and further out, remains peripheral. In this circumstance it has much in common with other mass relocation schemes, such as Easterhouse on the edge of Glasgow.

A second factor is the zoning of the site, in keeping with conventional planning practices in which cities are zoned for single uses, with a central district of civic or corporate buildings, monuments and spaces. Thamesmead is fragmented by the assignment of single functions to each part of the site, in contrast to inner city streets and neighbourhoods of mixed use. This leads into the third factor: that whilst Thamesmead was seen, in the late 1960s and early 1970s, as a progressive solution to the housing problems of London, in which planners and designers sought to learn from the shortcomings of earlier schemes[5], Robbins argues that rationalisation in design and manufacture is linked to mechanistic thinking in planning (Robbins, 1996:286–7), tracing the mismatch of intention and outcome to a divergence, at the root of planning assumptions, between sympathetic and pejorative ways of describing inner city neighbourhoods, and a negation of people's capacity to shape the built environment for themselves. So, from their inner-city labyrinths, the supposedly grateful poor were decanted to margins of new, high-density housing as out of sight as Victorian lunatic asylums.

People whose lives had previously revolved around the multi-dimensional spaces of the inner city were moved to Thamesmead as part of a process of social reconstruction and rebuilding which began in the late 1940s; still in a political climate of regeneration, the GLC dedicated large budgets to new housing in the late 1960s, mainly to rehousing populations to allow the demolition of older, dilapidated streets[6]. For the GLC policy-makers and designers, Thamesmead offered the latest in housing form and social possibility, providing a clean, well-ordered, safe, functionally delineated and segregated, and well-defined space into which people would come and build meaningful and happy lives. (Robbins, 1996:287). This is reminiscent of a middle-class idea of appropriate behaviour, of a neat and orderly life with everything in its place; and the original plan for Thamesmead included a marina to attract middle-class families, who never arrived, preferring to move further out to greener suburban developments in Kent. This ideology is perhaps central to the failure of Thamesmead, indicating an attitude on the part of professionals towards the poor which sees inner-city, low-income neighbourhoods as dilapidated, over-crowded, noisy, polluted and, because they are irrationally planned, ripe for clearance; from another position closer to street level, however, they are lively, have a supportive social fabric and accommodate a diversity of spatial uses (Robbins, 1996:284–5). Different words code the same actualities in opposing ways. Robbins writes:

> What appears to be the very chaos of the street is its attraction. Cacophonous though these streets may be, shared understandings of the rules of engagement make the street a most ordered and organized place. (Robbins, 1996:286)

Jane Jacobs came to similar conclusions in *The Death and Life of Great American Cities*, seeing safety in the continuous use of streets in zones of mixed use (Jacobs, 1961:29–54)[7]. And from a study of graffiti in the New York Subway in the 1970s, geographer Tim Cresswell concludes that the meanings of place, as well as its uses, are ambivalent[8] Also writing on New York, Rosalyn Deutsche argues against the designation of sites according to a single spatial function (Deutsche, 1991b:159), claiming that by naturalising such meanings, the dominant city becomes immune to questioning.

For Robbins, the inner city streets in which Thamesmead's residents formerly lived are key social spaces, complex but not disorganised; he argues that for families living in confined spaces, the street becomes a domestic space in which the evidence of confinement is not visible; people might fight in the street, but usually within structures of family or social group, whilst children seeing the diversity of street life were able to pick up its codes and 'learn about growing up' (Robbins, 1996:285–6). These activities, and the spaces they articulate, are gendered, though this is not a focus in Robbins' critique; but he sees the segregation of functions at Thamesmead as evidence of a 'deeply felt anti-urbanism' and distrust of people's ability to order their own lives (Robbins, 1996:289). So the spaces of 'middle-class familialism and individualism' replace those of 'working-class solidarity and sociality'; and residents are 'told through the design' that they belong to a class which needed to be moved out of its old environment, whilst their class origins are reinforced through the functionalising design and imposition of the new environment (Robbins, 1996:290). The crux of Robbins' critique is that the scheme offered an ordered space for dwellers, rather than an ordering of space by dwellers. The poor are not allowed to arrange their lives in the multi-dimensional spaces with which they are familiar, not because multi-functional zoning cannot fit the planning process, but because they

Figure 3.3 *Thamesmead: security at the health centre (photo M Miles)*

are seen as incapable of such organisation. Spontaneous social organisation is then replaced by social engineering which, despite its progressive aims, inhibits the sense of personal ownership given by unplanned use and casual adaptation. Design compounds the problem in that, in a set of spaces as regular as Thamesmead, any adaptation is likely to be seen as defacement, and street life as transgression in an environment in which most functions are set in the internal spaces of buildings; one consequence is an increasing presence of surveillance and addition to the original design of a vocabulary of security (Figure 3.3). Despite the good intentions of planners and designers who, Robbins notes, saw themselves as socialists, Thamesmead, then, fails due to the ideological assumption underpinning its planning: that the physical environment conditions behaviour, and an ordered environment produces orderly behaviour.

The first problem with this assumption is not that the built environment does not condition behaviour, which it obviously does by prescribing certain possibilities, but that the process is seen as operating only in a top-down direction, and excludes the mutability of space which is a site for the construction and expression of identities[9]. The second problem is that order is not natural but cultural, and its manifestations seen in different ways by different groups in society so that there is no given definition of orderly behaviour, nor of appropriate use of space. Hence the active life of the street, in which spatial boundaries are fluid, and which may include graffiti as a means of stating an emotional ownership of space, is seen from a viewpoint of civic authority as a transgression of social norms. But if zoning and street activity are two kinds of order, though they may seem incompatible, the point is to ask who determines what constitutes order, and Cresswell argues that the notion of place, as distinct from space, follows from tensions between the meanings attributed to it by different publics. Some meanings appear incompatible with others, though all constitute layers of reality, but the dominance of one meaning over others, he argues, is not inevitable. Instead, the designation of incompatibility follows from an interest in preserving a particular meaning:

> Within a particular discourse (say the discourse about graffiti in the New York press), a network or web of meanings is created. These meanings are created by direct reference (the meaning of Central Park is X, the appropriate behaviour in the subway system is Z) or . . . by metaphors and descriptive terms applied to perpetrators of transgressions against the favoured meaning of places (dirt, madness, disease, obscenity, and so on). The discourse creates a set of associations with its subject (disorder with graffiti). (Cresswell, 1996:59)

So, descriptions produced in a dominant culture, such as the association of inner-city streets with dirt, colour incompatible elements in negative terms. Inner city streets thus become slums to those who see the behaviour which takes place there as deviant. They remain, of course, homes to those who live in them; but their occupants are outside the dominant structures of power. Given histories of social upheaval, and perceptions of history on the part of the dominant class, such neighbourhoods are not just dirty but dangerous.

Robbins sees a mutual relation of policy and design: housing policy is embodied in spatial design, and the production of urban space is a way of making as well as delivering policy. The planning of Thamesmead translates a policy for social improvement into (literally and metaphorically) concrete; and those concrete forms impose a view of legitimate behaviour which constitutes an unwritten policy. In one way, this extends in a more humane form the disciplinary thinking behind the post-Enlightenment prison, or panopticon, as discussed by Michel Foucault, in which prisoners behave according to the requirements of an architecture of observation[10]. The design of a housing project is not a means of overt control, even when security cameras ensure constant surveillance by unknown others, but the model is still one of imposition. Robbins concludes by pointing to the irony of the situation: Thamesmead fails because its designers espoused progressive ideological positions, yet translated them in terms of *spatial* rather than *social* form.

Unlike other social housing projects such as Broadwater Farm, Thamesmead has seen no riots, and levels of vandalism, litter and graffiti are no higher than in many places, but there is a mild air of desolation, a sense that Thamesmead is not emotionally owned by anyone. Yet it is the product of professional expertise, and as well as issues of remoteness, functionalisation and ideology, there is that of how professional discourses and methodologies condition the design solutions professionals produce. Conventionally, such solutions utilise kinds of knowledge reserved to an elite class which, historically, is almost exclusively white, mainly male and largely from middle- or upper-class origins. The genuine wish for social improvement, then, on the part of planners and designers at Thamesmead was from the outset affected by this history. A similar conclusion might be drawn from a study by Henk ter Heide and Danny Wijnbelt from the University of Utrecht of the Bijlmermeer high-rise development to the south-east of Amsterdam (ter Heide and Wijnbelt, 1996). The two developments are not identical in purpose or form, Bijlmermeer being more a site for overflow housing in a city the central areas of which are still densely populated, and being entirely high-rise. But whilst ter Heide and Wijnbelt see Bijlmermeer as an extreme case, they attribute the scheme's failure (even before its partial destruction in an air disaster) to the rejection by a tightly-knit design team of the knowledges of users (ter Heide and Wijnbelt, 1996:79), arguing that designers are unable to comprehend social space because their notion of expertise precludes it by privileging planned space. The researchers see the privileging of one kind of knowledge over others as also impairing communication within a multi-disciplinary design team. This matters because Dutch urban design and town planning in the post-war period has become a multi-disciplinary field of geographers, sociologists, economists, demographers and policy analysts, all of whom have a significantly different training from architects[11]. The study finds a mutual lack of understanding between professionals from social science and design backgrounds: to social researchers, design methodology is enigmatic, and the ability of designers to integrate different kinds of knowledge is seen as minimal, though designers see themselves in exactly such a role, which is, too, that of power-broker. Ter Heide and Wijnbelt see social research through surveys as a means to indicate a community's 'prevalence of economic and of cultural lifestyles' (ter Heide and Wijnbelt, 1996:88), but note that although studies have been carried out and published, designers tend to avoid them, in part because they see social research as undermining the intuition which they regard as a key element in their creative practice (ter Heide and Wijnbelt, 1996:83)[12]. If, however, intuition marks design as a creative practice, to what extent does this permeate the literature of urban design? Or are there cases in which social research is also used? In the next part of the chapter, two contributors to the literature of urban design – Kevin Lynch and William H Whyte – are briefly considered to ask what relative weight each gives to design and social process.

Space and Process in Urban Design

Lynch[13] and Whyte[14] were both prominent figures in urban design in the English-speaking countries in the 1980s, both voiced concerns for the liveability of cities, and both used empirical methods of investigation, Lynch through interviews and Whyte through time-lapse photography. In his time, Lynch was progressive in his concern for the centres of cities, and for the legibility of city form through landmarks and pathways; Whyte, too, looks at downtown public spaces, particularly corporate plazas and small parks in Manhattan. But although the object of both their investigations is the space of users, do their methods and conclusions contribute to a conventional approach in which cities are primarily arrangements of architectural form, or to a more radical approach in which it is use itself which conditions readings of space?

Lynch describes his research methods in *The Image of the City*. He writes that 'analysis of existing form and its effects on the citizen is one of the foundation stones of city design' (Lynch, 1960:14). To this end, Lynch studied the central areas of Boston, Jersey City and Los Angeles, cases offering a range of distinctive types, exhibiting strong form, formlessness and newness, respectively. A team of researchers interviewed a sample of about 30 users[15] of each location, using a standard list of questions. A parallel study of each site was made by a professional observer, noting landmarks, pathways and any instances of what the observer saw as success or difficulty to compare with user perceptions. Lynch, then, allows users a role in defining good city form, but also prefigures his conclusions by defining landmarks as key elements of the built environment, and drafting a set of questions which foreground such visible elements (Lynch, 1960:141–2). His first question asks interviewees what, for them, symbolizes the city[16]; possible answers could include non-visual impressions, from the sound of foghorns to the surface of cobble-stones, the taste of a particular local food or the smell of drains. But Lynch adds a rider to the question accentuating the city's form, so that the interviewee is led from the outset to name the landmarks Lynch has already mapped. The next question asks interviewees to draw a rough map of the area, and the third to describe routes from home to work. Most of the questions concern navigation through the city, and the final (informal) question asks 'What cities of your acquaintance have good orientation? Why?' (Lynch, 1960:142). For Lynch, in 1960, cities are made of paths and junction nodes, given identity 'not only by their own form . . .' but also by '. . . the regions they pass through, the edges they move along, and the landmarks distributed along their length' (Lynch, 1960:84) – a list which does not include people. Lynch asserts that a highly legible city '. . . would seem well formed, distinct, remarkable; it would invite the eye and the ear to greater attention . . .' (Lynch, 1960:10); but if the ear as well as the eye is intrigued, the term 'legible', like the invitation to remember landmarks, replicates the viewpoint of distance in which the visual sense is privileged and the city seen as a unity.

Whyte is concerned with how people use streets, but less for navigation than for passing time in a variety of informal ways. In his seminal *The Social Life of Small Urban Spaces* (Whyte, 1980), he arrives at a concept of 'triangulation' described as the process by which a view or a human action, such as street entertainment, links people in unplanned dialogue. He writes that the quality of a street performance is less important than its ability to bond people (Whyte, 1980:96). Whyte's studies find high levels of use in small, open but contained spaces such as Paley Park and Greenacre Park, in which the physical elements rather than entertainment provide the attraction, and use consists more of contemplation or conversation with acquaintances than of spontaneous dialogue. Both parks have most of the elements which for Whyte constitute good public space: a variety of spaces in terms of sun and shade, surface and level, running water, trees and plants, availability of refreshments, and moveable chairs and tables (Whyte, 1980:73)[17]. Whyte's method was to mount cameras on the second or third floors of buildings overlooking plazas and street corners[18]. Using time-lapse super-8 photography, a large volume of data was collected through which to plot the use of spaces – how many people, singly or in groups, for how long, occupied the space – and from this read the success of spaces in terms of levels of use (Whyte, 1980:102–111). There is a possible anomaly here: although Whyte's work is about people's use of space, his method is that of the fixed viewpoint of linear perspective and his material is visual. Whilst this enabled him to gain insights into why some spaces were empty and others full, his conclusions pertain to city form, eventually given official status requiring developers to provide a specified quantity of public space, trees and seating, and his work goes little into the underpinning causes of patterns of sociation, tending to focus on a downtown public domain which is gendered in a way he ignores[19].

Perhaps Whyte and Lynch share what were innovative agendas in the 1970s, but have been superseded as critical frameworks from feminism, cultural studies and environmentalism reshape the discourse of urbanism. In his later work, however, Lynch grants more importance to the occupation of space as a social process. In *Good City Form* (Lynch, 1981), a summing up of his ideas, he defines a settlement as 'the spatial arrangement of persons doing things, the resulting spatial flows of persons, goods and information, and the physical features which modify space in some way significant to those actions . . .' (Lynch, 1981:48). He adds that cyclic changes and the control of space are also part of the description, though 'raids' upon the territories of 'social institutions' and 'mental life' (Lynch, 1981:48). This definition follows from a comparison of planning theory, functional theory and normative theory; these explain the methods of taking public decisions, the alignment of city form to function, and the relation of city form to structures of value. After rehearsing eight objections to any normative theory of urban design, Lynch argues for rationality[20]; he criticises the planning strategy of stating general aims against which it is hard to argue, such as good health, and then leaping as if logically to detailed decisions which may be healthy only for some recipients. His solution is a set of performance indicators in a middle range, by which good city form can be recognised: vitality, sense, fit, access and control, and two 'meta-criteria', efficiency and justice (Lynch, 1981:118). But, despite the utility of a mechanism for measuring cities against the needs of inhabitants, for Lynch, the determination of needs and the process of measurement remain professional affairs. His emphasis on spatial arrangements and flows, and interest in social institutions and mental attitudes limited to that '. . . most directly linked to that spatiotemporal distribution, and which is significant at the scale of whole settlements' (Lynch, 1981:48) objectifies cities and links his work more to histories of city form than dialogues of everyday life. When issues of reception are seen at a city-wide level, perceptions become generalised, and generalisation tends to obscure difference; yet it is difference which is the pervading condition of a city, characterising encounters in, and attachments of value to, urban spaces. Difference is what makes the feeling of certain spaces unlike each other, enabling dwellers to construct identities through the production of space in acts of occupation.

The Production of Space

If the god's eye viewpoint of the city plan is a metaphor for a position of power, and if progressive writing on urban design, which accommodates but does not grant power to dwellers, affirms this position, then urban planners and architectural or urban designers hold a position of real power to conceptualise the city and translate the concept through the work of civic institutions. The dominance of professionals over non-professionals is enhanced by the opacity of the planning process, the exclusivity of technical language and unavailability of information in an appropriate form to likely objectors. Jurgen Habermas argues that bureaucratisation does not spread power or create transparency, but increases the autonomy of professionals as experts (Habermas, 1991:233). Lefebvre, too, sees the production of space as where contending ideologies determine city form and as such a ground for struggle (as in Paris in May 1968). In *The Production of Space*, he sets out three categories for the discussion of space, which are restated in different ways a number of times in the book but retain a common terminology. The categories have been widely interpreted since (and before) the appearance of the English translation of this work in 1991[21], and are set out below.

Every society, Lefebvre argues, has a characteristic *spatial practice* which provides insight into its values. This practice, at which it arrives slowly, in a dialectic interaction[22], informs the relations of city to village and countryside, and monumental to domestic sites. It is an ordering and categorisation of spaces particular to a society's form of social organisation[23]. The spatial practice of ancient Rome, for instance, is to link the city and the country by straight roads, and allow the city to assert its centrality. Gates mark the thresholds of *urbs* and *orbis*, the city and its margins of subjected territories, and in the domestic realm the Roman house reveals a relation of private and political life, and a structure of the family (Lefebvre, 1991:245)[24]. Spatial practices under capitalism include the relation of local to global, the everyday to the symbolic, and the visible to the metaphorically invisible, so that: 'Operating-procedures attributable to the action of a power which in fact has its own location in space appear to result from a simple logic of space' (Lefebvre, 1991:289). This leads to benefit for some and exclusion for others, and often to a naturalisation of negative impacts, enabled through what Lefebvre terms the violence intrinsic to abstraction which 'manifests itself from the moment any action introduces the rational into the real, from the outside, by means of tools which strike, slice and cut' (Lefebvre, 1991:289). Whilst Lefebvre writes theoretically, accounts of gentrification linked to the symbolic economy of New York – by artist Martha Rosler and sociologist Sharon Zukin, as well as Rosalyn Deutsche – might serve as cases (Rosler, 1991; Zukin, 1989 and 1995; Deutsche, 1991a). And just as the relation of centre (city) and margin (countryside, provinces and empire) is an element in Roman spatial practice, so it is in other terms (enclave and margin) in that of late capitalism.

Lefebvre weaves his arabesque-like text around two complementary ways in which societies produce space. Firstly, through *representations of space* which are conceptual: 'the space of scientists, planners, urbanists . . . the dominant space in any society (or mode of production)' (Lefebvre, 1991:38–9), and which inscribe a pattern on the natural world through practical means such as pathways, place-names and markers[25]. And, secondly, through *representational spaces* of experience, the space which is lived rather than thought: 'hence the space of "inhabitants" and "users" . . . the dominated – and hence passively experienced – space which the imagination seeks to change and appropriate' (Lefebvre, 1991:39)[26]. These spaces of lived experience overlay those of design, are produced not so much physically as by association; they are the spaces given meaning by habitation, and tend towards non-verbal expression[27]. In Rome, for example, conceived space produces the duality of the grid of perpendicular streets, and the round arch; lived space takes the dual forms of men's authority and place in certain rooms of the house, and the repression of women's space into other, more hidden rooms, and the abyss of the cold, damp earth where seeds germinate (Lefebvre, 1991:245)[28]. Representational spaces, then, overlay physical spaces, lend them a certain feeling. Lefebvre does not see the two kinds of spatial practice as mutually exclusive, and points out that when a new economic order in Tuscany in the thirteenth century produced a new spatial ordering through linear perspective, a device soon translated into art and architectural practice, townspeople and villagers did not abandon 'the traditional emotional and religious manner' of experiencing space 'by means of an interplay between good and evil forces at war throughout the world' and in spaces of special import such as those around the body, or in the house, the church and the graveyard (Lefebvre, 1991:79). Neither are the two kinds of space put forward as produced exclusively in the psychic or somatic realms, since the conceptual space of a landscape inscribed with named places depends on physical as well as mental acts, and experiential encounters in spaces of desire involve projection of meaning[29]. But, Lefebvre argues, representations of space, which abstract or reduce the world, are dominant in capitalism.

For Lefebvre, the Italian city state is a location of a new way of representing space through perspective, to which architecture and city planning come to conform[30], and of a new economic relation in which the countryside produces, as a farm, for the town, and in which wealth is accumulated as money, the equalising medium through which all goods can be exchanged. Money is itself a representation, an abstraction like the measurement of hours by a clock or of space by regular units of distance. Capitalism is produced by this possibility of exchange and surplus, and increasingly reproduces the abstractions on which these depend. Lefebvre links capitalism also to roads, airports and information networks (Lefebvre, 1991:53 and 86). But the new economic order did not proceed only through exchange, but 'according to a model' of spatial arrangement (Lefebvre, 1991:78) through which it permeates everyday life; Lefebvre describes the new landscape of a house from which cypress-lined paths radiate to cottages, organising the land in a way 'evocative of the laws of perspective, whose fullest realisation was simultaneously appearing in the shape of the urban piazza . . .' (Lefebvre, 1991:78).

What are the implications of a dominance of representations of space, of the conceptualisation of space over experiences in space? One is the marginalisation of ordinary dwellers; another the construction in a particular way of subjectivity, of a subject gazing on an objectified world which becomes as if a fantasy. Lefebvre sees architecture as depending on visual representation, an abstraction which is implicitly if passively violent. He writes that the architect, within the spatial practice of modernity:

> . . . ensconces himself [sic] in his own space . . . bound to graphic elements – to sheets of paper, plans, elevations, sections, perspective views of facades, modules and

> so on. This *conceived* space is thought by those who make use of it to be *true*, despite the fact – or perhaps because of the fact – that it is geometrical, because it is a medium for objects, an object itself, and a locus of objectification of plans. Its distant ancestor is the linear perspective developed as clearly as the Renaissance: a fixed observer, an immobile perceptual field, a stable visual world. (Lefebvre, 1991:361)[31]

From this viewpoint, 'users' are marginalised even in language, associated, as Lefebvre points out, with the realm of things, of utility and exchange. Yet the use of space by dwellers is not confined to its utility, but is both 'concrete' and 'subjective', its origin in childhood, '. . . with its hardships, its achievements, and its lacks' (Lefebvre, 1991:362).

Edward Soja, drawing on several of Lefebvre's works including the first two (of three) volumes of his *Critique of Everyday Life* (Lefebvre, 1962 and 1992 cited in Soja, 1996:41), sees the importance of his work in, firstly, its focus on the spaces of alienation, and, secondly, its dwelling on the everyday[32]. The everyday, he argues, is where Lefebvre sees the struggle for social justice and against alienation played out, extending the work of Gramsci and the Frankfurt School by interrogating the institutional structuring of life[33]. Space matters because it is in spatial organisation and experience that social existence takes on concrete form: 'There are no aspatial social processes' (Soja, 1996:46). Soja argues that critical thinking about space is an alternative to the traditional Marxist attempt at making history[34]. Rob Shields cites Lefebvre, Benjamin and Lenin as the only commentators on the spatial dimension of capitalism, and Lefebvre's *Production of Space* as a decisive factor in the reinvention (and politicisation) of geography by Harvey (1989) and Soja (1989) (Shields, 1999:150).

But if the production of space is a location of alienation, and opens a possibility for the reaffirmation of the practices of everyday life, Lefebvre alludes several times to the representation of space as an extension of Cartesianism. This opens the question of what kind of subjectivity produces (and is produced in) modernity, and Lefebvre posits a relation between representations of space and the rational subjectivity of Cartesian dualism (Lefebvre, 1991:277). Cartesianism makes a separation between the subjectivity in which representations of space are conceived – that of the philosopher in a study, or the planner and architect in their professional office – and the objectivity thereby assigned to whatever occupies space. Ken-ichi Sasaki, in a critique of western aesthetics, links Cartesian space to visuality, citing Descartes' well-known passage from the *Discours* of 1637 in which he contrasts the merits of buildings designed by a single architect with the mess of old cities adapted by many hands. Sasaki writes: 'The essence of the Cartesian city consists in the geometrical principle which unifies and dominates the totality of the city, and which excludes all forms of contingency from its urban space' (Sasaki, 1998:44).

Lefebvre sees a contradiction when the thinker of the seventeenth century sees his role as other than work in an ordinary sense, whilst only appearing to be outside the social division of labour: 'In reality they were prisoners of the separation of manual and intellectual work' (Lefebvre, 1992:30); Descartes, he notes was an army officer. And this effort to put a mental realm above a physical realm leads to an abstraction of space in which contradictions can be falsely reduced to coherence. The cancellation of difference in the distant view of a skyline is an example of this. Lefebvre links abstract space to other media of exchange:

> It is in this space that the world of commodities is deployed, along with all it entails: accumulation and growth, calculation, planning, programming. (Lefebvre, 1991:307)

This is not to condemn abstraction, which allows critical distance, but to point to its limitation when separated from concrete reality. It is in constructing a new relation of the two that Lefebvre sees the importance of Marx and Engels: 'By refusing to leave the real world for the exile of a world beyond . . . the Critical Reason of Descartes and Kant becomes concrete, active and constructive' (Lefebvre, 1992: 142). But the space in which the architect is ensconced, of plans and drawings, constitutes a separate mental realm of abstraction, and it is this which enables a reduction of the world, or the urban fabric, to a blank ground (Lefebvre, 1991:361). Dwellers are then recoded as users. For many planners and architects of modernity, such as Robert Moses in New York (Berman, 1983), the conceptualisation of the city is (as if) real whilst the street, in which spaces are given meaning through the lives of dwellers, is (as if) unreal. The ground of the city plan or the architect's drawing is, then, a space constructed without value, whilst, outside the still air of the studio, the spaces of the street are filled with the contending values of people who live in and pass through them. Lefebvre sees the space of modernist architecture as homogenised, denying the orientations of the whole body and its senses. Any project for a post-modern spatial practice implies, then, a construction of a post-modern (post-Cartesian) subjectivity, a subject able to reflect critically on the world, yet at the same time be embedded in it.

Modernity – the Drawing of a Line

Several writers see Descartes as the founder of modernity. Claudia Brodsky Lacour writes of 'a commonplace in histories of Western philosophy and culture that the *Discours de la methode* marks the beginning of modern thought' (Lacour, 1996:18). Stephen Toulmin states that the 'chief girder in this framework of Modernity . . . was the Cartesian dichotomy' (Toulmin, 1990:108) and Wolfgang Welsch that 'modern architecture is actually Cartesianism in built form' (Welsch, 1997:109). Descartes uses the metaphor of architecture to articulate his idea of a world of mathematical certainty. His philosophy draws a line (in a way, literally) under the past, and under the impressions of the senses and knowledge gained from travel or book-learning which he distrusts. Only mathematics and geometry exist in the purity of an internally regulated system. He states, in the passage of the *Discourse* which begins with a reminiscence of his sitting in a stove-heated room (which is the passage cited by Sasaki):

> Thus one sees that buildings which a single architect has undertaken and completed are usually more beautiful and better ordered than those which several architects have attempted to rework . . . Thus these ancient cities, which having been only large villages, became great cities with the passage of time, are normally so poorly proportioned, compared with the well-ordered towns and public squares that an engineer traces on a vacant plain according to his free imaginings. (cited in Lacour, 1996:33)

The image of the engineer (or architect) drawing freely is a metaphor for the process of thinking, just as the space of the stove-heated room might act as a metaphor for the enclosure which enables and in turn characterises Cartesian subjectivity. In that enclosed space, free imagining in the form of a logical discourse is possible without reference to sense impressions or the actualities they denote[35]. Lacour writes:

> The act of architectural drawing that Descartes describes is the outlining of a form that was not one before. That form would combine reason . . . with imaginative freedom . . . It is not only new to the world, but intervenes in a space where nothing was, on a surface . . . where nothing else is. (Lacour, 1996:37)

In the twentieth century, technology and the alliance of capital with planning regulation allow fantasies of new cities to be realised, usually as enclaves within old cities, such as Canary Wharf. In Canary Wharf, histories of work and sociation generated by the industries of the London docks were obliterated, and residual industries which did not fit the glamorous image projected for the new Docklands were left out of the picture (Ghirardo, 1996:193) – a blank ground.

Descartes argues that the course of human history, as a process towards civilisation, consists of faltering steps which are insignificant compared to the 'ordinances made by God alone', and prefers the 'simple reasonings which a man of good sense can make naturally concerning things that present themselves' above the accumulated works of the natural sciences (cited in Lacour, 1996:90). Space exists only because it is sustained by divine thought; its laws are mathematical and laid down by God, and geometrical space is the sole element of nature (Lefebvre, 1991:283). Allied to such reasoning, and by implication the perfection of God's ordering of the universe, are the engineer's inscriptions of regular places. Lacour summarises:

> The proportional 'places regulières' drawn by an architect acting in complete autonomy are the manifestations of a rapid, mental continuity discontinuous with autobiographical or any human history. They are forms produced on an empty plain

> whose use is uninhibited by the remains of years and millennia that are historical memory. (Lacour, 1996:92)

So, regularly proportioned forms, in drawings or extended into plasticity, have a reality of their own. Architecture and town planning are thus fields of autonomy like modernist art. Yet abstract space, Lefebvre argues, is 'a product of violence and war', instituted by a state and institutional. It 'serves those forces which make a *tabula rasa* of whatever stands in their way . . . in short, of differences' And these forces, likened to a bulldozer or tank, 'grind down and crush everything before them' (Lefebvre, 1991:285).

Returning to Thamesmead, the functionalisation of space criticised by Robbins takes place in abstract space, as signs drawn on a blank sheet of paper. The social process which is repressed by the design, through denial of the multiple uses of the street characteristic of inner city areas and communities, takes place in, and produces, representational spaces. Marx, in 1844, called for the senses to become theoreticians in their own right (Lefebvre, 1991:400); and in 1845, in the 'Theses on Feuerbach', criticises Feuerbach for not conceiving sensuousness 'as a practical, human-sensuous activity' (Engels, n.d.:73). Lefebvre's formulation of representational spaces (of everyday life), whilst set in a dominated relation to the space of plans, opens a possibility to reclaim the value of such spaces, approached through human, sensuous activity, within a discourse of urban futures.

Notes

1. The reference is to Patrick Creagh's poem (1980) *Lament of the Border Guard*, Manchester, Carcanet: 'Railings divide nothing from nothing . . .' (p 9).
2. The allusion here is to Martin Heidegger's discussion of building and dwelling, and association of the verb to build with the noun neighbour, in 'Building, Dwelling, Thinking' in Heidegger, 1975:143–62.
3. A proposal for innovative, mixed-income housing in the Millennium Village on the south bank beside the Dome at Greenwich was diluted to the point that, in June 1999, the architects (Hunt Thompson Associates) withdrew. Although press reports emphasised disagreements over materials – steel and prefabricated concrete, or a cosmetic facing of brick – a deeper issue is the separation rather than mixing, as envisaged by the architects, of rental and owner-occupier housing. These are now separated out to enable developers to capitalise on the exclusivity of owner-occupation – see reports by Peter Hetherington and Jonathan Glancey, *The Guardian*, 30 June 1999. Comparison could be made with the dilution of diversity in the development of Battery Park City – see Deutsche, 1991a.
4. See Bird, 1993:120–35, and Ghirardo, 1996:176–94 for critical accounts of Docklands. Ghirardo sets the limit of Docklands on the south bank at Surrey Docks, a boundary since extended by the Dome at Greenwich, but still west of Thamesmead.
5. Robbins notes that a Greater London Council report of 1971 states criticism of tower blocks on social grounds – see GLC, 1971:13, cited in Robbins, 1996:206.

6. Between 1965 and 1969, the GLC allocated £150 million to provision of 26 000 dwellings. A sum above this was anticipated for Thamesmead's proposed 17 000 dwellings (GLC, 1969, cited in Robbins, 1996:286).
7. Jacobs writes of fears of 'barbarism' in city streets, but adds that 'The barbarism and the real, not imagined, insecurity that gives rise to such fears cannot be tagged a problem of the slums. The problem is most serious, in fact, in genteel-looking "quiet residential areas" . . .' (Jacobs, 1961:31). She concludes this chapter: '. . . We are the lucky possessors of a city order that makes it relatively simple to keep the peace because there are plenty of eyes on the street. But there is nothing simple about that order itself . . . [its components] unite in their joint effect upon the sidewalk, which is not specialized in the least. That is its strength' (Jacobs, 1961:54).
8. Cresswell, citing Rosalyn Deutsche, notes in his introduction Mayor Koch's efforts to evict homeless people from Grand Central station. For Koch, stations are for transportation alone. As Cresswell points out, his assertion denies that other kinds of people frequently use the station as a place to meet, eat oysters, buy flowers or study architecture, but these are not deviant uses because the users are middle class not homeless people. Cresswell links homelessness to the kinds of urban development taking place in New York, and continues: 'By divorcing the homeless issue from a wider context and referring instead to a single place, [Koch] removes the issue from the realm of the social and the political and simply asserts the out-of-place nature of homelessness. Indeed nothing could seem more natural. . . . Here geography and ideology intersect' (Cresswell, 1996:5).
9. Monica Degen, in a paper to the Sociology, Environment and Architecture working group of the British Sociological Association, at the University of Westminster, 19 June 1999, observed that in recent development in Barcelona, new apartment blocks were without the balconies on which people hang out washing and bird-cages in more traditional streets of the city; she saw this as a form of aestheticisation conforming to notions of a northern European city. The city's new identity is thus moulded by design in conformity with wider (dominant) cultural patterns, and contradicts acts of occupation which previously gave the city an aspect of its spatial character and, for many, charm. This is noted again in Chapter 8.
10. See Foucault 1977:195–228. Foucault sees the prison, which substitutes discipline for bodily torture, as indicative of an aspect of modernity in which life is increasingly institutionalised and abstracted. For example: 'Power has its principle not so much in a person as in a certain concerted distribution of bodies, surfaces, lights, gazes; in an arrangement whose internal mechanisms produce the relation in which individuals are caught up. . . . The Panopticon is a marvellous machine which, whatever use one may wish to put it to, produces homogeneous effects of power' (1977:202).
11. Ter Heide and Wijnbelt report that the training of architects leads them to interpret town and country planning as art; they are, they claim, influenced by the work of Geddes, Abercrombie and Unwin in England, and Sitte and Baumeister in Germany (Ter Heide and Wijnbelt, 1996:75).
12. Ter Heide and Wijnbelt suggest that the gap might be filled by behavioural research, market research and perception-based research including psychological studies. They also cite the activity patterns used by geographers, and the lifestyle theory of Pierre Bourdieu (Bourdieu, 1984) which compares economic (consumption-related) and cultural (knowledge-related) expressions of status. See also Cresswell, 1996:21 on Bourdieu. Ter Heide and Wijnbelt, however, restrict their own research method: their interviews and workshops involve only professionals; and the only study in which dwellers are involved is covered in one paragraph at the end of the article and concerns only a passive role in selecting one of two plans already prepared by professionals.

13. See, for examples, Lynch (1960) and Lynch (1981). The status of *The Image of the City* (1960) is suggested by its frequent reprinting, at least to the twentieth edition in 1990.
14. See Whyte, 1980.
15. Lynch admits that professional and business people are over-represented in the sample, and that this prevented understanding of a 'true "public image"' (Lynch, 1960:15)
16. 'What first comes to mind, what symbolizes the word "Boston" for you? How would you broadly describe Boston in a physical sense?' (Lynch, 1960:141).
17. Whyte notes that one of his, and the New York Urban Design Group's, proposals for amendments to the city's zoning regulations which was unpopular with local planning boards was that developers should have an option to provide spaces like Paley Park as a planning gain. The other proposals were accepted by the Board of Estimate in 1975 and incorporated in the city's zoning code in 1977 (Whyte, 1980:74). See also Whyte, 1988:132–40 on water, etc. and 1988:141–55 on the management of spaces (including provision of food and art).
18. Whyte states 'For a street corner, for example, this means a second- or third-storey perch on the other side of the street, most likely an office' (Whyte, 1980:104). His usage is North American, meaning by second storey what in England is the first floor.
19. Louise Mozingo questions Whyte's concern for men's urban experience, characterised as 'front-yard', or the experience of watching others in public spaces, rather than the more enclosed ('backyard') spaces she maintains appeal more to women (Mozingo, 1989:46).
20. 'Since decisions about the form of cities affect many people, they must at least *appear* to be explicit, and rational. More than that . . . public decisions should be rational in fact' (Lynch, 1981:107).
21. See, for examples: Massey, 1994:250–5; Harvey, 1996:272–4; Soja, 1989:numerous references; Soja, 1996:25–82 and other references.
22. 'The spatial practice of a society secretes that society's space; it propounds and presupposes it, in a dialectical interaction; it produces it slowly and surely as it masters and appropriates it. From the analytic standpoint, the spatial practice of a society is revealed through the deciphering of its space.' (Lefebvre, 1991:38). And (amongst other extensions): 'Spatial practice thus simultaneously defines: places – the relationships of local to global; the representation of that relationship; actions and signs; the trivialised spaces of everyday life; and, in opposition to these last, spaces made special by symbolic means as desirable or undesirable, benevolent or malevolent, sanctioned or forbidden to particular groups. We are . . . concerned here with . . . places of a purely political and social kind' (Lefebvre, 1991:288–9).
23. Soja glosses this as 'perceived space . . . open . . . to accurate measurement and description' (Soja, 1996:66).
24. Lefebvre references Vitruvius *Ten Books*, Book VI, chs 7–8, for a description of the Roman house.
25. '. . . traversed now by pathways and patterned by networks, natural space changes . . . practical activity writes upon nature, albeit in a scrawling hand, and that writing implies a particular representation of space. Places are marked, noted, named. Between them . . . are blank or marginal spaces' (Lefebvre, 1991:118).
26. Soja contextualises his interpretation of these three terms in Lefebvre by reference to illusions of transparency (or innocence); he uses the terms 'Spatial Practice . . . perceived space'; 'Representations of Space . . . conceived space'; and 'Spaces of Representation . . . lived space'. Soja interprets the third as 'encompassing' the others, whilst being to an extent intractable and a location of resistance (Soja, 1996:65–7).
27. Lefebvre links representational spaces to Bachelard's spaces of revery (Bachelard, 1969:xxxiv, cited in Lefebvre, 1991:121).

28. Soja writes of conceived space as 'intellectual, abstract, "cool", distanciating.' and lived spaces as 'passionate, "hot", teeming with sensual intimacies' (Soja, 1996:30). This discussion could be compared with Sennett's of hot and cool bodies in the thought of classical Greece (Sennet, 1994:40–82).
29. Lefebvre notes, though sees as restrictive, Heidegger's identification of dwelling and being, and linking of building and thinking, in *Poetry, Language, Thought* (Heidegger, 1975). Lefebvre sees nostalgia as one reason for a retention of currency in Heidegger's absolutism and use of images – the jug, the hut, the Greek temple – close to nature and thus far from modernity (Lefebvre, 1991:121–2).
30. Drawings of ideal cities in fifteenth-century Italian art are, at the same time, demonstrations of perspective systems, and new conceptualisations of city form enabled by such devices.
31. See also Lefebvre, 1996:153: 'Architects seem to have established and dogmatised an ensemble of significations . . . functionalism, formalism and structuralism. They elaborate them not from the significations perceived and lived by those who inhabit, but from their interpretation of inhabiting. It is graphic and visual, tending towards metalanguage.' Cf. remarks by Ter Heide and Wijnbelt (1996) on the intuition of designers.
32. Shields suggests that, although Lefebvre saw his work on the everyday as his major contribution to Marxism, it is his work on space which is more influential, crossing disciplinary boundaries and opposing technocratic specialisation (Shields, 1999:141).
33. See Soja, 1996:42–3 for Lefebvre's influence on the Paris uprising of 1968 and subsequent withdrawal from Parisian intellectual life. It is in the years following this that Lefebvre wrote *The Production of Space*, first published in France in 1974. During the same period (to 1970), Roland Barthes produced *Empire of Signs*. The books are vastly different, one large and meandering, the other short and consisting of a series of succinct and enigmatic narratives; yet each concerns urban space – Barthes writes, for instance, on the lack of street names and numbers in Tokyo, though he rejects that the book is about Japan rather than a statement of a 'possibility of a difference'(Barthes, 1982:33–7 and 3). See Shields, 1999:106–8 on Lefebvre's experience of May 1968 and link to Situationism.
34. See Massey, 1994:249–55 for discussion on the roles of space and time in her own and Ernesto Laclau's work. Massey argues, citing Lefebvre, that spatial practices are not a realm of stasis but implicated in the making of history.
35. Welsch argues that, for Descartes, the new city stands for the new science, and that to merely improve things from the past makes no sense: 'One had to begin from the start according to one's own order and create everything anew' (Welsch, 1997:109).

Chapter 4
Hajj Paintings in Upper Egypt

Introduction

This chapter, the first of three concerned with specific cases of decorative acts which convey identities, concerns paintings made on the external walls of houses in villages in upper Egypt to celebrate the return of the householder from the pilgrimage to Mecca (the *hajj*)[1]. Today the paintings are most often made by local artists, though the older practice of decoration by family members continues. The vocabulary varies, but generally includes a boat or aircraft, representations of the pilgrimage sites in Mecca, texts from the Koran and the date of the pilgrimage. This is a vernacular tradition dating back perhaps for a century, which has flourished in recent years as a growth in tourism has generated increased incomes, enabling more of those connected to tourism to make the great pilgrimage. The paintings are outside any mainstream of contemporary art, Egyptian or European, and would seem to constitute a case of everyday decoration. The villages, too, largely retain the vernacular of mud-brick, although tourism leads increasingly to the import of non-local technologies for houses, apartment blocks and hotels in towns, and notions of what constitutes an affluent lifestyle everywhere.

Hajj paintings are a frequently encountered sight in upper Egypt, but why in a religious culture which prohibits figurative representations of the sacred, is a sacred journey celebrated pictorially? From where are the images derived? To what extent do stylistic variations proliferate within the genre? And what, beyond the fact of a journey, is stated in these paintings – how do local (and non-local) people construct meanings in them? There are also questions about how western academics construct meanings in works for which their habitual frameworks of criticism are inadequate: when it is asked from a European perspective whether *hajj* paintings are aesthetic or functional, for instance, both terms are problematic. The advantage, however, of extending the scope of a framework is that its limitations are then exposed, and attention redirected to reflection on the assumptions underpinning it.

This chapter begins by linking the categories of the aesthetic and functional in European thought to colonial attitudes to the cultures of others. It asks if decorative acts seen by westerners as functional might support an aesthetic content. Nubian house decoration is then taken, through the account of Marian Wenzel, as a comparative context for *hajj* painting[2], which is investigated in terms of stylistic variation, the sources of imagery and the construction of meanings. Finally, the reception of the work in a traditional culture is considered, as a means to question the applicability of European categories of beauty and use, and of the characterisation of spirituality and worldliness as inner and outer realms.

The Functional and Aesthetic

The marginalisation of acts of decoration, including those in vernacular traditions and the crafts, follows from the independence, or exclusivity, of the true, good and beautiful in western thought from the useful; art allows personal experiment, expression and engagement in intellectual enquiry, whilst craft is required to demonstrate skill in the replication of objects. In the neo-classical discourse of the eighteenth century, the intellectual pleasure of contemplation is differentiated from the vulgar joys of recognition and sensation[3], and preserves as well as demonstrates the privileged status of the cognoscenti; it is this inheritance, amongst others, which conditions colonial attitudes to the visual cultures of subject peoples. Just as the privileged class in Europe, first aristocratic then bourgeois, affirmed their status through the cultivation of aesthetic knowledge, pleasure and taste, so such capacities were denied to societies elsewhere, because to accept an aesthetic sensibility on the part of subject peoples would equate their stage of development with that of European society, contradicting the rationale of colonialism as the spread of white civilisation to beings enjoying a more savage state.

African sculptures, masks, costumes, spears, bows, drums, chairs and other objects of colonial pillaging were thus grouped collectively as the utilitarian artefacts of a continent. Annie Coombes writes of a punitive raid by British soldiers on the city of Benin in 1897 and theft of a large quantity of bronzes and carved ivory belonging to the royal court, some of the ivory dating from the sixteenth century. She suggests that the influx of material denoting a high culture with its own specificities and historical progression might have changed European perceptions of Africa and its place in history, but that in fact: '. . . what the Benin example demonstrates is precisely the extent . . . [to] which such contradictory beliefs could be maintained' (Coombes, 1994:9). Coombes shows that in the emerging disciplines of ethnography and anthropology, the forms of non-European art were seen as degraded abstractions, reductions of form to schematic rendering[4].

The categorisation of African art as functional objects, however, still contained complexities. Moving, in the 1890s, to a more scientific basis, in part to raise their professional standing, and influenced by theories of evolution, ethnographic departments in museums became increasingly involved in taxonomy. Whilst national collections tended to adopt geographical categories based on the colonial map, classification by type of artefact was seen as appropriate to local museums. At the Pitt Rivers Museum in Oxford, objects from all geographical sources were grouped according to function (Coombes, 1994:118). This conveniently allowed lessons to be drawn on human progress, and African artefacts to be compared with weapons and tools from the European stone, bronze and iron ages. The categorisation of African culture as a set of functional objects, still, affirms the assumption that such objects lack aesthetic value, and are of interest to collectors and museums for the scientific knowledge they impart rather than for enjoyable contemplation.

That this assumption retained currency well into the twentieth century is suggested by Arnheim's *Art and Visual Perception: A Psychology of the Creative Eye*. Arnheim asserts that what he calls 'primitive' art is not derived from 'detached curiosity', nor from an autonomous creativity; this kind of art is 'not made to produce pleasurable illusions' but is 'a practical instrument for the important business of daily living' (Arnheim, 1960:103, cited in Faris, 1972:5). Arnheim may see everyday life as worthy of study, but does not endow its utensils with an aesthetic dimension. This is challenged by anthropologist James Faris, following research on Nuba body decoration in Sudan in the late 1960s. Faris responds to 'traditions [which] deny the "primitive" art for enjoyment or for purely aesthetic or decorative reasons' by documenting 'an artistic tradition that is chiefly motivated by aesthetic and decorative factors' (Faris, 1972:6). He shows that Nuba body art has a vocabulary and structure of regulation, for example in the ages at which certain colours can be used (Faris, 1972:40); and that, whilst it denotes social and physical status through scarification, hair style and colour[5], it has a diversity of forms showing considerable personal invention not connected to totemic powers (Faris, 1972:47–9). Faris links the aesthetic of Nuba body decoration to bodily health, seeking to establish a dimension of meaning for design in social relationship. But it seems also that the Nuba display themselves through playful, decorative practices which involve ingenuity and individuality, or free imagination.

This free imagining, and play, which is evidently a fusion of what western thought differentiates as aesthetic and functional elements in culture, is threatening to more than the categorisation of cultural objects (or their relative market values). It suggests a model of integration not unlike Lefebvre's model of an interplay between the spaces of plans and those of experience, and, since this disrupts a structure of dominance by reclaiming value for the dominated, threatens a whole structure of power. If the higher status accorded artworks, as objects of aesthetic value, compared to the merely useful products of craft[6], derives from the classical separation of the good, the true and the beautiful from the useful, then the higher status of society's institutions rests on an equally contestable footing; that it is contestable is demonstrated by the fact that the division itself, of beauty and use, is historically specific and was produced in an aristocratic society the strata of which it mirrors.

Herbert Marcuse, in his 1937 essay on 'The Affirmative Character of Culture' (Marcuse, 1972:88–133)[7], begins by asserting that no such differentiation is found in early Greek philosophy; on the contrary – 'The doctrine that all human knowledge is oriented toward practice belonged to the nucleus of ancient philosophy' (Marcuse, 1972:88)[8]. He traces a history of the division of knowledge from utility to a cause, recurrently stated in European philosophy, of perceived insecurity in the world of work and necessity. In a society in which the common good is incompatible with that of the individual[9], and the things which offer happiness are outside the control of the individual who seeks them, and when the Enlightenment promise of universal liberty is denied by the operations of capital, art offers an aesthetic land of dreams. An effort to reintegrate thought and action (or practice) is therefore revolutionary, and Marcuse writes also (in the same issue of the *Zeitschrift*) of a need for critical theory to retain an 'interest in the liberation of human beings' (Marcuse, 1972:152–3)[10]. He attributes to Aristotle the normalising notion that the distancing aspect of knowledge – a standing-back from practicality – is necessary because courses of action in the world are not always obvious and require reflection, which seems like common sense; but Aristotle states the duality of knowledge as a relation in which one aspect, pure thought, is privileged:

> He ordered them, as it were, in a hierarchy of value whose nadir is functional acquaintance with the necessities of everyday life and whose zenith is philosophical knowledge. The latter has no purpose outside itself. Rather it occurs only for its own sake and to afford men felicity. (Marcuse, 1972:88)

A hierarchic society, then, produces a superiority of the contemplative knowledges of beauty, leisure and peace over the necessary, useful and practical knowledges of business and war. Marcuse argues that the privileging of thought above other activities negates the original demand that thought be directed at practical knowledge, and that this leads to 'a development that abandons the field to the materialism of bourgeois practice' and 'appeasement of happiness' through culture (Marcuse, 1972:89).

The separation of thought from action and beauty from use has, then, an ideological basis, reflecting and consolidating a division of classes and labour. Adorno argues that the separation of work and pleasure, a related duality through which pleasure is allied to beauty and thought, follows when work becomes alienating (hence pleasureless) toil[11]. Adorno, in 'The Stars Down to Earth', cites a children's poem as evidence of the normalisation of the split:

> Work while you work, play while you play.
> This is the way to be cheerful and gay. (Adorno, 1994:71)

The unquestioned demarkation of work and leisure in the astrology column of the *Los Angeles Times* provides his evidence that everyday things are imbued with ideology[12]. Play thus becomes a compensatory activity remote from practical solutions to the contradictions of society. Similarly, Marcuse argues that the separation of knowledge from practice results, in the bourgeois epoch, in the idealisation of 'the world of the true, the good, and the beautiful' (Marcuse, 1968:90) and segregation from everyday life of a mental and spiritual world as an independent realm of value (Marcuse, 1972:95). From the value structure out of which bourgeois society fashioned its privileging of the aesthetic, as denoting status but, more to the point, offering a realm of escapism through which the misery of alienation might be compensated but not ended, came also the relegation of craft, and the cultures of other societies, to a secondary level. From it also came a polarised vocabulary of cultural evaluation, separating the aesthetic and social as end-points on an axis; what is interesting, then, is to see how such a polarity defeats the appropriate understanding of a phenomenon such as house decoration, which is both at once. And when the framework defeats insight into the object of its scrutiny, it is the framework itself which crumples.

House Painting in Nubia

The case of Nuba body art reveals that a tradition of a kind hitherto regarded as purely functional is, in a more careful analysis, both functional (in that display of the body has a social purpose) and aesthetic (in that the forms of decoration are freely determined within a given vocabulary), simultaneously and without contradiction. Neither term, of course, could be translated as such into the Nuba language. House decoration, too, could be seen as having a social function, but its ingenuity and diversity of style suggests it also has an aesthetic aspect. House decoration in Sudanese Nubia, north and south of the town of Wadi Halfa, flourished in the 1940s and 1950s. The walls of the mud-brick houses were painted, sculpted in low relief, and decorated with ceramic saucers pressed into the mud[13]. The walls, like those of Egyptian houses discussed below, consist of a core of bricks made from earth, dung and pulverised chaff and dried in the sun[14], and a surface layer of fine mud and sand plaster on which the decoration is applied. The surface layer weathers and cracks, requiring replacement every few years, so the decoration is not permanent. House decoration in Nubia was applied to exterior and interior walls, the latter being either painted or decorated with pages from magazines, drawings and saucers (Wenzel, 1972:43–4). The tradition ended when the local population was deported, mainly to the remote town of Khashm el-Girba, east of Khartoum[15], following construction of the Aswan High Dam and flooding of many villages in 1964. At this point it was documented by art historian Marian Wenzel[16], who notes some examples of *hajj* painting and house decoration in Egyptian Nubia. Egyptian architect Hassan Fathy, whose work in mud-brick forms the basis for the following chapter, also saw examples of house decoration on a visit to Aswan in 1941 (Fathy, 1989:6)[17].

In Egyptian Nubia, Wenzel records, most decoration was done by builders or women in the family of the house-owner, but, in Sudanese Nubia, by (male) plasterers working as assistants to the builder, who became locally known for their artistic skills. She lists the work of 44 decorators, though not all were still working by 1964, nine of whom were interviewed (Wenzel, 1972:177–92). Some artists were active as long ago as the 1920s, though still working in the 1960s; at least one had also been a labourer on archaeological sites, and another a railway worker and bus conductor, and many had other sources of income as builders, plasterers, carpenters or tin-cutters. Nubian house decoration has a wide vocabulary of motifs, both geometric and representational, denoting the personal styles of artists. Where most of the decoration is in relief, geometry predominates, with repeated rows of a dog-tooth pattern in white interspersed with circles, some including a star or star set within a circular moon, some being formed by saucers. The distinction between figuration and abstraction does not easily apply, when some images are themselves geometrical, notably the crescent moon (ubiquitous in Muslim countries above the domes of mosques). But mud relief ornament is not devoid of representations of the natural world, such as lions, birds and crocodiles. Other images include a schematic water wheel between two trees (Wenzel, 1972: colour plate 10), cars and occasional human figures. When decoration is painted, using a broad range of colours in ordinary house paint bought in markets and towns, plants and flowers appear alongside geometric patterns and animals. Whilst there is a common vocabulary, it is possible to trace the styles of individual artists, their development over time and the influence of one artist on another[18]. Some local explanations of imagery are available; a lion carrying a sword, for example, may denote Farouk, King of Egypt and the Sudan in the 1940s. The lion motif seems to have been introduced from Egypt by the artist Ahmad Batoul, who used red glass for eyes and bits of porcelain for teeth, and worked from images in newspapers (Wenzel, 1972:110–1). Wenzel records that a rival of Batoul's, Jabir Bab al-Kheir, painted a lion with a gun as a sign of superiority, then images of men shooting lions and crocodiles. (Wenzel, 1972:110–1). She also notes that the lion with sword stands, in Shia imagery, for Ali Ibn Abi Taub, the cousin of the Prophet and husband of the Prophet's daughter Fatima. The Nubians are not Shia, but the image of Ali is widespread in prints sold in markets. Wenzel records that there was some confusion amongst local people as to the meaning of the lion, some taking it to represent Arab hero Antar, others King Farouk, and others the British lion (Wenzel, 1972:161). Further motifs were derived from material culture; the circles, for instance, may replicate on exterior walls the effect of rows of basket-lids used to decorate house interiors (Wenzel, 1972:28).

One plate, illustrated by Wenzel and set above a house doorway, appears to date from the late nineteenth century, depicting a white lady with a flowery hat and ribbons. Some elements of this material culture, then, were colonial cast-offs. Allick Potter, professor of architecture at Khartoum University from 1957, describes a meeting with Wenzel in Khartoum; during their conversation she describes the work of Hasan Arabi and divides his interior decoration into two phases – the first of geometric shapes and long-legged birds, close to his exterior relief decoration; the second resembling European art deco in its use of superimposed cones, rays and

Figure 4.1 Hajj *painting, Luxor, 1997 (photo M Miles)*

Figure 4.2 *Exterior of a bakery, Luxor market street, 1997 (photo M Miles)*

bands of colour. This she traces to the imagery of Huntley and Palmer Christmas biscuit tins, of the kind cooks in Cairo might send home once the tins were discarded by their white purchasers[19]. Such designs were produced for tins until 1940, whilst Arabi's art deco style dates from 1943 onwards, but Wenzel takes this as an appropriate time-lag for the tins to filter through to Nubian villages (Wenzel, 1972:150; Potter, 1984:175–7). Wenzel shows a sketch of a biscuit tin, and graphic images from Egyptian and French newspapers showing a cinematic projector and camera, plus an art deco style advertisement for ties from an Egyptian paper of 1935, all of which have visual similarities with motifs used by Arabi in the 1940s[20]. She argues that in the 1950s newspaper and magazine imagery replaced that of tins, at which point images of cars appear (Wenzel, 1972:151, fig.44a and h). What emerges is that, whilst some images, such as wild animals, relate to local folk lore (Wenzel, 1972:159) and others derive from material culture, yet others are free adaptations of visual sources from the worlds of the town and colonial power incorporated into local culture, where they take on new, more playful, meanings.

HAJJ PAINTING

In the villages of upper Egypt, along the Nile from Luxor to Esna and Aswan, a tradition of *hajj* paintings goes back to at least the 1920s, and is thus contemporary with house decoration in Nubia. The tradition continues today, independently of tourism[21]. Some of the most exuberant cases are found in Gourna, near the Valley of the Kings, although a few can be seen in Luxor, in the small streets leading off the market (Figure 4.1), and on the Corniche[22], and in Karnak. In towns, *hajj* imagery tends to be small-scale, or incorporated with other signs, for example on the facade of a baker's shop (Figure 4.2), whilst in villages it frequently occupies the whole front of a house. But then, many town dwellers do not live in houses but in apartments. *Hajj* painting differs from Nubian house decoration (for which there is no equivalent in Egypt beyond the painting of an exterior wall in blue or yellow[23]) in having a specific subject-matter – the pilgrimage to Mecca which is the fifth pillar of Islam and culmination of a life of faith. On return from Mecca, the *hajji* (or *hajja*) sees his (or her) house decorated as a mark of celebration and new status[24], the decoration being an element of the festivities, not a permanent monument. Winifred Blackman, in an account of travels in upper Egypt published in 1927, recalls that:

> The house-doors are often decorated with a china plate or saucer fixed into the masonry above the lintel, as a charm against the evil eye. A house may also be decorated with coloured line-drawings of camels, boats, trains, trees, and other objects, some hardly identifiable. Such artistic effort denotes that one or more members of the family . . . have performed the pilgrimage to Mecca, the design representing the various objects seen by the pilgrim on his way . . . (Blackman, 1927:30)[25]

Parker and Neal claim the custom of *hajj* painting 'was established well over a century ago', citing a source of 1878[26]. Examples more than a decade old, however, seldom survive, given the regular replastering of walls which obliterates previous decoration. The cost of the paintings, whilst significant in terms of the local economy, is modest when compared to that of making the journey to Mecca, today usually by air, and staying for several days in the sacred sites whilst providing for a family at home[27]. The cost of decoration varies, but is something around the price of ten chickens[28]. Wenzel records the practice as carried out by women (Wenzel, 1972:47), and *hajj* paintings are still sometimes done by family members, in which case the only expense is that of the paints, but most are now made by professional (male) artists. But because the pilgrimage takes place at a fixed time each year, the work is seasonal and does not constitute a permanent living; most painters therefore earn money from other sources including work in the tourist industry, whilst some are teachers[29].

The paintings are usually made with industrially produced paint bought in towns, in a full range of colours, and include a mix of text and imagery – the date of the journey, Koranic verses, and images such as a camel, a boat or, more often now, an aircraft, the minarets of the mosque at Mecca, and the *Ka'bah* covered with the *kiswa*, or robe of black cloth embroidered with a band of Koranic verses and made new each year – arranged in a narrative from right to left. On two-storey houses there may be two layers of narrative, one above the other. Wenzel describes a narrow range of images in a style of blue and white line drawings[30], and until perhaps the 1980s *hajj* paintings retained a limited vocabulary. Many, in villages south of Qurna, and in New Qurna, are still painted in a simple, linear way, though not in blue and white[31], but in Gourna, most of the more recent decorations use broad planes of colour and a more flamboyant technique. Many can be attributed to named artists, whose visual language is distinct. *Hajj* painting seems, then, to have become a specialist profession, as increased wealth derived from tourism has enabled more local people to make the pilgrimage and commission an artist to decorate their house.

As the frequency of occurrence has increased, so the imagery of *hajj* painting has become more complex. In Gourna, several one- or two-storey houses are used as alabaster workshops with living space for an extended family above or behind; these houses are often quite large and built in concrete rather than mud, and are painted with *hajj* and other images on pink, white, yellow or blue grounds to advertise their craft in a competitive market (mainly for identical products, since little working of alabaster is now done on site and most of the goods on sale are plaster replicas of museum objects). The workshops are family businesses, and family members may carry out several tasks including making and selling objects, or acting as guides, according to demand. Some have been trained at the Decorative Secondary School in Luxor (see below), and others taught within the family. In some cases the workshop facade is decorated by a member of the family who shows particular skill in painting; in others, a painter is employed. Two artists, Ahmed

Figure 4.3 Alabaster workshop, Gourna, 1997 (photo M Miles)

Figure 4.4 Luxor, exterior of a fruit and vegetable shop, 1997 (photo M Miles)

el-Tauib Mohmed el-Naggar and Mohammed Ahmed el-Malk have painted several such workshops, covering the whole facade, during the 1990s. El-Tauib places images of lions and figures of women carrying water jars on their heads alongside those of the *hajj*, whilst el-Malk introduces scenes of music and dancing, with borders of flowers and garlands (Parker and Neal, 1995:143). The vocabularies are not dissimilar, though each artist has a personal style, el-Tauib using saturated colours and precise drawing on a plain ground, whilst el-Malk places more softly drawn figures within pale green and blue landscapes with horizons. Apart from working as a painter, el-Tauib is employed making archaeological drawings, which relates to the precision of his style (Parker and Neal, 1995:147). In one case (Figure 4.3), he has placed images of an aircraft and the Ka'bah alongside and above women carrying water jars and dancing figures; each secular image is framed by a border, and a winged solar icon, the sign of Horus, is placed over the door, in the position it might occupy in a temple court. A figure in the white costume of the pilgrim and holding a green umbrella stands to the left of the door. In an enclosure to the side, where younger members of the family demonstrate alabaster working, he has painted a lion and a man in blue jeans ploughing with oxen.

The workshops are a particular case within *hajj* painting. The presence of pharaonic images, not confined to el-Tauib's work, may be significant: the villagers of Gourna, many of whose houses are built above tombs, have for generations made a living from copying such images and guiding people around sites; this has given them a familiarity with a figurative tradition within a wider culture in which there is a prohibition, as in Judaism, of sacred imagery. Whilst the prohibition does not apply to decorative motifs derived from natural forms, like the flowers in Iznik tiles used in mosques, geometric design predominates in the decoration of mosques. On the other hand, the painted trucks of Afghanistan, and the pictorial towels, rugs and calendars sold in markets throughout the Islamic world, denote a popular culture replete with figuration. Shop facades, too, are often decorated. A fruit and vegetable shop, for instance, may be advertised by paintings of trees and flowers, and even display some words in English, as an example from Luxor shows (Figure 4.4).

The skill of painting has a wide market, then, though *hajj* painting is becoming a specialism within it through which certain artists have made personal reputations. Some of them were trained in art techniques at secondary school level or beyond, and have in turn passed on their skills to others. At least one house painter – Hassan el-Shark – has since become an artist exhibiting in galleries in Cairo and Europe (Abdel-Messih, 1994)[32]. The development of *hajj* painting as a specialist profession (with appropriate fees) makes it distinct from local crafts, such as the cutting of horse hair to create intricate geometric designs (Figure 4.5), or pottery, which is largely undecorated earthenware. The potter's skill is passed on through the male lineage within families of potters, but the tuition involved in painting tends increasingly to be within an institution, and to involve a dimension of invention as well as the tacit knowledge of making, from which it derives a higher

Figure 4.5 *Luxor, decorative cutting of horse hair, 1997 (photo M Miles)*

Figure 4.6 *Luxor, the Decorative Secondary School, 1997 (photo M Miles)*

status. The Decorative Secondary School in Luxor, on the market street, teaches painting alongside carpentry, marquetry, leatherwork and other crafts, to children of secondary school age (Figure 4.6). The models of art employed seem, from the evidence of large paintings on board in the courtyard, to include western, figurative imagery. Perhaps the notion of the artist's status has been imported along with European notions of art; yet Egyptian society has its own social hierarchies, based not least on education. The school is one of several specialist institutions within an extensive state education system, others being a Hotel Secondary School for boys and a Commercial Services Secondary School for girls in Luxor, and a Secondary Technical School at Esna.

The non-traditional sources of imagery available to house painters today include advertisements using a modernised script[33], and modern art seen in books. Ahmed Mahmoud el-Senosy has taught at Esna and, exceptionally for a *hajj* painter, graduated (in 1971) from the School of Fine Arts in Cairo; he cites Picasso and Matisse amongst his influences and comes from a family which includes another painter and a sister who teaches music (Parker and Neal, 1995:137–41)[34]. His style uses flat planes of colour and interlocking curvilinear shapes, and personal motifs such as a dove (representing peace) and a water jar, as well as traditional images. His technique differs, too, in using oil-based paints on a prepared surface. Senosy uses preparatory drawings on paper, as does el-Tauib (who studied under Senosy at the Secondary Technical School at Esna), and both begin by applying a white ground to give their colours maximum luminosity. Senosy works in Esna, but has influenced el-Tauib's work in Qurna, particularly in the latter's use of precise, flowing line and planes of strong colour; an example is a house painted with a blue ground in 1996. Again, a man in the pilgrim's white costume holds a green umbrella, standing before the Ka'bah (Figure 4.7); other images on the facade include an aircraft, a boat and dancing figures (Figure 4.8)[35]. The decoration continues inside the house with figures and garlands in the same style, again on a blue ground, and represents the current stage in the development of *hajj* painting, differing from earlier cases in the extent to which the whole building becomes a ground for imagery, and in the distinctiveness of an individual style. This follows increased prosperity on the part of clients and mobility on the part of artists in Gourna.

The Reception of *Hajj* Painting

If a proliferation of styles, widening range of sources and establishment of personal reputations affirms the increasingly professional status of *hajj* painters in upper Egypt, questions remain as to how such imagery is received. This depends on the social and cultural background – local, city or tourist – of the observer. To a tourist, the pictures may signify local colour within expectations of the exotic. They make the workshops more visible, but few tourists walk around village streets, and most

Figure 4.7 *Gourna, detail of house facade with* hajj *painting, 1997 (photo M Miles)*

Figure 4.8 *Gourna, house facade with* hajj *painting, 1997 (photo M Miles)*

will never see the simpler pictures in villages south of Luxor and Gourna, or in New Gourna; nor, for the most part, do they recognise the structures of style, invention and professional reputation which characterise the recent development of *hajj* painting along lines found in equivalent structures in the art of the affluent world (with the exception that no galleries, dealers or critics are involved).

Egyptian villages have settled, conservative patterns of spatial organisation based on family structures (Fathy, 1989:54–8), and their inhabitants participate in a collective religious identity. For villagers, who are participants in rather than observers of the work, the depiction of the pilgrimage, with whatever elaboration, is part of a shared as well as dominant culture; and in a village society of extended families[36], the narrative may be understood through personal contact with either the *hajji* (or *hajja*) or the painter. The feast which welcomes back the pilgrim will be a semi-public affair, and the painting is another element of that celebration, and the paintings remain for a few years to remind other villagers of the pilgrim's status, derived from both devotion and wealth. The paintings, then, have a function of denoting individual identity in village life, and are collectively elements in a wider cultural identity for village society. They also offer employment to artists. Around Luxor, this employment is contextualised by tourism (which provides the money but not the subject-matter), and by past efforts, including those of Fathy in the 1940s, to encourage craftwork as an alternative livelihood to tomb-robbing[37], in effect to subsume villagers' livelihoods to a more regulated lifestyle.

For city people, village traditions may seem unsophisticated, or what they have left behind in a search for employment in Cairo[38]. Yet the community of believing Muslims – the *umma* – is '. . . a powerful force for unity, bringing together rural and urban . . . into the brotherhood of Islam'. (Fluehr-Lobban, 1990:17); Farha Ghannam emphasises the importance of the shared space of the mosque for people relocated to new settlements in Cairo:

> Religion, rather than nationalism, neighbourhood and the village of origin, became a powerful discourse in articulating and socially grounding the various identities of different groups . . . all find commonality in religion that is expressed in practices such as a dress code and the decoration of houses and shops. (Ghannam, 1997:129–30)

Being part of a collectivity was stated, especially by women, as a reason for going to the mosque, where people of all levels are integrated in a common faith and practice of everyday life. In the village that practice includes *hajj* painting.

The relation of *hajj* painting to a national identity as promoted by state culture seems less clear. Today, the national style in architecture, as in the new Nile Bridge south of Luxor, guarded by granite figures of Horus, and several granite-faced railway stations, is Pharaonic not Arabist, and built to last. There was, however, a link between vernacular as well as Pharaonic art in the construction of a national culture preceding and after the 1952 revolution. In the 1940s and 1950s, a school of folk realist artists rose to national prominence, using folk subjects to express an

Egyptian character not moulded by the colonial powers or European culture of the ruling class. Amongst them was Abd al-Hadi al-Jazzar (Karnouk, 1988:47–57), whose work reflects his childhood in the medieval streets of Cairo through a social realism imbued with myth[39]. Hassan el-Shark, who began as a *hajj* painter, continues in this tradition (Abdel-Messih, 1994). But for the most part, *hajj* painting is part of village life and travels to towns or to Cairo with immigrant populations.

The public for *hajj* paintings, then, is the pilgrim, his or her family and other villagers; the street is a well-used, though gendered, social space, especially early and late in the day. It extends for men into the front rooms of houses, where they (and foreigners invited in) engage in conversation, watch television and drink tea. The paintings have a function in stating identity, but identity is a complex intellectual process, not a simple utility. They also offer pleasure, and part of this is in the particularities of style and invention. Wenzel associates a rise in the status of Sudanese house painters with 'a predisposition of the local inhabitants towards art' (Wenzel, 1972:47)[40], and there is no reason to think Egyptian Nubians today less open to such enjoyment than Sudanese Nubians then. To deny villagers such pleasures, or to see them restricted in scope to an unsophisticated delight in bright colours, would in any case be to divide the images from their meaning just as nineteenth-century collectors and ethnologists categorised African art as a set of utensils for domestic or ritual purposes. The paintings are celebratory acts; a European analysis of them in terms of function and aesthetic quality, or use and beauty, breaks down, just as it does for popular culture in the affluent world. These images are both aesthetic and functional, their religious and social meanings indivisible from their forms and from everyday life. The inclusion of images from other traditions and cultures, such as the Pharaonic, is based equally in everyday life, in that, for the villagers of Gourna, the tombs are part of it, in fact are for many its economic basis. But could a similar analysis not be applied to Centenary Square in Birmingham? Its function is to denote the city's cultural identity and status, and its design is taken as aesthetically pleasing and derived from a wider culture. The difference, perhaps, is that the recoding of Birmingham as a cultural city is imposed from above, popular adoption of its monuments taking the resistant form of names such as the 'fluzie in the jacuzzi', whilst house decoration is an art dependent on popular demand. And if Birmingham's reinvention aestheticises the city centre as a realm of cultural value, the street in which *hajj* paintings are made is a realm of dwelling which is not aestheticised, but given an added layer of meaning.

Notes

1. The author made visits to villages near Luxor in 1997, particularly Qurna and New Qurna.
2. Another possible comparative case is house decoration amongst the Ndebele in South Africa. This is a recent tradition, its motifs derived from beadwork and weaving, using

mainly geometric motifs but also images from the encroachment of affluent technologies, such as cars and light bulbs. See Schneider, 1985; and Courtney-Clarke, 1986. The popularity of Ndebele decoration outside South Africa is illustrated by, for example, an exhibition in Auckland Art Gallery, New Zealand, at which visitors were invited to 'Experience first hand the colour and culture of the Ndebele as four African artists bring a decorative mural to life', and by a visit to the Ndebele territory by fashion designer Kaffe Fassett reported in the travel section of a newspaper (*The Guardian*, 1 May 1999).

3. See Joshua Reynolds' 'Discourse III': '. . . The wish of the genuine painter must be more extensive: instead of endeavouring to amuse mankind with the minute neatness of his imitation, he must endeavour to improve them by the grandeur of his ideas; instead of seeking praise, by deceiving the superficial sense of the spectator, he must strive for fame, by captivating the imagination' (cited in Eitner, 1971:37).
4. See Coombes, 1994:48–51. Coombes illustrates her argument with drawings made as an experiment by Henry Balfour, to show that continuous copying of a realistic image leads to its debasement and illegibility; and with a plate from Augustus Lane-Fox Pitt Rivers (1907) *The Evolution of Culture and Other Essays*, showing the deterioration of ornamental paddles in New Ireland from figuration to abstraction. Balfour also proposed that an absence of two-dimensional art in Africa represented a lower sensibility, on the grounds that 'We know that solid shapes appeal more readily to the lowly cultured mind . . .' (Balfour, H (1894) 'Evolution in Decorative Art', *Journal of the Society of Arts*, vol XLII, 27 April, pp 455–71, cited in Coombes, 1994:52). Coombes cites Gottfried Semper's theories on the origin of architecture in the material culture of weaving, in which the natural variations of woven matting are reproduced and elaborated in woven cloth, as an antidote to the degenerationist approach (Coombes, 1994:49, and see note 19, pp 232–3 for sources on Semper).
5. For example, youths of a certain age can use red ochre, orange, grey and blue, the latter purchased from Arab merchants; at the next level of progression to maturity is marked by a change of hair style and access to rich yellow pigment for body decoration. Rich black is available after a further two years (Faris, 1972:40).
6. For a summary of prejudices against craft knowledge, see Dormer, 1994:8.
7. The essay was first published in the *Zeitschrift für Sozialforschung*. The Institute for Social Research moved in 1934 from Germany to Columbia University, New York. Marcuse taught in Geneva during 1933–34, then joined Adorno and Horkheimer in New York in 1935; he states that the essay, in volume VI, was prompted by remarks by Horkheimer on modern culture's false idealism in the previous volume of the *Zeitschrift* (1936) p 219. (Marcuse, 1972:277, note 1).
8. Marcuse takes this as given, supposing an original unity of theory and practice, for which the beautiful and the useful might be seen as a metaphor, as a ground for their reintegration in his efforts to reconstruct Marxism in face of the rise of fascism in Germany. Marcuse studied with Heidegger at Freiburg between 1928 and 1932, and the proposed reintegration, introducing the sensual aspect of daily life to social theory, is perhaps a response to the predominance of ontology in Heidegger's thought; it responds, also, to Lukacs' *Geschicte und Klassenbewusstsein* [History and Class Consciousness]. Katz writes: 'The dualisms of both academic philosophy and vulgar Marxism, which had in effect removed man [sic] from the world of objects and experience and this limited his power over it, were explicitly attacked throughout *History and Class Consciousness* . . .' (Katz, 1982:62).
9. See also Horkheimer on Kant: 'The idealist tradition linked with Kant elaborated the meshing of autonomous reason and empirical individualism'. Horkheimer notes Fichte, and continues: 'The eternal Ought . . . originates in the depths of subjectivity. The medium of philosophy remains that of self-consciousness. But Hegel liberated this self-

consciousness from the fetters of introspection and shifted the question . . . to the work of history . . .' (Horkheimer, 1991:2).

10. From 'Philosophy and Critical Theory' (1937), in Marcuse, 1972:134–58. McCarthy notes Marcuse's insistence on the transcendant aspect of theory, as its ability to see beyond circumstance to transformation. Marcuse, cited by McCarthy, continues that critical theory's interest in liberation 'binds it to certain ancient truths . . . universal propositions whose progressive impetus derives precisely from their universality' (Hoy and McCarthy, 1994:20). The link between critical theory and liberation can be seen alongside critical theory's other central concern, to be critical of its own assumptions.
11. Work is pleasurable when it is not alienating. French utopian socialist Charles Fourier, whose ideas were influential on the painter Gustave Courbet in the 1850s, posits a libidinisation of work, on which Marcuse writes in *Eros and Civilisation*: 'the possibility of "attractive labour" . . . derives above all from the release of all libidinal forces . . . pleasurable co-operation' (Marcuse, 1956:217).
12. Adorno also sees astrology as a 'feeding on paranoid dispositions . . . a symptom of regression of society as a whole . . . a recurrence of the unconscious, steered for purposes of social control which is finally irrational itself' (Adorno, 1994:123).
13. Wenzel states that mud relief ornamenting began in c.1927 (Wenzel, 1972:25); but lists sources which document the use of saucers in house decoration in Nubia since the late nineteenth century: in particular, '. . . the omda of Dehmit in Egyptian Nubia, is quoted as saying that saucers were introduced into his region by Nubian servants working in hotels and European houses, from about 1895" (Blackman, 1910:29, cited in Wenzel, 1972:199, n30).
14. For a general account of mud-brick building, see Denyer, 1978:92–5. She records: 'In the far west of the Sudan zone [meaning Mali and Mauritania] sun-dried bricks were made using wooden shutters. The bricks were cemented into place with more mud and the outsides of the walls were plastered over with a mud mixture' (1978:93).
15. Wenzel states that Egyptians displaced by Lake Nasser were moved to Kom Ombo, between Luxor and Aswan. This could suggest a link between the Nubian and Egyptian practices, if any of the painters continued working in their new location, expanding or being absorbed into a local tradition (Wenzel, 1972:10, map).
16. Wenzel made two visits to Sudan in 1964 under the auspices of the Sudan Research Unit at the University of Khartoum. She records that local people had already begun to discard external decoration by the late 1950s: 'The custom of making painted or relief decoration outside the house is becoming old, and people are now satisfied with decoration inside the house only' (anon. source cited in Wenzel, 1972:175).
17. Fathy records that the provincial architecture of Aswan lacked interest, but that on going to Gharb Aswan (on the west bank) he found '. . . a whole village of spacious, lovely, clean, and harmonious houses each more beautiful than the next. There was nothing else like it in Egypt; a village from some dream country . . . each house decorated individually and exquisitely around the doorway with claustrawork – mouldings and tracery in mud' (Fathy, 1973:6). Fathy illustrates his book with two photographs (plates 1 and 2) of houses in Dahmit, Nubia, each richly decorated with circle and triangle motifs in low relief.
18. Wenzel notes that Dawud Osman worked as assistant to Hasan Arabi on a facade in 1942, and produced decoration of his own but resembling it on another house the same year; and that Abdu Batoul made a lion motif in imitation of those by his brother Ahmad Batoul (Wenzel, 1972:138–9 and 111 respectively). She also cites the work of Arabi as a case of a recognisable and sustained style: 'Hasan Arabi's facade formula allowed for variation within a set arrangement, resulting in an overall impression of

similarity . . . The invariable features were, first, the lengths and placement of three pairs of columns . . .' (Wenzel, 1972:128).

19. Wenzel's own account does not differ from Potter's recollection of their conversation – see Wenzel, 1972:147–50).
20. Wenzel correlates motifs by Arabi with various art deco motifs, but also with biscuit tins in more traditional designs showing flowers within geometric borders. She recalls Arabi himself saying she might look at biscuit tins, and at Egyptian towels of the 1930s (which she considers would not have survived by the time of her research) (Wenzel, 1972:146–51).
21. Although tourism is the area's main industry, the writer found no evidence that local guides attempted to show the paintings to tourists, or thought they would be interested. Guide books seldom mention *hajj* painting, and then only in passing. At the same time, there was no resistance to showing them, and house owners were usually pleased to see their decorated houses admired by a white person.
22. Rashid Bahaga went to Mecca in 1996 at a cost of around LE2000. He works at the airport, and made the painting himself on his return, on the facade above a small cafe and tourist shop owned by his family, who also have a house in a village a few miles away. He is one of seven brothers (conversation with Rashid's brother, May 1997).
23. Responses to the author's question 'Why do people paint their houses blue?' tended to be of the kind 'Because they like it'. Other explanations favoured by westerners include to keep off the evil eye and to keep off insects. Denyer links the use of potash and mimosa mixed into mud plaster to wealth (Denyer, 1978:93). Wenzel suggests that women painting houses in northern Sudan used washing blue, whilst men (who control money) bought paints in the market. She cites enjoyment as a motive: 'He decided to decorate his house because he felt like doing so, and because he enjoyed colour and wanted to have it around' (Wenzel, 1972:53), which suggests that 'because they like it' might be a correct answer.
24. In 1980, the researcher saw local people running towards an aircraft to touch the garments (white) of a returning *hajji* at Luxor. Europeans were asked to wait at one side while this happened.
25. Wenzel cites this page in W S Blackman (1927) (Wenzel, 1972:200, note 7), and Blackman (1910) as noting saucers used as decoration since 1895 in Sudanese Nubia (Wenzel, 1972:199, note 30). The mention of trains, an image seldom seen today, may relate to the Hejaz railway which, until destroyed by Arab volunteers under British command in the 1914–18 war, was the principle means of travel to Mecca. This is supported by a reference in Parker and Neal (1995) to an account by E Ludwig in the 1930s, which refers to 'the curious old-fashioned [train] their father took on his pilgrimage . . .' (Parker and Neal, 1995:8). Blackman (1927) also includes a photograph of a tomb of a sheikh decorated with line drawings including a figure on a camel, geometric designs and calligraphy (Blackman, 1927:85, fig.39).
26. Parker and Neal cite G Ebers (1878) *Egypt: Descriptive, Historical, and Picturesque*: 'Over many of the doors we see some modest decoration . . . a painted picture of a camel or steam-boat on which the master of the house performed his pilgrimage to Mecca across the desert and Red Sea' (Parker and Neal, 1995:8).
27. The *hajj*, which is open to women as well as men providing women from more than three miles distance from Mecca are accompanied by their husbands or other (sinless) companions, involves a series of rites lasting several days. The costs of a pilgrimage quoted to the writer in 1997 ranged from LE2000 to LE5000. One of eight conditions for the undertaking of the *hajj* is that the pilgrim has the necessary means to both make the journey and provide for the subsistence of a household. This money must be

legitimately gained. For a detailed account of the rites and associated religious law see 'Performing the *Hajj*', www.ummah.org.uk/hajj.

28. In 1997, the author found the most frequently quoted figure for painting a house exterior was LE100, equivalent to about £20 or $32. For comparison, a field labourer might earn LE10 a day, and a chicken cost LE10–12 in the market at Luxor (conversation with Hamed, a carriage driver, Luxor, May 1997). Parker and Neal report that the cost of a painting can vary according to the wealth of the family commissioning it, but that the average charge (up to 1995) is equivalent to two days' work, though this presumably means in some station above field labour, which is the lowest-paid occupation (Parker and Neal, 1995:27). Wenzel records that Hasan Arabi, one of the most accomplished house painters in Nubia, was paid £3 to decorate a whole house, which took five days, equivalent to two weeks' wages for a servant in a white household (Wenzel, 1972:146).
29. Amongst the artists on whom Parker and Neal comment individually, Ahmed Hassan Farahot is a teacher in El Shurufa; Ahmed Mahmoud el-Senosy is a teacher; Ahmed el-Tauib el-Naggar, from Qurna and a previous student of Senosy, is a full-time artist, but undertakes calligraphy, bus and truck decoration, and other similar work in times of the year there is no call for *hajj* painting; and Ali Eid Yasean of Silwa Bahari, between Luxor and Aswan, also works full-time as a painter, having previously been an employee of the telephone company (Parker and Neal, 1995:129–58).
30. Wenzel writes: 'It was thought propitious for the returning pilgrim to gaze upon the colours of blue and white, representing purity, as he re-entered his house, and its doorway surround was prepared for his arrival by being painted in these tones. The background was always white while blue paint was used to write some Quranic phrases, sanctifying the pilgrim's entrance, over the door. It was also thought desirable to remind him of his journey by painting pictures of what he had seen on his trip, such as the Kaaba shrine . . . as well as the different means of transportation . . . Ritual objects used for purification were there, too, such as prayer mats, basins and ewers for cleansing before prayer, along with flowers and foliage' (Wenzel, 1972:54). Wenzel notes that in one Egyptian village, West Degheim, where the entire male population went to Mecca in 1961, 'multi-coloured pictures of boats, boatmen and the house-owner at prayer' were depicted, and that the Egyptians (Kenuzi people) had their own artists who used the human figure (Wenzel, 1972:56). One such artist, Sabri, whose background was in commercial art, was working in Dongola, Sudan, and Wenzel argues that *hajj* painting may have widened the traditional vocabulary of Sudanese house decoration.
31. New Qurna is the village planned and designed by Hassan Fathy in the 1940s, discussed in the following chapter, to which the Egyptian government attempted to move the (resistant) inhabitants of Qurna. Its inhabitants seem to have little link to tourism, making a living more from the land. This may explain the relative simplicity and less ubiquitous occurrence of paintings there compared with (old) Qurna.
32. Hassan el Shark exhibited at the Dr Ragab Gallery, Cairo (1988), Ifa Gallery, Stuttgart (1989), Goethe Institute, Munich and Berlin (1990), Al Shoumi Gallery, Cairo (1992) and Schloss Burgfarmbach, Furth (Germany) (1994). A catalogue was produced in 1994, with text in Arabic and German by Dr Marie Therese Abdel-Messih of Cairo University (Abdel-Messih, 1994).
33. An example of modern script in *hajj* painting is seen on the house of Abdul Alebbi in Karnak (1996). Abdul Alebbi paid an artisan LE100 for the work (conversation with worker in a juice bar across the alley, May 1997).
34. Parker and Neal state that Senosy is head of the art department at the Secondary Technical School at Esna, but elsewhere that he took up a four-year contract to teach in Qatar (Parker and Neal, 1995:137 and 141).

35. The author was unable to determine the artist's name from the house owner, but the style corresponds with that of Ahmed el-Tauib, as in the facade of a workshop described above, and other work illustrated in Parker and Neal (1995: illustrations pp 105, 143 and 147). The closest similarity is with an unattributed image from Qurna (1995:42) which shows an identical figure holding an umbrella, though on a yellow ground, standing before Mecca, with a kneeling figure reading a Koran to the right. The figure holding the umbrella resembles closely that by the door in the workshop. Another illustration in Parker and Neal which is attributed to el-Tauib shows a kneeling figure in the same pose and with many closely corresponding details to that of the unattributed painting (1995:88). The authorship of the blue house seems clearly, from these two links, to be el-Tauib's.
36. 'The extended family represents both genealogical and physical closeness in rural Egypt because close kin not only are related by blood and marriage but also are one's closest neighbours or even co-residents of a single house. . . . Family origin determines to a very great extent one's occupation in life as well as one's marriage partner. Marriage of cousins is strongly preferred . . .' (Fluehr-Lobban, 1990:24).
37. Fathy proposed craft workshops and a market for New Qurna, which never materialised. He records weaving and pottery as extant crafts (Fathy, 1989:62–5)
38. According to Fluehr-Lobban, 55% of Egyptians live in villages, but 'the pace of urbanization has been phenomenal, resulting in basic social change' (Fluehr-Lobban, 1990:20).
39. The composite imagery of workshop facades is similar to the following description of Egyptian folk tales: 'composed of fragments of *Arabian Nights* stories, African legends, Greek myths, and Pharaonic mythology. Over time, the meaning and origin of these stories were forgotten as they were transformed by the fantasy of each narrator' (Karnouk, 1988:67).
40. Wenzel states that: 'The members of Sudanese households who encouraged the hiring of professional artists to decorate their homes were frequently artists themselves. Alongside the art made by professional decorators there also existed an art made by members of the Nubian family which was not unlike some of the women's painting in Egyptian Nubia. Women, men – who were either house owners, grown sons, or bridegrooms marrying into the family – and boys, all had their own kinds of wall painting. Anyone in the family might do an additional painting, designed to be seen by persons returning from the pilgrimage to Mecca' (Wenzel, 1972:48).

Chapter 5
Architecture for the Poor

Introduction

This chapter considers the mud-brick architecture of Hassan Fathy, in particular his project for the village of New Gourna in upper Egypt. To some extent, New Gourna shares the social context of *hajj* painting, though Fathy's work there dates from the late 1940s, before the days of mass tourism. But whilst the previous chapter looked at the decoration of structures this chapter concerns their building. In (old) Gourna, cultural and social identities are given visibility through acts of decoration within existing spaces constructed without plan or design by local builders within a vernacular tradition. To what extent, then, can a new village be designed so that its spaces are permeated with those identities from the beginning? And, given the gradual processes through which vernacular architecture evolves in keeping with the requirements of occupation and terrain, can its feeling be reproduced when a village is designed in one piece (or designed at all)?[1]

The question is not straightforward. The meaning of the term design is rooted in a division of labour in industrial society which privileges the conceptualisation of a building over its construction – in a hierarchy mirroring that of beauty over use. But building in mud-brick is an improvised process in a non-industrial society, in which the householder is closely involved; it is less dependent on drawings and plans, or the autonomous language of signs which Lefebvre, as noted in Chapter 3, calls representations of space (Lefebvre, 1991:39). But if building in mud-brick constitutes a practice of the architectural everyday, the experiment at New Gourna remains a product of Fathy's intervention. So, whilst the categories of planning, design and building as normalised in the industrial world do not apply to building in mud-brick, Fathy reconstructs them, acting as planner and social researcher.

The chapter begins by describing Fathy's efforts to build the village of New Gourna, partly from his own account in *Gourna: A Tale of Two Villages*[2]. The project, seen by Fathy as a solution to Egypt's housing problem, is discussed in terms of his affirmation of traditional values against those of international modernism, contextualised by the emergence of an Egyptian national culture. His attachment to tradition may derive from a romanticisation of rural life as an antidote to the corruptions of the city; but whilst cultural and social values are shared in a village, offering a common ground for living, they also bind, especially for women. A further question is the extent to which Fathy formalises the vernacular, and how the intervention of an architect changes the traditional relation of builder and dweller. Despite its difficulties, though, does New Gourna offer a radical alternative to conventional schemes for housing in non-affluent countries?

New Gourna

Hassan Fathy was employed by the Egyptian government's Department of Antiquities from 1945 to 1949 to design and supervise the construction of a village in which the inhabitants of Gourna, many of whose homes were built over ancient tombs in the Theban necropolis of the west bank, opposite present-day Luxor, were to be rehoused. The traditional source of income for the Gournis was the sale of objects found in tombs; additional sources included acting as guides, being labourers for European archaeologists, or guards at archaeological sites. They were known for an ability to spot slight variations in the landscape which might denote an as yet undiscovered tomb, but also for their dexterity in removing the contents of tombs. Today, the manufacture of objects has supplanted their discovery. Fathy records, however, that thefts (or finds, to the Gournis) had, in the early 1940s, reached a scale unacceptable to the authorities[3]. A site of 50 acres was bought from a landowner by compulsory purchase (in the days before land reform) to provide homes for up to 7000 people. The project was, from the outset, a way to clear out a nuisance population whose livelihood represented an unofficial exploitation of an archaeological heritage which the Egyptian government and foreign experts wished to appropriate in their own, to them more legitimate, ways. Fathy hoped to persuade the Gournis to move voluntarily, recognising the complexities:

> All these people, related in a complex web of blood and marriage ties . . . a delicately balanced social organism intimately integrated with the topography, with the very bricks and timber of the village – this whole society had, as it were, to be dismantled and put together again in another setting. (Fathy, 1989:17)[4]

Fathy researched the patterns of spatial occupation in the existing village, based on a structure of extended families, and sought to improve access to water[5]. But he seems, in his book, to think of the Gournis as peasants, that is, an agricultural class, whilst for the Gournis the tombs provided a better living than the land. He writes of the peasant house as holding 'a large variety of bulky stores and the owner's cattle as well . . . [with] hens running in and out among the dust and babies . . .' (Fathy, 1989:92), which is less sympathetic than Winifred Blackman:

> In the better houses there is generally a flight of steps leading to an upper story, where there may be a sitting room . . . The flat roof is a pleasant place on which to sit and watch the life in the streets below; it also serves as a hen-run, dog- and cat-run, a drying ground . . .' (Blackman, 1927:27)[6]

Fathy sets out, then, to improve the lot of a peasantry to which the Gournis, whilst occupying traditional mud houses, belong only in part. A family whose male members work in the archaeological sites might see themselves as having needs somewhere between those of a peasant family and the inhabitants of the town, their patterns of sociation still traditional but beginning to be modified from those of agricultural society. Fathy, perhaps, sees village society in romantic terms, remaining himself a member of an urban professional elite[7].

The Gournis, sensitive or not to such nuances, refused to give up their livelihoods, and most continue today to live in the old village[8]. But if Fathy's interpretation of village life was coloured by a romantic perspective, social research was also part of the project's inception. Fathy writes that he would have liked to work with a team of socio-ethnographic researchers, but that the government would not make such a team available; he relied, therefore, on his own observations from conversations with village elders, some of whom he found quite wily, recording at one point an incident over a 'huge, soggy pie, which gave me food poisoning just to look at it' (Fathy, 1989:53 and 158–9). His research determined the spatial organisation of New Gourna at two levels: that of the family and that of the badana, or group of families headed by a sheikh, within a clan structure[9]. This translates, in the village plan, into the levels of individual houses and groups of houses around a shared courtyard. There is a third level of planning relating to the provision of public buildings and elements such as craft workshops to encourage new industry, but these relate more to Fathy's imaginative projections of a renewal of village life than to his observations of its present state.

In the old village, spread over a wide area with open space between clusters of buildings, Fathy found five badanas occupying four specific geographical areas. These four clusters are preserved but brought into geographical proximity in the plan for the new village, as four quarters (roughly one of which was built)[10]. Within each quarter houses are arranged in sub-groups around shared courtyards. In the old village, Fathy noted, each badana had its own café, barber and grocer, whilst all families in a badana had access to the oven of any member baking bread, and participated jointly in feasts for weddings and circumcisions (Fathy, 1989:58). Fathy retains this collectivity, but formalises the arrangement; the shared courtyards, and the houses grouped around small squares linked by streets which have detours to discourage strangers, are a spatial representation of a perceived social order. Thresholds of public and private space follow a hierarchic gradation – from the large square around which the village's public buildings are grouped, to the streets, shared courtyards, houses and front rooms in which the men drink tea, talk and (today) watch television, to the interior rooms of houses where the women spend much of their time. Within this system, the courtyard is a pivotal space between the worlds of individual and extended families, though such spatial arrangements are not found in the old village.

Fathy sees the courtyard as important for family life, in terms both of individual families and extended families, though to his critics it is an aspect of city architecture – specifically that of Cairo in the fourteenth to sixteenth centuries – imported into the village[11]. Fathy's description of a courtyard lends it an aesthetic autonomy:

> In an enclosed space, a room or a courtyard, there is a certain quality that can be distinctly felt, and that carries a local signature as clearly as does a particular curve. This felt space is in fact a fundamental component of architecture, and if a space has not the true feeling, no subsequent decoration will be able to naturalize it into the desired tradition. (Fathy, 1989:55)

To aestheticise something is also to generalise it, and his discussion of the courtyard follows from his equally generalising attachment of a symbolic value to the house, as a refuge from the desert and a mirror of cosmic order[12]. The courtyard is 'the owner's private piece of sky' (Fathy, 1989:56) and actively replenishes the spirituality of the house whilst its rooms can offer at best a sense of calm and security.

In New Gourna (Figure 5.1), the houses are grouped in irregularly shaped spaces, so that each is slightly different and has a different outlook from the others. Fathy sought to overcome the standardisation of mass housing projects by this device, which was not a response to an irregular terrain, since the site is flat. The design of the houses, in Fathy's account, expresses the properties of mud-brick. Each, with minor variations in proportion and layout, is based around a domed space off which are alcoves for a bed on one side and a cupboard on the other. Fathy describes this as 'a great improvement on the usual peasant room, which is a small, dark, ill-ventilated place' (Fathy, 1989:96). A baking oven is sited outside the kitchen, which is at the back of the house and leads on to a courtyard; and each house has its own latrine.

Of the public buildings designed by Fathy, the mosque, the theatre and the khan remain; the school for boys has been destroyed (and a large concrete school building constructed between the mosque and the fields); the market area, in which Fathy imagined animals sheltered by rows of trees, is neglected and contains piles of scrap. The school was an important element in Fathy's concept of the village, education being seen as a means to offer the Gournis a way of life beyond tomb-robbing. This is contextualised by a government drive in the late 1940s to build 4000 schools, many of them in villages (Fathy, 1989:81)[13]. Fathy sought to encourage learning through designing a sympathetic environment, and writes of his own memories of secondary school:

> . . . unexpected corners, odd-shaped open spaces, halls and class-rooms of all shapes and sizes, and lovely gardens. The casual surprises of the architecture must have quickened the imagination and sensibility of many schoolboys . . . Yet the building was not designed as a school at all; it was an old palace. (Fathy, 1989:85)

Deciding to build schools for both boys and girls rather than wait for the government programme to reach Gourna, Fathy designed each around courtyards.

Figure 5.1 *New Gourna, houses opposite the theatre (photo M Miles)*

In the boys' school, the entrance courtyard has a fountain, and four (of eight) domed class-rooms look on to the main courtyard, on the adjacent side of which are the dining room and school mosque, the latter lit by small apertures in the dome. Ventilation was to be provided by square towers above each room, with north-facing openings to catch the cooler air, which could then be filtered downwards over trays of wet charcoal – a form of *malkaf*, or wind-catch, derived, like the courtyard, from his studies of medieval houses in Cairo and vernacular architecture elsewhere (Fathy, 1986:56–60; Fathy, 1989:87 and fig. 93–4; Steele, 1988:33–43)[14].

The mosque, one of the first structures to be completed, is modelled on Nubian building types seen by Fathy in 1941. The building occupies a square, the maximum dimensions of each perpendicular axis being equal, yet appears as a long horizontal mass leading to the minaret. The main, covered space is a rectangle of five units by eight with a domed prayer-space, into which a central, open courtyard is partly inserted; there are two external courtyards, one for washing. The prayer space follows the demarkation of the village in offering distinct areas for the residents of each quarter. The interior is a sequence of pointed arches and circular domes, creating a many-faceted whilst plain and tranquil space in which light is filtered gently (Figure 5.2). The courtyard garden with its trees and well-watered plants contrasts with the dust of the square outside (Figure 5.3), and the sides of the prayer hall are articulated by large open-work screens (Figure 5.4). These allow breezes to pass through the building whilst deflecting the glare of the sun, like the wooden lattice windows of houses in old Cairo. The mosque is 'an enclosure to shelter worshippers during their prayers', those worshippers needing no intermediaries between themselves and god, nor 'to interpret him by means of symbols' (Fathy, 1989:73–4). In a society largely observant of religious obligations, which include both prayer and alms, perhaps the space of the mosque, though set apart by its tranquillity, is also a space of everyday life[15].

The theatre (Figure 15.5) was intended to revive vernacular drama and support traditions such as stick-dancing. It has stepped seats on three sides, and a stage with a balcony, a door and a window as a permanent set suggesting both interior and exterior spaces, like a house with a courtyard. Perhaps Fathy saw village drama, like village crafts, through a romantic glaze. He writes that, for instance, at weddings bands perform, and men challenge each other with quarterstaffs, and that this sport goes back to Pharaonic times. He sees it as '. . . a better entertainment for spectator and player than any that the town provides' such as cinema or radio: 'Only in a theatre or watching a real game can the audience feel that it is a single spirit . . .' (Fathy, 1989:79). But, as he also says, theatres are not a customary element in Egyptian villages; so is its provision a way of regulating popular tradition by setting aside a designated space? Lacking other models, he designed the theatre on the lines of Greek and Elizabethan types. The plays, on the other hand, did not follow European models, but were improvised, involving mime and dancing as well as narratives of village life performed by local people. But the theatre, more than

Figure 5.2 *New Gourna, interior of mosque (photo M Miles)*

Figure 5.3 *New Gourna, courtyard of mosque (photo M Miles)*

Figure 5.4 *New Gourna, courtyard of mosque, with guardian, showing openwork screen (photo M Miles)*

Figure 5.5 *New Gourna, wooden door to theatre (photo M Miles)*

other buildings, raises the question as to how much a vernacular culture can be designed or whether its facilitation needs to be less interventionist.

New Gourna is perhaps both a success and a failure: a success in demonstrating that a village built entirely in mud can last and provide homes and public buildings for a stable community, which it does today; a failure in that the community for whom it was intended refused to live in it, and because the plan was from the outset a coercive gesture on the part of a government bureaucracy behaving like a colonial power towards its own non-urban citizens. More interesting than the question of Fathy's complicity in that coercion on the part of a bureaucracy with which his relations became increasingly strained, is the question as to how far he saw design as a means of engineering a new, or renewed, village society at Gourna. His efforts, for instance to provide buildings for education and drama, and his interest in a craft revival[16], go beyond the replication of a traditional village, and the architectural types by which he is most influenced are those of the region around Aswan rather than Gourna. Is New Gourna an idealisation, a translation of an image of the vernacular into a utopian design? One implication of such questions is the relation of Fathy, who champions traditionalism in architecture, to modernism, which, whilst using industrial technologies, also entails the design of environments for the production of a new society.

The project at New Gourna was abandoned unfinished in 1948, and for several years stood empty. Government bureaucracy had increasingly undermined the project through delays, financial constraints, corruption and, eventually, disinterest. Fathy was unable to find a government ministry sympathetic to it (probably because it offered no route for advancement for civil servants, and denied profit to those with an interest in imported construction materials). His efforts to promote mud-brick building through official competitions in Cairo were also frustrated when his winning design was funded but not built, and then, despite agreement from the Building Research Centre to test a mud house next to one in concrete, only the concrete house was erected (Fathy, 1989:184). After three years of work at Gourna, dissuaded that further progress was possible, Fathy decided to work with the firm of Doxiadis in Athens on a project for rural planning in Iraq, staying there for five years.

New Gourna is still Fathy's best-known project, though, in 1967, he began work on a second new village at Baris near Kharga, in the western desert. In this case the 250 families for whom the settlement was intended were not identified, at a time by which migration from villages to Cairo had reached very high levels. Fathy's research here concerned the use of mud-brick forms and natural energy to reduce temperatures, contributing to his (1986) *Natural Energy and Vernacular Architecture*. Construction stopped during the 1967 war and was not resumed (Steele, 1997:197). Fathy's final experiment for social housing took place in New Mexico, despite his concern that Nubian forms might be inappropriate (and were hardly those of the Navajo), but this, too, remained unrealised. Only the mosque and religious school, of a planned range of public, educational and domestic buildings, were constructed by the time of Fathy's death in 1989, and use a concrete-coated form of mud-brick (Steele, 1997:142–55). The significance, however, of what might superficially seem a record of unbuilt dreams, may be in the model it proposes of a new relation between architect, builder and householder and in the possibility Fathy demonstrates for the use of local materials and technologies in place of imports from industrial countries. Both are potentially empowering, though questions remain as to the extent to which Fathy gives up or retains the power of the architect, and to what extent, in keeping with that, he constructs a radical alternative to modernism, rather than another, vernacularised, kind of modernism.

A Wider Context

Fathy saw his experiment at Gourna, for all his difficulties with the Egyptian government, as a prototype for a new kind of social architecture evolved from specifically Egyptian models – whether the village houses and mosques of Nubia or the medieval courtyard houses of Cairo. Where he makes wider references, for instance to wind-catches in Sind, they are within the world of Islam. In his writing he proclaims not only the desire for, but also much of the detail of, a renewal of traditional architecture as an alternative to international modernism. This can be understood in two ways: on one hand, Fathy's romantic image of rural life, derived from his childhood, is a source of an idea of vernacular architecture, taking it from a practical to a conceptual level; on the other, his social concern seems genuine and his projects highly practical, mud-brick representing what he calls a 'no-cost' solution to Egypt's housing problem (Fathy, 1988:16). The two are not exclusive; his idealisation of the vernacular is linked, paradoxically perhaps, to a wish to improve the quality of life for the peasantry, and the translation of his ideal into real (if unfinished) projects, for which considerable persistence was necessary, is a contribution to development outside the limitations of colonial structures. What links these aspects of his support for tradition is the background of Egyptian nationalism. From the demise of Ottoman rule until 1952, Egypt was, with Sudan, a puppet state under British domination. It had a notionally independent constitutional monarchy, and a political organisation, but little freedom. Fathy's model of mud-brick architecture is a post-colonial solution, in being independent of the power, knowledge and technologies of colonial states and corporations. There is a certain irony, in that Fathy himself belonged to an elite whose taste was informed by European cultural hierarchies, but this does not invalidate his rejection of the corruption of rural life he perceived when those values were applied to it.

Political nationalism had cultural equivalents – like the school of folk realism noted in the previous chapter, and the work of al-Jazzar (Karnouk, 1988:47–72). Other Egyptian artists trained (often abroad) in the early twentieth century, such as Muhammad Naji and Raghib Ayyad, had painted rural themes as part of an intentionally nationalist approach (Karnouk, 1988:25–7). Naji's mural *The Renaissance of Egypt* (1935), for the Senate in Cairo, depicts a Pharaonic goddess (presumably Isis) carried on a bullock-cart amongst a crowd of peasants in front of a palm grove. The gestures of the figures have something of the quality of a Holman Hunt, and the horizontally layered perspective suggests Italian art of the fifteenth century. The only figure whose head is above the skyline, as if able to foresee the future, is Isis. This is a hybrid style, Egyptian in subject-matter but European in language and technique. Other artists, notably Mahmud Mukhtar, chose a Pharaonic language, as in his *Egyptian Awakening* (1928) for Cairo University – a female figure looking to the distance beside a sphinx, in pink granite. Naji, who advocated public mural projects on the model of Mexican revolutionary art, was forced to resign from a government post after making the following statements in Prague in 1928:

> I see ourselves affected by a spleen without remedy. Disillusioning travels would only drive us to exasperation.

and

> When the health of a society runs out, it is up to the people close to the nourishing origins of the civilisation to feed it through its inexhaustible resources (Naji, 1958:11, cited in Karnouk, 1988:26).

The language of the first remark is reminiscent of Baudelaire, but the sentiment of the second is clearly nationalist, and aimed at the corruption of a Europeanised monarchy. The difficulty for Egyptian artists is in determining what strata of Egyptian culture and society constitutes those nourishing origins. Is it Pharaonic art, despite that only the Nubians of the south and not the Arabs of Cairo are an indigenous people, and that any link made over two millennia is problematic? Is it folk art, in which case does a non-mainstream art retain its authenticity if incorporated into the mainstream? Or is it a wider Islamic art, the commonalities of which would be defined by the design and decoration of mosques, and hence non-figurative?[17] The decorative geometries of Islamic art were influences on European modernists including Klee, Kandinsky, Macke and Matisse, and some Egyptian artists argued for a cross-fertilisation in the other direction. The Art and Freedom movement, for instance, was linked to French surrealism, and Hamid Nada's paintings are influenced by the two-dimensional, decorative quality of Klee's work (Karnouk, 1988:32–3 and 67–9). But by the time of New Gourna, the folk-realists were probably the most influential group, though, in contrast to the generation of Naji and Mukhtar, who were overtly nationalist, they had little contact with political life (Karnouk, 1988:47)[18].

That political life was complex, divided between nationalist, Islamist and communist groups[19], but unified in efforts to free Egypt from British control and dislike of an overtly corrupt Farouk. British rule was more at arm's length than might be found in a colony as such, though Egypt's monarchy was an implanted

European institution[20]; but an incident during the 1939–45 war indicates the way in which the arm's length principle was operated by the British: following unconfirmed reports that Egypt sought to hinder the war effort, Farouk was forced more or less at gunpoint to sign a paper replacing his prime minister with a British nominee, after which the British government confirmed its policy of 'sincere collaboration' (Hopwood, 1982:16–17). Farouk and his reformist ministers continued to chart a course of compromise between acceptance of their puppet status and illusions of power displaced in luxurious living. Meanwhile, popular uprisings took place in 1945 and 1948; and land remained in the ownership of an urban elite whilst the rural poor became further impoverished by a fall in the price of cotton following the slump of the 1930s (Hopwood, 1982:17–19). The Egyptian bourgeoisie, many of whom were European, established new industries to produce in Egypt items previously imported, contributing to a migration of peasants to the towns, where their conditions were not much improved but their traditional patterns of sociation threatened. It is against this background that Fathy's promotion of a vernacular style can be set and his interest in the preservation of village life be seen to be radical within Egypt's professional class[21].

TRADITION AND MODERNITY

Fathy's relations with the government during the 1940s have been shown to be uneasy, leading him to go to Athens in 1948 and return only after independence. Many of his statements carry an overtone of anti-colonialism, whether political or economic. They also touch on the question of corruption, with which the Egyptian upper class was identified and which Fathy sees filtering down through the professional class to a local level. He is critical, for instance, of architects who replicate imported design:

> . . . the work of an architect who designs, say, an apartment house in the poor quarters of Cairo for some stingy speculator, in which he incorporates various features of modern design copied from fashionable European work, will filter down, over a period of years, through the cheap suburbs and into the village, where it will slowly poison the genuine tradition. (Fathy, 1989:21)

The implication is that an acquired vocabulary of modernism is not just second hand and debased, but also an aspect of the way a colonial power (generalised as the industrialised world) assimilates, but at a distance, the elite of the subject state. Later in the same passage he writes of diagnosing the disease of Egyptian architecture and attacking its root causes; here Fathy brings the argument to a level of personal choice:

> The cultural decay starts with the individual himself, who is confronted with choices that he is not equipped to make, and we must cure it at this stage. (Fathy, 1989:22)

This applies to individuals at every level of society, for all of whom the exercise of choice is self-expression. For western intellectuals and the elite class in Egypt, assuming the autonomous subject of modernity, self-expression is a possible concept. In an Egyptian village, there is no equivalent sense of a self which is not part of the same organisation of society and belief as other selves, and Fathy, accepting this, sees tradition as dealing, for the villager, with certain levels of choice in order to afford freedom in others:

> Tradition is not necessarily old-fashioned and is not synonymous with stagnation. Furthermore, a tradition need not date from long ago but may have begun quite recently. As soon as a workman meets a new problem and decides how to overcome it, the first step has been taken in the establishment of a tradition. (Fathy, 1989:24)

Tradition is contrasted to modernity, then, not as a constraint, but as a safeguard, preserving a structure of value whilst allowing adaptation to circumstances. Is this another version of the privileging of thought over action, in that the villager's freedom is to find new solutions to practical rather than philosophical (or architectural) problems? Tradition, however, is vital to Fathy's argument, because it is at the level of individual choice that corruption sets in. The argument seems to be that the peasantry need the safeguard of tradition because they are unable to distinguish for themselves between the baubles offered by industrial society and the worth of their own inheritance. This does not apply in towns, where 'the public and the surroundings can take care of themselves'. Fathy states that to wilfully break a tradition in peasant society is 'a kind of cultural murder', and that architects should respect the traditions they invade (Fathy, 1989:25).

But does this approach affirm Fathy's power as a professional able to make distinctions for those unable to do so for themselves? And, if Fathy's position is predicated on an assumption that the peasantry cannot take care of themselves[22], does he differ as much as he believes from modernists (and, until recently, European or North American governments) who make assumptions about the inner city poor not being able to manage their lives – as viewed critically by Edward Robbins in his commentary on Thamesmead (see Chapter 3)[23]. Fathy, however, unlike the European modernists, sees a naturalised vocabulary in traditional architecture, as in the right size for a window, which the architect 'has no right to break with his own personal whims' (Fathy, 1989:26). It seems, also, fair to see him as critical of his own class from within it. At the same time, perhaps Fanon's comment on the isolationism of emerging national cultures sheds another light:

> . . . the native artist who wishes . . . to create a national work of art shuts himself [sic] up in a stereotyped reproduction of details. These artists . . . turn their back on foreign culture, deny it and set out to look for a true national culture . . . But these people forget that the forms of thought and what it feeds on . . . have dialectically reorganised the people's intelligences and that the constant principles which acted as safeguards during the colonial period are now undergoing extremely radical changes. (Fanon, 1967:181)

Could Fathy's emphasis on the vernacular to the exclusion of foreign influences be like this? Or an effort to protect the rural poor from foreign interference? Fanon continues by saying that what intellectuals in emerging nations need to do is to '. . . realise that the truths of a nation are . . . its realities' and that they should seek '. . . the seething pot out of which the learning of the future will emerge'. Fathy, no doubt, would have argued that he did exactly that, setting aside the corruptions of the city for the realism of the village, and seeing in vernacular architecture a form of knowledge out of which the learning of tomorrow would be born[24].

He would have some justification. Much of Fathy's criticism of architecture refers to the import of costly and inappropriate technologies and materials from the colonial states. This is partly on the grounds of exploitation, and the corruption it breeds within the recipient nation when a chain of intermediaries in the public and private sectors add their bribes, fees and profits to the cost of the material for a development project, but also on the grounds that local materials – particularly mud in a hot, arid climate – are more effective in solving the problems of building. He argues that the built environment alters the microclimate, that 'the configuration of buildings, their orientations, and their arrangement in space create a specific microclimate for each site' to which are added elements including materials and surface colours. He continues: 'These man-made elements interact with the natural microclimate to determine the factors affecting comfort . . .' (Fathy, 1986:38). His early experiments had demonstrated both the feasibility of mud construction, as in his prototype house at Bahtim for the Royal Society of Agriculture in 1941 (Fathy, 1989:5–6; Steele, 1997:24 and 190)[25], and its efficiency in moderating temperatures (though his proposed tests in 1947 and 1948 were not carried out). Until the completion of the Aswan High Dam, mud was freshly deposited annually by the Nile flood, and was a plentiful and free resource, as was the dung and straw with which it was mixed to bind it in bricks which were then baked in the sun. Mud had been used in Egypt since Pharaonic times, and Fathy illustrates in his book the (partly still-intact) vaults of the granaries at the Ramasseum (Figure 5.6). Reflecting on the mud houses built by peasants, Fathy writes:

> . . . here, in every hovel and tumbledown hut in Egypt, was the answer to my problem. Here, for years, for centuries, the peasant had been wisely and quietly exploiting the obvious building material, while we, with our modern, school-learned ideas, never dreamed of using such a ludicrous substance as mud for so serious a creation as a house. But why not? (Fathy, 1989:4)

Fathy's view of the peasant house as a hovel is unflattering, and offers scope for professional intervention through design, but he also cites the mud-brick architecture of Nubia as 'standing proof that uninstructed peasants, given the necessary skills, can do far better than any government housing scheme . . .' (Fathy, 1973:29). He implies that building is a matter, not of intellectual, but of tacit knowledge,

Figure 5.6 *Ramasseum, granaries from the nineteenth dynasty (photo M Miles)*

learnt by example. Mud is also a social leveller, as appropriate for the country house of a landowner as for that of a peasant.

Today, Fathy's traditionalism might be criticised for its acceptance of gendered space in the Egyptian village. Although he saw his role as improving house design, for example by bringing water sources nearer, Fathy did not seek to intervene in social patterns, but replicated their traditional gendering. He gives more attention to the design of the boys' school than the girls', and expresses the gendering of space as an aesthetic principle:

> The inward-looking Arab house, made beautiful by the feminine element of water, self-contained and peaceful . . . is the domain of woman. . . . Now it is of great importance that this enclosed space with the trembling liquid femininity it contains should not be broken. If there is a gap in the enclosing building, this special atmosphere flows out and runs to waste in desert sands. (Fathy, 1973:57)

As with his writing on courtyards, aestheticisation is a form of generalisation and normalisation; there is also a sense of sexual imagery underlying the text (as if it is the seminal fluid which might run out) which makes matters worse. But, even if the confinement of women to domestic interiors was commonplace, the point this leads to is the abstraction of Fathy's description. By reducing women and houses to signs for an aesthetic principle, Fathy, as a product of the Beaux-Arts tradition (Steele, 1997:183), echoes the sentiments, and sentimentality, of the modernists, notably Le Corbusier. Building in mud-brick, on the other hand, is a matter of skill and knowledge gained in immediate and practical ways, and quite unsentimental. Perhaps there is a contradiction between the post-colonial aspect of Fathy's architectural thought and his traditionalism in respect of gender, though he does not share Le Corbusier's orientalism[26].

Mud

Building in mud, in which the construction of the vault is the most skilful aspect[27], requires improvisation and is the province not of the architect but the mason. Fathy describes a traditional arrangement in which the design of a house is a process of mediation between the owner, who, for superstitious reasons will delay its completion and alter details of its construction[28], and craftsmen from the same neighbourhood who interpret the owner's intentions, showing what is possible, setting out, as he says, 'subtle variations in three dimensional design that could never be represented on an architect's plan' (Fathy, 1973:28). Fathy, of course, made a plan for the village of New Gourna and controlled the allocations of plots as well as the groundplan for each house; but many of his drawings for buildings use eclectic styles, from Persian miniatures to tomb paintings (illustrations, Steele, 1997:34, 60, 69, and 82) and seem artworks rather than specifications. In one, the ancient goddess Hat-Hor, in the form of a cow, appears over a desert represented, as in the tombs, by a pink ground dotted with red ochre; a stylised sycamore tree stands for regeneration. On either side are house plans and elevations. But how does his insistence on 'the intelligent participation of the client' (Fathy, 1989:40), and reluctance to interfere in the traditional relation of householder to builder, fit with his view that the Gournis were unable to articulate their views on architecture?

Firstly, Fathy's role at New Gourna was as social researcher and facilitator, as much as designer. As a member of a professional elite from Cairo, Fathy had the potential power – and to him responsibility – to push through the project, despite its break with the conventions which suited those who gained financially from the import of materials. The villagers, and even less the landless fellaheen who made up a majority of Egypt's rural population, had (and have) no such power. That Fathy was, after three years, unable to secure the project's future does not detract from this argument. Secondly, Fathy does not invade but supports the role of the Nubian masons and employs them both to build and to teach their skills to others. Thirdly, there is an element of pragmatism, in that the power of consumerism and the image it presents of an affluent society, now spread by the television sets which appear in peasant houses in many countries, including Egypt, is difficult to resist, and Fathy's intervention lends, by his status, a credibility to the vernacular. Fathy saw New Gourna as more than an isolated experiment, indeed, as an answer to the housing problem brought about by Egypt's rapid population growth:

> What aspects of the problem does it solve? First, that of money. It is built entirely of mud and costs nothing. Second, that of space . . . there is no limit to the size of the house; ten rooms are as cheap as one. Third, that of hygiene. Space means health, both physical and mental, while the material, mud, does not harbour insects as thatch and wood do. Fourth, that of beauty. The demands of the structure alone are almost sufficient to ensure pleasing lines. (Fathy, 1989:129)

And despite its frequently rehearsed difficulties[29], New Gourna may be a model of development which, if viewed critically, has implications for social housing in the affluent as well as non-affluent worlds[30]. The relation of architect or builder to dweller implicit in the vernacular of mud-brick challenges the conventional power of the architect and opens a possibility for the knowledge of non-professionals to be taken as seriously as that of professionals.

Today the argument can be extended, as the assumption that rural communities (or the urban poor) cannot work out their own solutions is discarded in a 'decolonisation' of the mind[31]; evidence that non-privileged people can produce appropriate and carefully managed spaces is seen in the informal settlements which grow around many cities in the non-affluent world. And whilst Fathy is willing to share the status of knowledge with Nubian masons, today it is the role of dwellers which is brought into the framework in the work of development architects such as Nabeel Hamdi, and through housing association self-build schemes (both discussed in Chapter 9). Turner writes of the potential power of people to reclaim the environment:

> Personal and local resources are imagination, initiative, commitment and responsibility, skill and muscle-power, the capability for using specific and often irregular areas of land or locally available materials and tools . . . None of these resources can be used by exogenous or supra-local powers against the will of the people. (Turner, 1976:48)

Perhaps, then, New Gourna's biggest failing remains its rejection by those for whom it was intended, who saw its whole inception as an act of coercion and still regard it with suspicion.

The present inhabitants of New Gourna migrated to the area as squatters from villages south of Aswan after the building of the High Dam in 1964, and make their livings for the most part outside the tourist industry, another way in which the new and old villages remain separate. If signs of conspicuous prosperity are absent, the village appears to support a stable community. The mosque is well cared for, and its small school room is still used for religious instruction (whilst secular learning takes place in the concrete school built by the government). Many of the houses retain their original design, though some of the domes have been replaced by flat roofs using timber, avoided by Fathy because it was a scarce and hence expensive material. This allows bedrooms to be constructed upstairs; in at least one case, that of Ahmed, who sells soft drinks and cigarettes from his front room using one of the alcoves for storage, additional rooms became necessary as his family grew up – the rooftop room is for an older son who spends part of his time in the town. A stall has also been added to the back of the house for a cow which provides the family with milk. But the addition is in mud-brick, and the original fabric has been well maintained. Only one house has a concrete balcony, resembling the houses of the emerging middle class in Luxor. Ahmed and the guardian of the mosque were aware of Fathy as the architect (or engineer), on account of whom a small number of foreigners now come to see the village. Ahmed was able to point out each element in his house designed by Fathy and each modified by himself[32]. Perhaps his case is unusual, but perhaps also the adaptation of the environment is an expression of ownership conducive to its sustainability.

NOTES

1. This question raises another: is Fathy's work a radical alternative to international modernism or is it a regional kind of modernism? The aspects of modernism it could be seen to share are the desire to make new and the belief in social engineering – making a better society – through design. These issues will be discussed below.
2. Later published as *Architecture for the Poor* (Fathy, 1973), with identical text, illustrations and pagination.

3. Fathy records that a sacred boat had been stolen from the newly discovered tomb of Amenophis II, enabling one of the guards to buy 40 acres of land (Fathy, 1989:15); and he mentions the unauthorised removal of a complete stone bas-relief as the immediate cause of the planned resettlement of the villagers (Fathy, 1989:16; Steele, 1997:61). Fathy is not unsympathetic to the Gournis, citing city dealers as the link with 'unscrupulous foreign buyers' and as exploiting the Gournis, who 'took all the risks, developed the skill, and did the hard work [whilst] the dealers sat in perfect safety, encouraging the vandalism . . .' (Fathy, 1989:16).
4. Steele gives an inaccurate version of this quote (Steele, 1997:61).
5. Fathy narrates his plan for a communal steam bath, noting that showers provided by the government in some villages remain unused due to a lack of a hot water supply and neglect by the government employees responsible for their maintenance; individual houses have washing facilities and lavatories, fed by a large ceramic water jar on the roof. Fathy argues against providing an individual water supply to each house, on the grounds that drawing water from a communal well or tap is an important social event (Fathy, 1989:87–9; 99–103).
6. Blackman does begin the paragraph by saying that peasant houses are in many cases 'mere hovels', and is not writing specifically about Gourna but about upper Egypt in general.
7. Fathy begins Chapter 1 of his book with a heading 'Paradise Lost: The Countryside', and writes how his father's avoidance of the countryside and mother's stories of tame lambs and self-sufficiency led him to see the countryside 'as a paradise', though one '. . . darkened by clouds of flies . . . bilharzia and dysentery' (Fathy, 1989:2). His arrival in Luxor, from the overnight train, confirms his urban status: '. . .I got off with all my suitcases, trunks, rolls and rolls of plans, instruments, gramophone, records, . . . for I was going to stay in Gourna for a long time . . .' (Fathy, 1989:152); and suggests that Cairo's professional class were not unfamiliar with aspects of the European (colonial) culture they also wished to reject in the cause of national liberation.
8. In c.1995–96, according to official reports following a storm and/or flood which damaged several houses, a small proportion of the villagers were moved to a second new village built on arid land near the Valley of the Kings. The author visited the site in 1997 by taxi; the driver, asked why people moved there, replied 'because they shouted at them'. The Gournis were, it appears from studies elsewhere in the non-affluent world, right to retain their homes. Turner describes the deterioration of living standards and health for a family '. . . after being rehoused from an informal settlement to a neatly built house with the usual facilities'. By contrast, he sees a family living in a shack as enjoying better food and health, greater proximity to work and social life, and a more secure existence. The case is also cited by Gilbert and Gugler (Turner, 1976:52–9; Gilbert and Gugler, 1992:119).
9. Fathy writes: 'The badana is a tightly related knot of people, consisting of some ten or twenty families, with a recognised patriarch and a close sense of corporate allegiance. The families live in adjoining houses and, though there are differences of wealth and status between the individual families, they follow a communal way of life' (Fathy, 1989:58).
10. Fathy does not say whether, when new houses were built in (old) Gourna they were in the same geographical area. Research associated with the excavations at Çatalhöyük, near a village in which there are three districts, shows that, today, new houses are built when a family becomes too large for the old house and may be in a different district. (http://catal.arch.cam.ac.uk/catal/Newsletter) 1996.
11. See Steele, 1988:74–5. In this, his earlier book on Fathy, Steele cites Andre Raymond (1984:85) as criticising Fathy's adoption of the courtyard and other attributes of what

he sees as the elite houses of Cairo. Steele writes that the adaptation of the courtyard for a village house (and other attributes) 'is unrealistic' (1988:75). In his later book, Steele is less critical on this point: 'While the appropriateness of his regeneration of typologies in general may be questioned, this is not why work on New Gourna stopped, or why the town was unoccupied' (Steele, 1997:83); though in his conclusion, framed by Said's critique of orientalism, he criticises Fathy for a methodology too dependent on typology (Steele, 1997:183).

12. '. . . in desert countries men [sic] try to bring down the serenity and holiness of the sky into the house, and at the same time to shut out the desert with its blinding, suffocating sand and inhospitable demons' (Fathy, 1989:56).
13. Amongst Fathy's later projects are schools at Fares and Edfu in 1957 (Steele, 1997:104–7 and 195). The government drive for education has, since independence, been successful – today nearly all Egyptian children go to school.
14. In *Natural Energy and Vernacular Architecture*, Fathy refers to and illustrates the use of wind-catches in a village in Sind, Pakistan (Fathy, 1986:fig.46).
15. See Ghannam, 1997:129–32, cited in the previous chapter, for discussion of the importance of an urban mosque as a space of shared identity for women in migrant and relocated communities.
16. See Fathy, 1989:35 and 62–9. Fathy planned a permanent crafts exhibition hall, as well foreseeing a sustainable market for weaving and pottery, both seen as alternatives to unofficial livelihoods for the Gournis.
17. Fanon writes of the tendency for the colonised to look to a remote past for legitimation of their desire for freedom. He sees this as unrealistic but perhaps necessary: 'I am ready to concede that on the plane of factual being the past existence of an Aztec civilisation does not change anything very much in the diet of the Mexican peasant of today. . . . But . . . this passionate search for a national culture . . . finds its legitimate reason in the anxiety shared by native intellectuals to shrink away from that Western culture in which they all risk being swamped.' He goes on to argue that the claim to a past culture also undoes the distortions of that past of colonial narratives. He cites the Arab world as an example (though in relation to Algeria). (Fanon, 1967:168–9 and 171).
18. Karnouk sees a 'massive desertion of intellectuals from the political arena', leading to a more populist (revolutionary rather than reformist) element in the growing national struggle (Karnouk, 1988:47).
19. The three movements are: Young Egypt, founded in 1938 and described by Karnouk as fascist and seeking to renew Pharaonic glories; the Muslim Brotherhood, founded in 1928, an anti-modernist and anti-western grouping; and the Egyptian Communist Party, founded in 1922, many of whose members were European residents in Egypt (Karnouk, 1988:29). Hopwood also mentions the more reformist Wafd, Saadists (an off-shoot of the Wafd), Liberals and Independents (Hopwood, 1982:21).
20. Hopwood writes that King Faud 'was not very popular and considered to be virtually a foreigner by the Egyptians. He had lived abroad for a long time and spoke Italian better than Arabic' (Hopwood, 1982:15).
21. Fathy remains a radical, better known outside than within Egypt. There is a strange hybridity in a web-site promoting Egyptian culture, which features Ramses Wissa Wassef. Wassef designed and ran a school for tapestry weaving at Harrania, which has become known by tourists, and, like Fathy, was a product of the Beaux-Arts system who turned to the vernacular. But the text attributes to him the discovery of 'the beauty of Nubian villages, where the houses are composed of mudbrick vaults and domes . . . This discovery revealed to Wassef the connection he had been seeking with the past.' The text continues to say that Wassef found 'bricklayers who could make vaulted roofs for

houses' and that he applied this as 'Gorna Architecture or architecture of the poor' (http://www.sis.gov.eg/egyptinf/culture/wessa).

22. Fathy writes, in another section: 'The Gournis could scarcely discuss the buildings with us. They were not able to put into words even their material requirements in housing; so they were quite incapable of talking about the style or beauty of a house. A peasant never talked about art, he makes it' (Fathy, 1989:40).
23. Gilbert and Gugler argue that the notion that the poor are unable to help themselves and must therefore have their housing problems sorted out by governments is passing; they cite Turner (1976) on the better solutions produced by self-help compared with government schemes (Gilbert and Gugler, 1992:118).
24. In this respect, Fathy's contribution to a national culture differs from that of, say, Hungarian architect Imre Makovecz. His church at Siófok (1990) has been described as fusing 'images from nature, Christianity, and Transylvanian mythology' (Pearson, 1994:136). Makovecz is identified with the political right in post-communist Hungary. His style, whilst having a relation to wood equivalent of Fathy's to mud and similarly dependent on research of local traditions, seems more eclectic, in parts reminiscent of Eisenstein's film *Alexander Nevsky* more than a historical past or real present.
25. Fathy's first effort to design a dome at Bahtim was unsuccessful – the first domes collapsed – which led him to go to Nubia to find masons still working in a tradition of mud-brick vaulting. This utilisation of a traditional technique underpins his whole future development of mud-brick architecture. See photographs in Fathy (1989) plates 7–18.
26. See Colomina for an account of Le Corbusier's interest in postcards of exotic ladies in Algiers, and the utilisation of this imagery in murals in a villa designed by Eileen Gray (Colomina, 1996:84–91).
27. Vaulting in mud-brick buildings is relatively unusual, though characteristic of archaic and rural buildings in Nubia. Myron Goldfinger, in his survey (or travelogue) of vernacular architecture in the Mediterranean, includes several cases from Morocco, all of which use timber for flat roofs. The vaulted structures he finds in Metameur, Ghoumrassen Hadada and Takrouna in Tunisia are stone-built (Goldfinger, 1993:122–49 and 158–71).
28. In some countries this is also, or more likely, for tax reasons, property taxes being applied only to completed buildings.
29. See Steele, 1997:83: 'It is generally assumed that Fathy somehow got it wrong'; and Ghirardo, 1996:15: 'New Gourna . . . evidenced profound conflicts in values and a host of underlying political and social issues only partially addressed by the architect . . .'. Steele, however, maintains that 'New Gourna still has enormous influence on all those contemplating similar projects' (Steele, 1997:192).
30. Ghirardo cites Fathy's *Gourna: A Tale of Two Villages* (1969) as one of four books which 'suggest the dimensions of the changes in attitudes towards architecture' signalling an assault on Modernism. The other three are Jacobs (1961); Venturi (1966); and Rossi (1982) (Ghirardo, 1996:13).
31. See Carmen, 1996:1–3. Carmen argues that the myth of development produces a feeling in the so-called under-developed that they are 'the problem'.
32. Conversation with the author, May 1997, conducted by Ahmed in Arabic and the author in English.

Chapter 6

Reclamation: Nine Mile Run Greenway

Introduction

The two previous chapters considered *hajj* painting and vernacular architecture in Egypt. This chapter describes a project to reclaim part of Nine Mile Run in Pittsburgh – a 238 acre wasteland produced by the dumping of slag by the steel industry – as green public space[1]. The contrasts are obvious: from a non-affluent to an affluent country, a rural to an urban environment, and from the built environment to an adjacent open space. But the three cases taken as the bases for Chapters 4, 5 and 6 compose a trilogy of decoration, building and reclamation. The case of *hajj* painting showed one way in which identities are stated within the built environment; and Fathy's intention at New Gourna was to translate the social identity of a village into buildings using traditional materials and technologies. Reclamation recodes existing sites, lending them new meanings in context of uncertain urban identities. Whilst house decoration and mud-brick architecture are cases from a pre-industrial society, reclamation denotes a post-industrial landscape and a post-modern set of contentions. The Nine Mile Run Greenway project is also an interface between the processes of urban planning and development, community organisation and art.

Acts of decoration take place in the industrialised world as well as the non-industrialised, but are marginal; stone cladding on terraced houses, for instance, signifies poor taste (or the taste of the recently poor), and graffiti is the mark of a mythicised underclass, a threatening presence of transgression (Sennett, 1990:205–7; Cresswell, 1996:31–61). These decorative forms are discussed in the following chapter in context of the architectural everyday; enough to say here that house painting, stone cladding and graffiti each have specific vocabularies, and that, in industrial (or affluent) societies, acts which state individual identities are more often confined to the decoration of domestic interiors. The vernacular is marginalised in a different way as an officially sanctioned historical or heritage category; in the UK this takes the form of model villages and half-timbered suburban cul-de-sacs, and stick-on Tudorbethan facades for supermarkets[2]. Reclamation of buildings and sites, on the other hand, is an increasing necessity in the cities of the industrialised countries, as rising populations and wealth put pressure on land for housing, consumption and leisure uses, while encroachment by development on to greenfield sites becomes politically and socially unacceptable. Even the Millennium Dome occupies a brownfield site, and it will be interesting to see how it is reclaimed 20 or 30 years ahead when its fabric disintegrates. So, two of the cases on which the middle section of this book is based are derived from a non-industrial society (and non-affluent country), and this third case involves the creation of a post-industrial landscape; none of the three belong to the world of industrial modernity itself in which the metropolitan cities of the twentieth century were produced. But while dominant concepts are normalised through the growth of such cities, it is sites such as Nine Mile Run which, as much as inner city dereliction, denote the destructive effects of the modern Utopia.

The chapter contextualises the project within the growth of environmental art; and in relation to the issues raised by other reclamation projects, such as the Earth Centre (on a disused colliery site near Doncaster, in Yorkshire) within a discourse of post-industrial cities[3]. The project's planning process is then investigated through the evidence of community workshops[4]; and the problem, raised by the artists themselves, as to whether reclamation work of this kind remains art, is taken as a form of the wider problem of the relation of art's aesthetic and social dimensions.

ENVIRONMENTAL ART SINCE THE 1970S

The end of modernity is a background of declining certainty, and it was against the increasingly evident and culturally represented contradictions of modernity and its market operations that environmental art emerged as an avant-garde category within mainstream art practice in North America and Europe in the 1970s. That mainstream itself, since the late 1960s, had widened to include art which no longer took the form of objects, but was conceptual. In the USA, in particular, sculptors began to reconstruct the landscape itself rather than put objects in it, for example by digging holes in the ground. Rosalind Krauss writes of a work by Mary Miss made in 1978:

> Toward the center of the field there is a slight mound, a swelling in the earth, which is the only warning given for the presence of the work. Closer to it, the large square face of the pit can be seen, as can the ends of the ladder that is needed to descend into the excavation. The work itself is thus entirely below grade: half atrium, half tunnel, the boundary between outside and in, a delicate structure of wooden posts and beams. (Krauss, 1983:31)

Beginning with description, Krauss then seeks a way to discuss holes in the ground within art criticism. She argues that critical operations engage with the unknown aspects of work which redefines art, but do so through known categories such as sculpture. Part of the problem is that sculpture, associated with monuments – for instance, Michelangelo's statue of Marcus Aurelius in the Campidoglio – breaks down with Rodin's *Gates of Hell* of 1880, which no longer claims a place in the public domain[5]. Krauss adopts a strategy of redefining categories by negation, plotting their shifting boundaries with other categories on which they border. Rodin's sculpture, then, negates the category of sculpture as monument by being siteless – by exhibiting 'an absolute loss of place' (Krauss, 1983:35). Miss, for Krauss, negates the kind of modernist category opened up by Rodin, which depended on the context of an aesthetic space in which art could claim autonomy. Looking at works by Robert Morris, Alice Aycock and Robert Smithson, Krauss goes on to declare a new critical territory for sculpture by mapping it in a series of diagrams as not-landscape and not-architecture (two categories still in a public domain). Hence an expanded field '. . . generated by problematizing the set of oppositions between which the modernist category *sculpture* is suspended' (Krauss, 1983:38). It is intriguing to speculate how other categories of professional work, such as urban planning or engineering, might be redefined using a similar model.

Digging holes was only one means to expand the field for sculpture. Others included, from the late 1960s, happenings, community art, auto-destructive art and conceptual art using the juxtaposition of image and text. One force behind much new art was a desire on the part of artists to free themselves from the operations of the art market, and the commodification of their work, as well as from the prevailing reductionist critique of art advanced by Clement Greenberg[6]. This move to non-art forms (in the sense of non-object art) was partly the voice of an avant-garde looking to a post-capitalist society and resisting the seductions of the gallery system – if artists ceased to make objects, then the art market would have nothing new to sell, nor critics objects of taste to interpret. Within this broad direction, some artists were directly motivated by political events, or the radical perceptions of class, gender and cultural difference introduced by the new discipline of cultural studies. Martha Rosler, for instance, produced collages from magazine pictures, protesting at the American war in Vietnam in a language of everyday imagery and using materials which lacked the privileged status of paint or bronze. In the UK, Victor Burgin made a series of poster-size photographic works on class differences; these, however, were sold by a London dealer at sums equivalent to a week's professional salary. The art market, like that of popular music, proved adept at colonising whatever set itself apart from it, including graffiti[7]. At the same time, art made in the desert, or which was ephemeral, could be represented in the gallery only by photographs and remained a challenge to the culture of the object. If the market was able to deal in it, and artists accepted complicity on the grounds of needing to earn a living, new art forms were able still to make visible some of the contradictions of late capitalist society, even if only for an art-world public.

But another factor in the new art of the late 1960s was a desire to reach new publics by using non-gallery settings, and this, too, conditions the growth of environmental art. Whilst the tradition of sculpture produced public monuments, these had, by the mid-twentieth century, lost their currency, and the world of the modern art gallery with its characteristic white walls denoting a so-called value-free space had become a preserve of the possessors of money or cultural knowledge[8].

Siting art in the street seemed to some artists an escape from the limitations of a critical discourse based on gallery experiences, just as happenings were a way out of commodification. For commissioning bodies, on the other hand, mainly city authorities supported by grants[9], and large corporations, public art was a means to imprint an identity of their own making on the built environment, a kind of logo[10]. Suzanne Lacy sees the move to public art as, in cynical terms, an expansion of the market for sculpture; but also identifies a new activism informed by Marxism and feminism, particularly the latter, leading to what she terms new genre public art (Lacy, 1995:26–7)[11]. Within this category, artists such as Dominique Mazeaud and Mierle Ukeles (Lacy, 1995:262–3 and 201–2) have engaged with environmental issues, Ukeles working with the waste disposal systems of New York and Mazeaud carrying out a ritualised and reflective cleaning of a river bed in Santa Fe. For Ukeles, walking the five boroughs of New York to shake the hands of garbage collectors in a work titled *Touch Sanitation* (1978–79), art activism integrated a refusal of commodification with a democratisation of the audience, and an invitation to that audience to become participants. Writing on this area of new art practice, Suzi Gablik, in 1991, asserted that the criteria by which art should be evaluated included its capacity to overturn the (Cartesian) way of thinking about the world which had produced environmental destructiveness (Gablik, 1991:26).

Land art, as in the work of Mary Miss, Nancy Holt, Robert Morris, Alan Sonfist, Walter de Maria, Robert Smithson and others in the USA for whom the land itself is their material, is a specific strand of art's wider dematerialisation[12] and quest for new audiences and contexts. Its response to a desire for alternative settings is mediated, perhaps, by an attraction to the open spaces of a vast land mass. This attraction is linked to the North American tradition of the log cabin and the pioneer, and to the self-sufficiency of Thoreau's *Walden Pond*. Wilderness landscape, and its juxtaposition with or absorption by landscapes of civilisation, is a persistent theme in north American nineteenth-century painting, and has been identified as a background element in the Nine Mile Run Greenway project's philosophy[13]. Just, then, as holes in the ground can be mapped as not-landscape and not-architecture, so land art can be thought of as not-wilderness. At the time land art became known, from the 1970s, other artists, mainly British and more in the area of conceptual than environmental art, walked the land and recorded their reveries in photographs and texts, or made slight interventions unlikely to disrupt an ecosystem (in the days before chaos theory's mythicisation of the butterfly's wing-beat) – Hamish Fulton, for example, and Richard Long. Their walks were often in remote places, from Peru to Tibet, and their interventions restricted to replacing a few stones or taking a photograph. Andy Goldsworthy's work is an extension of this reuse of materials found on site, producing striking rereadings of landscape, though at the point where journeys to the North Pole become involved, the level of intervention becomes unsympathetic, and a critique (by two geographers) of Goldsworthy's identification with place in his project for 100 sheepfolds links his likely place in future cultural history to the possibility of a Goldsworthy trail[14].

From its beginnings, however, land art had a practical aspect, and involved for some artists the reclamation of industrially pillaged landscapes[15]; projects were not always successful – Robert Morris, for instance, contributed to the further erosion of an abandoned gravel pit near Seattle in 1979–80, by removing trees in a gesture designed to foreground the industrialisation of the site. Perhaps, too, Robert Smithson's *Spiral Jetty* of 1970 in Utah, and his later (unrealised) proposals for sculpting mining wastes in Colorado, could be seen as colonising the land for art-space[16]. Here, land art becomes not-mining and not-playing with earth-moving equipment. Fulton argues that art which reconstructs the land in this way lacks respect for it, though it could equally be argued that there is, in Europe at least and perhaps over most of North America outside the desert, very little nature which remains unreconstructed by agriculture. Land art is not, in any case, confined to remote or rural areas. Alan Sonfist planted native species of tree to recreate the original landscape of a vacant lot on the north edge of SoHo (1965–78); more recently, playing on readings of nature and culture within urban streetscapes and the artificial landscape of parks, Eve Andrée Laramée constructed a series of three installations of flora on the back of trucks. Made for the Natural Reality exhibition in Aachen (1999), these were driven through the city, texts on the truck sides stating, for instance, the volume of greenery required to counteract the atmospheric pollution produced by driving such a truck. Another states: 'Reality must take precedence over public relations for Nature cannot be fooled' (Figure 6.1)[17].

Reclamations

Reclamation art, dealing specifically with sites of dereliction in cities or surrounding areas, has the same potential range of relations to site as other forms of non-gallery art, from aesthetic statements to projects which link land use to democracy, but has increasingly moved towards social concern, if not activism. One instance is the work in Boston of a group called Reclamation Artists, co-ordinated by Joan Brigham; between 1990 and 1995, the group organised five temporary installations of work in the sites of a neglected and polluted inner city landscape when the demolition of a raised freeway system opened access to the margins of land beneath the freeway. Some of the work had a specifically ecological theme, creating access to bodies of water or referencing the diversity of plant and bird life which survived almost secretly on the sites, whilst, more generally, the presence of art drew public and press attention to issues of site, ownership and access in relation to the Central Artery Project. Brigham writes 'We are dedicated to attempting to ensure that the adverse impact of CAP's plans can be mitigated by the adoption of some of our proposals to preserve the land for common use. Meanwhile, we "reclaim" land for increased public awareness and for public debate . . .' (Brigham, 1995:385).

Figure 6.1 *Eve Andrée, Laramée,* Parks on Truck *(detail), 1999, Natural Reality exhibition, Ludwig Forum, Aachen (photo M Miles)*

Reclamation art, then, takes place in the context of the reclamation of ex-industrial urban sites for new uses, and seeks to influence the determination and character of future use. Its range of possible responses is conditioned by the scope and status of reclamation itself, whether of land or redundant buildings. But the reclamation of buildings has both condoned and transgressive forms associated with differing levels of abundance and official sanction. A disused factory transformed into high-rent lofts is not perceived in the same way as an empty house squatted by homeless people, though both are reuses of empty space for domestic purposes. The difference is less in the legality than in the coding: either as urban development denoting the spread of the affluent society, or regeneration associated with the efforts of the non-affluent to help themselves. For the interests of capital, self-help of this kind poses two threats: it draws attention to the uneven distribution of the benefits of development, and it indicates that social groups marginalised by development may help themselves to more than empty buildings; they may take back their right to the city[18]. Reclamation art, too, recodes spaces and lends them new associations and meanings, most often with official agreement, which will be perceived according to the same structures of difference as the reuse of buildings. Artists, as a social category, are in a borderland position; on one hand the concentrations of artists in redundant warehouses and factories in east London, Birmingham's Custard Factory or the dockside in Bristol, do not represent wealth – most rent studios there because the rents are low (and for the company of other artists); on the other, some specific artworks, and more often the culture of resistance, as in road protest, do seek radical social change. But the recoding of districts for art is part of a wider redetermination of the city and its symbolic economy in which, as Sharon Zukin demonstrates in relation to New York (Zukin, 1995, 1996), cultural value, as in the delineation of cultural quarters, plays a central and affirmative role[19].

The possibilities for reclamation differ, then, according to the agendas of which they are part. These agendas may be commercially driven or involve dwellers in the regeneration of local economies and patterns of sociation. The Nine Mile Run Greenway project involves local people in the regeneration of open space, and the non-productive (in capitalist terms) use of a site for the conservation of biodiversity. Most urban development, however, responds to agendas in the private sector, not confined to the circumstances of individual cities but linked to transnational networks of capital. This kind of development has little use for regeneration[20], but increasingly involves the recoding of commercial and industrial buildings and sites as cultural zones; examples include the Tate at Bankside in London, and Tate of the North at Albert Dock in Liverpool, the wholesale redevelopment of Cardiff Bay as a set of waterside vistas, the zoning of Temple Bar in Dublin as a cultural quarter, and proliferation of cafes, bars and clubs in Castlefield, Manchester. Other cases, such as South Street Seaport in New York, the harbour area of Baltimore and gas-light district in San Diego, Pioneer Square in Seattle, or Wigan Pier and Ironbridge in England, are zones of heritage and tourism. For developers, these two, overlapping kinds of reclamation – for culture and for tourism – are a pioneering element in urban renewal which rescues sites from dereliction and invites consumption. From another perspective, cultural zones aestheticise the city and increase its polarisation into areas of affluence and deprivation, whilst the narratives carried by heritage and tourism are seldom critical and frequently part of a homogenisation of culture in keeping with the dreams of world domination conveyed by companies such as Disney.

In contrast, experiments in social organisation and economic self-sufficiency, such as Tinker's Bubble in Somerset, Crystal Waters in Australia (based on permaculture), and the occupation of a disused brewery site in south London renamed Pure Genius[21], suggest that reclamation, as occupation of land, can also take the form of very local solutions which by virtue of that specificity go against the grain of globalisation. Perhaps one of the more interesting roles for reclamation art is, then, to give form to ideas for alternatives to development on the global pattern, reclaiming sites and cities for dwellers and for the fragile but sustainable ecologies which are incompatible with fantasies of an ever-expanding economy. This is a more specific definition for reclamation art, and it is in this context that artists have increasingly turned, since the 1980s, to work in spaces of industrial waste, such as Nine Mile Run, or have taken the issues of environmentalism and ecology as subject-matter. Reclamation, in this sense, means reclaiming more than space, taking back the power to shape a possible future, and realising that, perhaps, the planet's human population does not have exclusive rights to that future.

But models of future worlds require, to be credible, evidence of possibility. In this respect, some artists have collaborated with other professionals to develop practical ways in which to heal damaged and polluted landscapes. Mel Chin's Revival Field, for instance, is a three-year pilot project begun in Minneapolis in 1989 (Lacy, 1995:210–11). Working on a poisoned waste site, Chin worked with an agronomist, identifying plants (called collectively 'hyperaccumulators') which take up toxins such as cadmium or zinc from the soil. The site was given a simple geometry of a circle within a square, divided into four quarters, each with different planting, bounded by a wire fence. Corn, bladder campion and pennythrift, amongst other species, were planted and duly harvested, and the pollutants removed by incineration; this was seen as a possible strategy for funding such projects when sufficiently valuable minerals are extracted. Chin has now proved the effectiveness of the technology, and at this point is prepared to hand over the idea, as science, for wider application[22]. European artists and arts organisations, too, have developed reclamation projects, including Hermann Prigann's projects for brownfield sites in Germany and Belgium (Prigann, n.d.). In 1999, nine artists from Europe and the USA were invited by the Mondriaan Foundation to design billboard works for the periphery of a landfill site near Breda, in a project titled Tales of the Tip. And in 1997 in Quaking Houses, a mining village in the north of England, a group of local people formed an environmental trust to create, in

Figure 6.2 *Earth Centre, near Doncaster: natural treatment of waste in reed-beds (photo M Miles)*

collaboration with scientists from Newcastle University, artist Helen Smith and the Artists Agency in Sunderland, a wetland to naturally cleanse local water sources of pollution from mining wastes[23].

Most artists' initiatives are independent of, though usually permitted and sometimes funded by, official bodies. This allows them to be more closely linked to local publics than is possible for top-down schemes such as the Dome. Most large-scale reclamation of brownfield sites, however, is within state or municipal control and operation. But the Earth Centre, an ecological exhibition and demonstration site in a disused colliery near Doncaster in Yorkshire, funded through the national lottery as a millennium project, is an unusual case. Opened in 1999, the site has been presented as an ecological theme park. But there are no rides or entertainments; it has a museum-style shop selling organic chocolate, natural cotton clothing and books on ecology, and a restaurant in which most food is organic and locally sourced. In its main gallery, Planet Earth Experience, images of earth, air, fire and water are projected through a series of moving panels representing, through semi-abstract forms, animals, fish, birds and people. The effects change according to people's movement through the room, shifting from states of purity to intimations of disaster. Outside, demonstration organic and dry-climate gardens, solar energy and growing willow shelters and fences are part of what might be described as a public education programme. The Earth Centre's publicity material states that it '. . . exists to provide inspiration and access to people and organisations that can help individuals make decisions . . . that will make a significant and positive impact on our future . . .' (Earth Centre, 1999). And it seeks to be a model of the good practices it promotes, minimising energy consumption, encouraging visitors to use public transport and operating open management. It remains to be seen whether the concept of a theme park can be subverted from within[24], but its use and treatment of water stands for its environmental policy – all water on the site, from rain, drainage and sewage, is reprocessed for re-use on the land. Visitors can see sewage cleaned by natural methods in Waterworks (Figure 6.2), where it flows through beds of reeds, willow and papyrus. A jug of the output is exhibited daily and, though not pure enough to drink, is colourless and odourless – in fact, the whole interior of Waterworks is free of odours other than those of the reed-beds. The Earth Centre, then, presents a series of alternative solutions, which it tries to practise as well as preach, for the reclamation of brownfield sites, though it has no interface with art.

Nine Mile Run and Community Participation

The Nine Mile Run Greenway project, which aims to reclaim parts of a 238 acre site of steel industry slag dumping for public space and biodiversity (Figure 6.3), is located in the genre of reclamation art, with its associated histories of land art and art for environmental conservation. It was initiated by five members – Bob

Figure 6.3 *Pittsburgh, Nine Mile Run Greenway: view from upper slope of slag heaps (photo M Miles)*

Bingham, Tim Collins, Reiko Goto, Richard Pell and John Stephen – from the Studio for Creative Inquiry at Carnegie Mellon University, Pittsburgh, and its philosophy owes something to that cultural history in which issues of wilderness and civilisation are represented; but equally to the ideas of practical experiment, inter-disciplinarity, negotiation and contingency which characterise Chin's work. Pittsburgh is today a post-industrial city, with redevelopment schemes for its redundant industrial buildings and open spaces. The Greenway is located in the web of shifting perceptions of the city and contestations of who has a right to the city, or to its reconfiguration in a post-industrial future.

Part of the Nine Mile Run site has been designated for new housing by a coalition of the city authorities and private-sector developers; some groups of local people would like to see it incorporated into a network of old parks and new waterfront trails, others to see it left to wildness (and wild turkeys); and the project, which aims to see a third of the site set aside as public space and a zone of biodiversity, is led by a team of environmental artists for whom it is an opportunity to create a post-industrial landscape. The Studio for Creative Inquiry is a research centre supporting cross-disciplinary work attached to the College of Fine Arts at Carnegie Mellon University, which began work on the project in 1996. Acting to bridge the agendas of competing interests, such as those noted above, through workshops using methods similar to those of action planning, and an education programme in local schools co-ordinated by Reiko Goto, the Studio is producing a detailed conceptualisation for the site which attempts to reconcile the needs and perceptions of dwellers, developers and city authorities, with scientific research on the requirements for sustaining wildlife and aesthetic sensibilities. Once a detailed proposal has been agreed, documented and given appropriate textual and visual forms (using digital imaging), the ideas will be handed over for others to put into practice. Like Chin, the artists seek no continuing authorship[25]. The team of artists do not propose to site conventional art in Nine Mile Run, nor to recode the site as art-space. In seeing their role as facilitators and intermediaries, they follow the methods of conceptual art, dealing with ideas rather than material; but they also depart from these methods, not only by participating in practical experiments for greening the site and monitoring biodiversity, but also in not privileging the artist's viewpoint within a critical discourse. A comparison could be made here with the work of Helen Mayer Harrison and Newton Harrison, who, since the 1970s, have combined conceptual art with research in areas such as science and ecology. In 1998, the Harrisons produced a series of large-scale maps of the area between the estuaries of the Humber and the Mersey, plotting the likely outcomes of free market development, and alternative futures including the re-creation of forests and introduction of protected zones of biodiversity. The Harrisons, although using an open studio technique, confer mainly with other professionals and maintain a top-down approach (epitomised by the viewpoint of the map), whilst the Studio generates proposals from more structured workshops with local people and professionals; and the Harrisons produce schemes for which they then seek political support, whilst the Studio begin with the kind of negotiation which implies support at a later stage, since they claim no ownership of the proposals.

The site Nine Mile Run takes its name from its distance from the confluence of the Monongahela and Allegheny rivers which join to form the Ohio. It consists of a stream valley bordered by mounds of slag, much of it dumped illegally but ignored by the city authorities – Pittsburgh was a steel town – and as high as a 10-storey building[26]. Steel slag is hard, grey and porous, and although it contains fewer toxins than some industrial effluents, it has no nutrients either and cannot hold water[27]. Where pockets of trees and undergrowth appear, it is in places where other kinds of material have been added to the dump, principally waste from building and demolition sites. This provides a soil in which roots can take hold and water be retained. Along the stream bed, vegetation is quite lush (Figure 6.4), and the valley was identified in 1910 by Frederick Law Olmsted Jr (son of Olmsted the planner of Central Park) as 'the most striking opportunity' to create a public park. Olmsted wrote:

> Its long meadows of varying width would make ideal playfields; the stream, when it is freed from sewage, will be an attractive and interesting element in the landscape; the wooded slopes on either side give ample opportunity for enjoyment of the forest, for shaded walks and cool resting places (Olmsted, 1910, cited in Simony, Brodt and Pryor, 1998:14).

Nine Mile Run is bordered to the north by Frick Park, a reminder of the philanthropy of the city's wealthy families in the nineteenth century. The park is a little run down, but efforts are being made to raise funds for its restoration, and the Greenway would create a green open space from Frick Park to the Monongahela River shore.

Green areas are seen as part of the city's future image, and the city authority has worked with the private sector to regain public access to several miles of waterfront. A trail for walkers and joggers (known as the Jail Trail because it begins near the city jail) now runs along the downtown (north) shore of the Monongahela River; another trail is planned to link Pittsburgh with Washington, DC. A nineteenth-century railway bridge no longer used for trains has been converted, with addition of access ramps, to pedestrian use as part of a waterside trail. On the downtown shore of the Allegheny River, landscape architects Susan Child and Stanton Eckstut have designed a strip of trees, grasses and cornflowers – very much the kind of constructed nature to which Laramée's trucks in Aachen drew attention[28]. But these are fairly conventional kinds of urban public space, with the usual provision of landscaping and seating. The Nine Mile Run Greenway project aims to go beyond such conventions, to 'identify, experiment and model the application of sustainable alternative approaches to urban open space . . .'[29]. In doing so it engages with three questions. Firstly, what are the strategies and

Figure 6.4 *Pittsburgh, Nine Mile Run: lush vegetation by the stream bed (photo M Miles)*

Figure 6.5 *Pittsburgh, Nine Mile Run: Tim Collins collecting old tyres from the site (photo M Miles)*

constituencies for defining and progressing the agenda? Secondly, given the complexities of a post-industrial city, what constitutes an identified public for the project? And, thirdly, given that the Studio for Creative Inquiry is part of a College of Fine Arts, is the work of the artists still art? The last question may seem the least important, or part of art's self-referential dialogue, but it links to wider questions as to the relation of the social and aesthetic dimensions of culture, and the intervention of artists in changing ways of thinking about the world which have led to the damage to the land which the Nine Mile Run Greenway project seeks to heal.

The project's stated philosophy describes it as 'an experiment in public discourse', and affirms a 'unifying theory' for reclamation 'as an integrated ecosystem restoration that embraces the complex goal of "nature" in the context of contemporary urban culture' (Simony, Brodt and Pryor, 1998:4). This is interpreted as retaining the needs of ecosystems, as in the stream bed, for survival, whilst equally recognising the ecosystems of people in housing areas, and accepting that what for non-human creatures is nature, for humans can also be culture in the form of recreational space. The statement continues: '. . . integration of the reclamation into the social fabric of the community is essential'; the rationale is that when a reclamation project arises from local support, and meets the needs of local people as well as those of natural systems, then it is more sustainable. A previous case at Sudbury, Canada, is cited in support, where 3000 people were employed in landscape restoration over a 15–year period[30].

This integration discounts any attempt to restore the site to its original condition, which would involve removal of the slag – a vast undertaking in itself, raising the question of where it could be put without causing another destruction of the landscape; and allows for selective import of plant species likely to prosper in the conditions of the site. The vegetation of Frick Park is taken as an indicator of what these might be. The grey slopes of the mounds, however, are not easy to green, and are steep, and in 1999 were sprayed with a mulch containing a mix of nutrients and grass seeds, to establish a thin surface green layer, to begin the process and help other life to survive. This will also make the site more aesthetically pleasing. Where material has collected on level surfaces, small trees representing 10 to 15 years' growth are found. A further aspect of the integration of the project with the social dynamics of adjacent urban and suburban areas is the creation of a sense of ownership of the site. As steel slag, it was legally owned by Duquesne Steel, and emotionally by no one. The evidence of litter, such as old tyres and televisions, indicates that for some local people it remains a dump. The artists seek to counteract this through participation, but also regularly remove litter to improve the visual aesthetics of the site (Figure 6.5). Aesthetic perception affects the site's public image, and the experience of Sudbury is again cited to support a strategy of using appropriate scientific methods within a cultural context[31]. Amongst the scientific methods are restoring soil-chemical balance, establishing initial stability for vegetation and enabling longer term biodiversity.

There are also specific methodologies in relation to the stream, the water of which is partly contaminated by the effluent from storm drains, whilst supporting some life and being visually quite clear. Part of the solution is to divert the sewage, open up culverted areas and protect the water quality; but equally important within the project's philosophy is to talk with people in the areas where pollution is produced, spreading awareness of how the stream becomes polluted and, in a wider ecological context, how urban settlements can use less water and put less poison in the drain. Similarly, an education programme in schools is intended to encourage interest in, and care for, biodiversity. The Studio has set up a trailer near the stream bed as an information point. It is also used as a base for meetings and keeping tools, and for making links to other local groups. The Studio, in addition, conducts walking tours along the stream bed.

One of the main roles for the team of artists is to mediate between the structures and languages of professionals and non-professionals, and those whose interests are vested in differing needs – such as citizens' groups, city health authorities, planners and developers. The upper reaches of the slag are zoned for new housing, which will involve levelling some stretches and further loss of vegetation. The developer's first plan was to cover the stream and impose an entirely cultured landscape on the site, replicating the generalised aesthetics of other sites and cities and importing both the plants and the surface layer of soil. Previous proposals for development had met with local opposition, as in 1982, when a proposal for a mall was successfully blocked, but in 1995 the city authorities reacquired the site and appointed a developer to work in partnership through an Urban Redevelopment Authority. The main strategy for enabling participation by local people, through 1997–99, was a series of meetings, workshops and round-table discussions. In July 1999, an exhibition was presented, articulating ideas through art and digital image technologies. Four specific themes were investigated by professionals from science, art and planning, local people and city officials. These were history, context and public policy; stream remediation; community and ecology – slag, soil, plants and wildlife; and sustainable open spaces. Local people were able, through this structure, to interact with city officials and developers, having added status as members of a workshop[32]. They also became informed, enabling a more focused approach and selectivity, as the ambience of the project became increasingly one of negotiation rather than confrontation. Some gains were made, from the Planning Commission's imposition of controls on the development after public consultation in 1997, to changes in zoning in keeping with the Greenway strategy in 1998. Much in the situation remains, at the time of writing, fluid. Fluidity, of course, is potential, though some things may yet be more potential than others.

A topic like stream reclamation might seem a specialist area, but this discussion group was an important step in communicating the diversity already in the site, and began with walking tours. Heavy rain the previous day conveniently produced storm drain outflows and a breakdown of the sewage system. An afternoon session began with 10-minute reports from specialist advisers, and an overview of precedents elsewhere in the USA. A total of 50 people participated, and were reminded of Article I, section 27 of the Pennsylvania Constitution:

> The People have a right to clean air, pure water, and to the preservation of the natural scenic, historic and aesthetic values of the environment. Pennsylvania's public natural resources are the common property of all the people, including generations yet to come. (Simony, Brodt and Pryor, 1998:69)

What the people who inherit this statement of Enlightenment values actually get is (according to the Allegheny Health Department) 'high concentrations of Fecal Coliform bacteria . . . potential for infection by viruses . . .' and so on (Simony, Brodt and Pryor, 1998:69). Comments in a following workshop included, to give a random and edited sample:

> An inherent conflict exists if political officials (who are elected for two-year terms) have authority over sewer maintenance . . .
> No one wants to make a commitment which costs money . . .
> By the report released by the URA themselves, that is a lie, a misrepresentation. There are additional hazards . . .
> I don't care about a greenway project. What we have to talk about here has to go forward with or without a greenway project . . .
> If we don't address the problems upstream, we are dealing with the symptoms rather than the cause. If you do that the cause continues to decay. I am not a fan of wetlands; it avoids the real problem, the sewers . . .
> (Simony, Brodt and Pryor, 1998:86–95 [remarks in original text are attributed])

What emerged from the workshop was an understanding that the causes of stream pollution were from outside the valley, that there was uncertainty as to responsibility for repairs and that perhaps fines were cheaper than repairs anyway, that some citizens' groups were familiar with and willing to use legal processes, and that the relation of the greenway project to the housing project was implicit rather than explicit in the discussion, but a reality.

Such findings are not in themselves an action plan, but establish a solidarity amongst (at least some of) those taking part. Collins calls this 'empowerment through discourse', in a society which has fragmented its processes of decision making into specialist areas, privileging quantitative analysis over lay experience. Collins continues:

> We have learned to leave our decisions in the hands of experts, yet at the same time we have learned to mistrust those experts depending on who is paying for their opinion. . . . brownfield sites provide an ideal environment to 'reclaim' the individual's role in the discursive public sphere. We need to reclaim our relationship to complex public issues. (Simony, Brodt and Pryor, 1998:6)[33]

The workshops, then, did not seek to mask complexity, including that of conflicting propositions and outcomes, nor to affirm a single identity for the site, but allowed diversity, aiming only to provide a common space for its expression. A key question is the extent to which the voices heard can be said to represent the total diversity of voices of local neighbourhoods. The answer to that kind of question is usually at least in part negative, in that no form of representation translates all voices into one voice. Realisation that all representation distorts is part of the reconstruction of values in post-modern thought, but it presents particular problems for a project of this kind, which is obliged to reconsider notions of community when it is evident that communities linked by common attachment to place are also increasingly seen as an aspect of world which has either gone or is going.

But is it art? Each of the artists comes from a background of making art in non-gallery sites, and uses a particular skill within the project: Bingham documents through video, Collins tends to be most active in the project's public presentation and Goto works through the education programme and on monitoring biodiversity in and around the site. Collins and Goto define reclamation art as '. . . an opportunity to beautify a devastated landscape, and as an opportunity to commemorate (through formal intervention) the aesthetic components of post-industrial landscapes'. But they see it '. . . plagued by two controversial arguments . . . '. These are firstly, that reclamation can provide solutions which make future devastation of the land more acceptable, on the grounds that most kinds of mess can be cleared up, and, secondly, that reclamation art ceases to be art (Collins and Goto, 1996:1). The former argument is answered when it is realised that destruction takes place within a context and a value-structure, and that a post-industrial approach to the land will not replicate the destructiveness of the industrial, not so much because there are no more heavy industries (light industries also pollute), but, more to the point, because cultural attitudes have shifted, reinvesting green space with value. For Mel Chin the latter was a real question, in that the National Endowment for the Arts withheld his grant of $10 000 for Revival Field project on the grounds that it was not art at all, but science. Chin responded that he used the traditional method of carving – to remove material (toxins) to reveal form (cleansed earth) – and persuaded the NEA to release the grant. Collins and Goto see the act of reclamation as itself an aesthetic experience, and their funding body, the Heinz Endowments, is not concerned about the infinite varieties of aesthetic category.

To sum up: one of the most effective ways to prevent future destruction of the land may be to change the way people think about it and the associations they lend it. This is a cultural process involving frameworks and knowledges from many disciplines, and those of dwellers. Sustainable solutions are likely to be those for which local people feel an ownership, rather than top-down solutions which are distrusted or seen as rhetorical. Reclamation artists act as communicators and researchers, and as intermediaries between those who have power and those who do not, a possibility derived from the autonomy claimed for art in the modern period, which allows critical distance and independence of viewpoint whilst,

Figure 6.6 *Pittsburgh: a dog-owners' Sunday morning parade, May 1999 (photo M Miles)*

through the strategies developed here, also, in the post-modern period, regaining a sense of engagement and interaction with diverse groups in society. What projects such as the Nine Mile Run Greenway show is that autonomy can be combined with access, and that it is not the artist's experiences of everyday life so much as those of diverse publics, no longer neatly cohering as communities rooted in place, which need to be given equal weighting to those of experts. Pittsburgh has many publics, including one of dog-owners, who paraded one Sunday morning in May through the city to the downtown waterfront (Figure 6.6). Nine Mile Run is theirs, too.

NOTES

1. The chapter is based on information provided by the Studio for Creative Inquiry at Carnegie Mellon University, during a visit by the author in May 1999.
2. Another form of the vernacular, in the USA, is the Disney town of Celebration (Florida). Houses are in a variety of older styles, with porches, weatherboard and picket fences; home owners are required to observe a catalogue of regulations from not mending cars in the street to having only white or beige curtains. See MacCannell (1999).
3. Discussion of post-industrial cities is resumed in more depth in Chapter 8, as a context for other kinds of intervention by artists in the built environment.
4. A series of four workshops is fully documented, with verbatim accounts, in Simony, Brodt and Pryor (1998).
5. For another reading of Rodin which places more evidence on his relation to radical ideas and the continuation of Realism, see Elsen (1985).
6. For a history of changing concepts of the avant-garde, see Crane (1987). Crane writes: 'Greenberg argued that the goal of the modernist approach was to establish the autonomy of painting as an enterprise by eliminating from its activities effects that were associated with the other arts. Thus, as Greenberg says, "modernism used art to call attention to art". Because the flatness of the pictorial surface was more characteristic of painting than of any other art form, he argued that "modernist painting oriented itself to flatness as it did to nothing else"'. (Crane, 1987:55–6, citing Greenberg, C (1961) 'Modernist Painting', *Arts Yearbook*, vol. 4, pp 101–8, quote pp 103–4).
7. Rosler writes: 'The anti-institutional revolt was unsuccessful, and the art world has now completed something of a paradigm shift.' She argues that patterns of behaviour in the art world increasingly resemble those of the mass media, replicating notions of celebrity status. She adds: 'In fact, the art world has been called a branch of the entertainment industry . . .' (Rosler, 1994:57).
8. For a critical account of the development of the white-walled gallery, from the Museum of Modern Art in New York, see Grunenberg, 1994.
9. The National Endowment for the Arts, in the USA, established public art as a funding category from 1967 – see Miles (1997a).
10. For discussion of some contradictory aspects of the establishment of public art as a category, see Phillips (1988) and Miles (1997a).
11. Lacy writes: 'Moving into the public sector through the use of public space . . . was inevitable for artists who sought to inform and change. Because of their activist origin, feminist artists were concerned with questions of effectiveness.' (Lacy, 1995:27).
12. The term 'de-materialisation' was coined by Lucy Lippard in her book *Six Years: The Dematerialization of the Art Object*, New York, Praeger (1973).

13. See Kirk Savage, 'Art, Science, and Ecological Inquiry: The Case of 19th-Century American Landscape Painting', paper published through the Nine Mile Run Greenway project website: www.slaggarden.cfa.cmu.edu. Lucy Lippard (in Lacy, 1995) refers to a contrast between the 'holistic, earth-centered' view of indigenous peoples in America and the 'conquered, exploited and commodified' landscape of white settlement (Lippard, 1995:117).
14. David Matless and George Revill carried out extensive interviews with Goldsworthy in 1995, noting his work in Grizedale Forest, his use of photography to record ephemeral replacing of natural materials, and more recent work to reconstruct a series of sheepfolds. They conclude: 'While he welcomes a popularity beyond a narrow art audience, and a place on school curricula, a popular place-based art can be double edged. If art, artists and locality are so bound up, then what better way to understand Goldsworthy than to visit his places?' This leads to a worry that one day a sign will read 'You are now entering Goldsworthy country' (Matless and Revill, 1995:444).
15. For an overview of art with an ecological content, see Matilsky, 1992.
16. For an anthology of critical writing on land art, see Sonfist (1983).
17. See Ludwig Forum (1999) pp 118–9. Tim Collins and Reiko Goto, two of the artists working on Nine Mile Run, undertook a project on Aachen's buried water sources for the same exhibition.
18. As some of them did on 18 June 1999 when demonstrations were held under the banner 'Reclaim the Streets' in the financial district of London; property belonging to banks and financial institutions was damaged.
19. That artists are in a borderland position is demonstrated by the contrasting histories of London Docklands, in which the presence of artists' studios was one of the first signs of coming gentrification, and Wanstead, where several artists were amongst the occupiers of short-life housing in the path of demolition for the extension of the M11. See Wall, 1999:74–9. For other accounts of the cultures of road protest see McKay, 1996 and Field, 1999 (in Jordan and Lent, 1999).
20. Byrne argues that (for the most part) in the USA, the poor no longer vote, and in the UK national policy is determined in relation to the interests of affluent groups. He adds: 'The poor are politically relevant only as a source of disorder and crime, and responses are designed around the exclusionary maintenance of order . . .' (Byrne, 1997:66).
21. For accounts of Tinkers Bubble, Crystal Waters and Pure Genius, see Schwartz and Schwartz, 1998:43–54; 124–141; 54–65 respectively.
22. Conversation with Chin, Aachen, June 1999.
23. For a range of accounts of this project, see Griffiths and Kemp, 1999.
24. At the time of writing, visitor numbers were below target; but, take-up from school groups has been high. Unrealistic target numbers for visitors were set by consultants during the initial funding negotiations for the project, which was established, like most lottery-funded projects, as a capital scheme without revenue support. Although a large number of local people (many unemployed since the closure of the pits) were employed, in July 1999 some were again made unemployed when visitor numbers did not rise in line with those unrealistic targets. The messages conveyed by the Earth Centre's exhibits, however, are not mediated by government rhetoric, and have nothing of the insipid, fake or banal feeling of a theme park.
25. The structure of the Studio requires that projects constitute research, and it works only at a conceptual level. This could be seen as a limitation, restricting embeddedness in local networks; but the Studio sees its autonomy, enabling it to produce thinking not conditioned by vested commercial or state interests, as part of its value.
26. The site was used in the nineteenth century for farming, a salt works, natural gas wells and a golf club, then designated for housing and some of the stream put into culverts; in

1923 the Citizens' Committee on Civic Plan, an elite group of citizens, proposed that Nine Mile Run be turned into a civic park with recreational facilities. But 94 acres had been purchased by Duquesne Steel in 1922, with further purchases following, and used for dumping slag. Dumping continued until 1972, filling much of the valley.

27. The steel industry produces a range of noxious substances and emissions, including sulphur oxide, carbon monoxide and nitrogen oxide, but these are emitted as gasses. A participant in one of the workshops identified zinc, chromium, lead and sulphur as found in the slag.
28. For Child's and Eckstut's work at Battery Park City, see Beardsley, 1989:150–4.
29. Tim Collins and Reiko Goto, October 1996, from website http://slaggarden.cfa.cmu.edu
30. The source given is Lautenbach et al. in Gunn, 1995.
31. Bradshaw A N, in Gunn 1995.
32. Local people were invited on the basis of existing structures of representation, such as community and residents' groups. To give one example from a round-table discussion: participants included six members of the project team (four from associated departments in the University, such as Engineering and Planning); two local government officers; and representatives from Citizens for Responsible Development, Squirrel Hill Urban Coalition, the Town and Country Alliance, and three residents of Squirrel Hill (Simony, Brodt and Pryor, 1998:40).
33. Collins – the lead artist – cites Habermas (1991) on the emergence of the autonomous self through participation in the shared discursive process.

Chapter 7
Architectural Everydays

Introduction

The case studies in Chapters 4, 5 and 6 offer understandings of how people relate to, and state identities in, the environments they inhabit. Two of the cases are in the non-industrial, or non-affluent, and one in the affluent world, yet some issues are common to the three. These include the relation of aesthetic languages and perceptions to social life, the roles of dwellers and professionals in determining the built or green environment and the significance of the incidental and the ordinary. None of the cases concerns the construction of monuments, even the public buildings of New Gourna being modest in scale, yet each establishes its meaning in terms of local conditions which reflect wider, even global, currents; *hajj* painting, mud-brick building and the designation of a zone of public space and biodiversity at Nine Mile Run are, then, elements of a world which is the site of everyday life.

Each case involves participation by non-professionals, from the commissioning of *hajj* paintings by house-owners in Egyptian villages, to the construction and occupation of vernacular architecture, and engagement of citizens in planning workshops. In the Egyptian village, engagement is mediated by tradition, whilst the workshops begin to define a new participatory democracy, perhaps constituting the extension of the public sphere proposed by Jurgen Habermas[1]. What links these cases is the ability demonstrated by people to condition their environments rather than being conditioned by them. The possibility to shape a specific, local future is, in face of the spread of globalisation, a radical proposition, which suggests a deconstruction of power. Chapters 1 and 2 began to suggest alternatives to the dominant view of the city, for instance in women urbanists' claim to a right to the city and its carnival of difference, and Lefebvre provides another point of departure for consideration of the architectural everyday – for the study of the uses, occupation and embodiment of space, and its recoding through memory, association and desire – in his formulation of representational spaces. From this it is possible to see an appropriateness rather than marginality in, for instance, allotments[2] and informal settlements[3]. But if appropriations of the environment arise from desires to state identity, suggesting new models of intervention by professionals, this raises other problems, not least the need to redefine terms such as place and community for post-industrial cities, which will be considered in Chapter 8 as a context for new, interventionist practices in art. Underpinning the case for intervention in the built environment, and the informal settlements and self-build schemes discussed in Chapter 9, is a critical and theoretical framework investigated in this chapter.

The chapter begins with a reconsideration of the literature of community architecture. Whilst conventional architecture replicates dominant conceptualisations of the city through its methodology and hierarchies, does community architecture empower dwellers through design? Or is the alternative to conventional critiques of urban development found in writing on the architectural everyday? This literature concerns the things people do to construct their surroundings for themselves – to take back the house, the street and the city, dissolving the zoning of space as public and private. The literature of the architectural everyday recognises, in contrast to modernist utopianism and community architecture's enthusiasm, a contended and perhaps unresolvable complexity in the determination of urban futures, both built and social. The chapter finally notes a range of practices of appropriation which state identity within an affluent society, including the sanctioned and unsanctioned, from stone cladding to graffiti and skateboarding. Each practice has its own codes and forms of regulation, though these may be invisible to people outside the social context in which the practice takes place; graffiti on a subway train is as affirmative of its social order as gnomes in a suburban garden of theirs. Each is an element of the architectural everyday, in which the concept of architecture is not inevitably tied to the design and production of objects. To consider the everyday is itself to begin to imagine futures other than those prescribed by a market economy.

THE LITERATURE OF COMMUNITY ARCHITECTURE

Jeremy Till writes, in *Occupying Architecture* (Hill, 1998), of attending a meeting of his local Labour Party in north London, at which the speaker '. . . sustained a half-hour diatribe, eyes glaring, which laid all the sores of society at the feet of the architect' (Till, 1998:62). The subject was community architecture, and, as he recalls, the audience was left in no doubt as to who, of conventional and community architects, was associated with right-wing politics and corruption and who was not. As an architect, he admits, he left the meeting furtively. Audiences at conferences on art and architecture during the 1980s were treated to similar invective in which community artists rather than community architects were the new folk heroes. Architects have not always been effective promoters of their cause, seeming to be elitist, overpaid members of a male-dominated profession; but Till's essay responds to the case presented for community architecture as an alternative movement, and is not a defence of the privileges of architects. One of the issues underlying his concern is that whilst community architecture has become a specialism within architecture and its institutions, from higher education to professional organisations, its advocates have polarised debate as if architecture might be incompatible with social responsibility.

Till seeks to reconstruct a socially responsible and receptive role for architects and to interrogate simplistic analyses[4]. He argues that, specifically, the book

Community Architecture: How People Are Creating Their Own Environment, by Nick Wates and Charles Knevitt, published in 1987, became identified with the media face of its subject-matter. The writers are preoccupied with apocalyptic episodes of inner city disturbance, and uncritically link conventional architecture to a collapse of social value. Within this version of the urban war story, Till sees the book's image of community as vaguely or misleadingly defined: 'The word 'community' is always suggestive but never fully defined . . .' holding a promise of 'interaction, mutual support and communality' which it cannot deliver (Till, 1998:63). He adds that the community architecture movement reached a peak in the Thatcher–Reagan years when traditional values of community were displaced by those of market forces and social atomism. The sense of loss of democratic power produced by right-wing, market-led policies (and the real deprivations caused by Reaganomics) was a factor in the growth of alternative structures of power, as in single-issue campaigns; but more often the outcome has been nostalgia and a search for compensation in aesthetic solutions, such as public art[5], or in community architecture. Community architecture in the UK thus shares with the Garden City movement a retreat into a past which includes notions of unity and social cohesiveness (Wilson, 1991:101–4), for which there is little evidence and which are, today, incompatible with understandings of social difference. In the USA, as Denise Scott Brown states in a lecture at the Tate Gallery in 1988, 'Planning is like a haunted house since we have had Nixon and Reagan'; she, unlike Till, identifies the shift to the right as detrimental to community architecture. Definitions, however, differ: in the UK, community architecture is seen as small-scale and concerned with social housing, but in the USA, it refers to large-scale projects using community participation in the determination of plans for city districts (Scott Brown, 1990:41)[6], and it is this element of participatory planning about which Scott Brown is pessimistic.

Provoked by his experience at the Labour Party meeting, and the simplistic attribution of social violence to conventional architecture and social cohesion to community architecture, Till seeks to rupture the illusion. His critique has wider implications, including the need to reconsider understandings of community in a post-modern and post-industrial world where rootedness to place has little currency. A second problem is the position of women, as dwellers and professionals, in the design of the built environment, mainly overlooked by Wates and Knevitt. A third, noted by Till, is that when associations are made between community architecture and specific architectural styles, these are over-invested with meanings not integral to their histories, just as historical references become signs for traditional values[7]. A fourth problem is the methodology of community architecture, and the extent to which it questions (or not) conventional ideologies and power-relations between architect and client, or client and the state.

Publication as a mass-market paperback of *Community Architecture* (Wates and Knevitt, 1987) marked the height of the community architecture movement in the UK. Showing the Prince of Wales on its cover, along with elderly ladies looking at plans and young people suitably active on a building site, it proposed an alternative to architects' crimes. In place of 'manipulators of people to fit the system' it calls for 'enablers'; in place of a 'doctrinaire' ideology, community architects show a 'pragmatic, humanitarian, responsive and flexible' approach (Wates and Knevitt, 1987:24–5). Till cites a passage dealing with gangs of youths wielding knives and petrol bombs against police on a north London housing estate (Wates and Knevitt, 1987:15, cited in Till, 1998:63), and another in which the authors link violence to a lack of control by people over their environment; he responds:

> The argument is never explicitly made, but the implication of this hysterical opening of social unrest is clear: traditional architecture . . . is the cause of social breakdown; community architecture . . . will overcome these ills. (Till, 1998:63)

Traditional architecture refers here to the conventional methodology of architecture rather than to revivalist styles, the latter being favoured by the Prince of Wales and seen as elements of a stable society. But how far does a pragmatic and flexible approach go in directions, associated with traditional social values, which may themselves be socially divisive?

Wates and Knevitt cite Lord Scarman's inquiry into street disturbances in Brixton in 1981; Scarman argues that 'Local communities should be more fully involved in the decisions which affect them' and criticises a top-down approach to urban regeneration, though he does not refer to buildings (Scarman, 1981:6,7, 6.42(iii) cited in Wates and Knevitt, 1987:16–17) and his remarks could be interpreted as applying to politics rather than design. But Wates and Knevitt claim this aspect of the report was overlooked at the time but brought into focus by the Broadwater Farm disturbances four years later, during which a community policeman was killed. Against this background of violence, community architecture is introduced as an umbrella term to cover design as well as aspects of planning and technical aid. Wates and Knevitt know the built environment is a mess – 'characterised by ugliness, squalor, congestion, pollution, wasteland, vandalism, stress and the destruction of communities . . .' – that conventional architecture and planning have failed, and that '. . . a handful of pioneering development projects all over the country have demonstrated that it is possible to escape from this disaster . . .' (Wates and Knevitt, 1987:17). Unpicking the rhetoric exposes contradictions: the terms used to describe the built environment resemble those of urban war stories, and carry a certain charge of adrenalin, but are also dismissive of an environment which is more complex than being simply a product of design and which, in almost any circumstances, includes traces of everyday occupation which are easily subsumed in negative descriptions. The causes of urban unrest include deprivation in health, education, employment, transport and access to culture, as well as housing[8]; and though poor housing is linked to poor health, as Robbins appreciates (see Chapter 3), the designers of the post-war estates for which Wates and Knevitt have particular scorn were not reactionary or elitist, but committed to a more socially just society (which is probably why they worked in the unglamorous area of social housing). To attack their work as conventional architecture misses the point. And whilst the emphasis on process in community architecture is a response to the failure of schemes which emphasise form, there is no guarantee that community architects are better equipped than conventional architects to undertake this, whilst the sweeping characterisation of the environments of the poor as squalid and ugly situates Wates and Knevitt in the same territory as more elitist critics. Squalor is, like beauty, in the eye of the beholder, and certain signs or voices of unrest, such as graffiti, might be appropriate (or the only possible) responses to disenfranchisement, and may have their own complexities of narrative. Yet broad perceptions of an urban wasteland ignore these traces of social process. Robbins' critique is more careful and less sensationalist; and Wates and Knevitt (like the speaker at Till's political meeting) probably occupy a similar political position to the planners and designers of Thamesmead.

Wates and Knevitt are not, of course, the only writers on community architecture, and their book should be seen in context of the marginality of the movement in the late 1980s. In a more recent survey, *Building Democracy* by Graham Towers (1995), greater reference is made to the experience of specific projects. Towers still offers an image of the urban wasteland which uses words such as 'homelessness, poverty, declining educational and moral standards, increasing crime and lawlessness, sporadic violent unrest . . .' and so forth (Towers, 1995:xiii). But he is less ready to lay these ills at the feet of architects, and takes a wider view than Wates and Knevitt, noting, for instance, the role of ecological design in providing alternative technical solutions and the spread of community architecture to rural areas. He also covers a longer historical development, from the construction of mass housing during the industrial revolution to the present, including a range of recent case studies such as the Lambeth Community Care Centre and the Jagonari Centre for Asian Women, both in London (Towers, 1995:198–203 and 123–28)[9]. His approach is otherwise related to (but critical of) that of Wates and Knevitt[10]. He uses brief descriptions of Glasgow, Toxteth in Liverpool, Manchester Moss Side, and other sites, as snapshots of urban degeneration; but in his analysis of Broadwater Farm he notes that amenities such as shops and a doctor's surgery were dropped from the scheme for financial (not architectural) reasons. He describes how the estate changed from being popular to being hard to let, so that 'those in the worst accommodation, the unemployed, single-parent households' were concentrated there, and how drug abuse led to an association of the estate with crime. But whilst Wates and Knevitt use Broadwater Farm to attack conventional architecture, Towers recognises the progressive intention of its design[11], links its failure to the technical inadequacy of systems-building and lack of resources, and recounts collaborative efforts by community groups, the local authority and health authority to revitalise the estate after 1985. Towers proposes, however, that high-rise blocks will never suit families with children, and should be redesignated for occupation by elderly people in sheltered units, students and single people (Towers, 1995:225).

In another account, informed by growing up in a British colonial territory, Denise Scott Brown gives a history of community architecture linked to currents emerging from modernism, in particular from brutalism. She writes that in the post-war UK, social idealism was a strong current in architectural education:

> The ex-service students . . . saw social housing as their first concern. When I entered the AA as a fourth-year student in 1952, I found there an invigorating air of high endeavour and a major focus on social concern. At that time the Smithsons were part of the Independent Group at the Institute of Contemporary Art. . . . before they became gurus to the profession, the Smithsons became architectural comrades-in-arms to a small band of AA rebels. (Scott Brown, 1990:31)

She adds that her understanding of the term 'active' socioplastics used by Alison and Peter Smithson was that architects should design for real situations regardless of aesthetics[12]. She sees this not as an abandonment of architecture, but its redirection towards social relevance. The Smithsons later designed the pedestrian walkways of estates such as Broadwater Farm.

In general, Towers and Scott Brown offer more historically grounded appraisals than Wates and Knevitt, whose interest seems to be in mythologising people like themselves:

> It has been a hard – and often heroic – struggle, marked by bitter campaigns and frustration. Those in the vanguard of change are rarely welcomed or appreciated initially . . . (Wates and Knevitt, 1987:18).

They add that the 'breakthrough' came with the Prince of Wales's speech in 1984 at the RIBA, in which he declared that 'Some planners and architects have consistently ignored the feelings and wishes of the mass of ordinary people . . .' (cited in Wates and Knevitt, 1987:19). The authors then present a table of the attributes of conventional and community architecture. The binary division suggests opposition, and the claim, for example, that community architecture is 'likely to be multi-functional' is simplistic; the schemes they illustrate, such as Black Road, Macclesfield or the Catholic University of Louvain, seem to be single-function schemes for housing and education, whilst a prominent case of a multi-function (if utopian) project is Le Corbusier's *Unité d'Habitation*. The drive towards multi-function zoning which characterises some recent projects for urban regeneration is absent from *Community Architecture*, and probably requires the power of a partnership between planning authorities, dwellers, developers and architects to be achieved[13]. The case of Coin Street is one example of multi-use within a site, where social housing, retail units and a restaurant occupy spaces in a combination of new-build and reutilisation of the redundant Oxo Building.

Returning to the table of attributes presented by Wates and Knevitt, the ideologies of conventional and community architecture are described as 'Totalitarian, technocratic and doctrinaire . . . survival of the fittest' and 'Pragmatic, humanitarian, responsive and flexible, small is beautiful, collaboration, mutual aid'

(Wates and Knevitt, 1987:24–5). There are several difficulties here, even allowing that the lack of complexity is related to the book's publication for a mass audience, itself an assumption like that of modern planners that the poor cannot organise their own lives. The difficulties include questions of community, the role of women, style and methodology, stated above, but also issues of to whom the case is addressed. Much of what the book targets is the work of urban and regional planners and government departments. Today, with the widespread adoption of design-and-build processes, it is project managers acting for the client in the public or private sector who control a scheme and to whom the architect is subcontracted. In the 1980s this was not the case, but much design, even then, was contingent on the technical properties of materials, planning controls and, in the public sector particularly, lack of money. Pragmatism would seem at least as much an attribute of conventional as of community architecture.

Marion Roberts makes a different case for alternative architectural practices, structured around issues of gender and class, in *Living in a Man-Made World* (Roberts, 1991). This book offers a critical view which could be applied to conventional or community architecture, and is informed by feminism and the work of all-women architectural practices. Roberts calls for an architecture which meets the needs of women in domestic and work environments, and sees the role of women as designers as crucial to meeting this[14]. Neither does she set her case against a background of burning cars and barricades. Her context is defined by the position of women in the labour market, government policies to encourage home ownership and changes in the perception of the family as the key unit of social life (Roberts, 1991:6–12). She notes, for instance, the derivation of the design of high-level walkways in tower blocks from a liking on the part of the Smithsons for the active streets of working-class neighbourhoods, mediated by their desire to order such activity: 'By building long flat blocks with elevated walkways . . . it was hoped to do two things – to separate pedestrians from traffic . . . and to recreate the working-class street at high level' (Roberts, 1991:145–6), but argues that the image of the working-class street which conditioned this image was no longer extant by the 1970s. Women were increasingly part of the workforce, commuting to jobs, and adopted dispersed patterns of sociation more metropolitan in character and less dependent on the proximity of neighbours than in the pre-war years. Indeed, she cites evidence that those most closely mixing with neighbours were likely to be the poorest and thus least likely to be moved into new rather than existing council housing stock such as the tower block estates, which were initially seen as prestigious developments (Roberts, 1991:146, citing Stacey, 1970). Roberts adds that suburban cul-de-sacs, too, were designed to encourage neighbourliness so that middle-class women might 'achieve the nebulous goal of community' (Roberts, 1991:146).

If the goal of community is nebulous, and if Wates and Knevitt have little to say on the male domination of architecture[15], another difficulty arises when these authors try to map the contrasts of conventional and community architecture on to style, proclaiming a community-based vernacular in place of modernism. Rural vernaculars denote a pre-industrial society, and their formal languages evolve slowly; but in the 1990s, ersatz-vernacular has become a sign of out-of-town supermarkets, as well as, using more expensive materials, Poundbury, the Prince of Wales's model housing development in Dorset, which extends the tradition of model villages such as Bourneville and Port Sunlight[16]. Wates and Knevitt cite an extract from the Prince of Wales's speech at the RIBA, including his remark that 'the architect must produce something which is visually beautiful as well as socially useful' (cited in Wates and Knevitt, 1987:38). The Prince continued by saying that architects had no monopoly of taste, and that ordinary people should not feel guilty if they liked 'traditional' designs identified as 'a small garden, . . . courtyards, arches and porches'. These might be found in Poundbury, yet are remote from most vernacular traditions. Till summarises the approach:

> There is an underlying assumption that a certain vernacular will emerge effortlessly from the process of collaboration because that is what people most naturally relate to. Thus the Prince can conflate an argument about social use with one about style . . . The Prince's later association with a set of architects who propounded highly conservative stylistic values compounded the problem and forever associated community architecture with a certain regressive vernacular . . . (Till, 1998:69)

Till sees this as part of a depoliticising of architecture; it can also be seen as masking a nostalgia linked to heritage, hierarchy and in general the position of the political right. Till argues further that community architecture's claim to '. . . have radically revised the relationship between the architect and user', perhaps its central methodological claim, is unconvincing on the grounds that the involvement of users in design is '. . . set in opposition to the system of normative practice in which the architect is assumed to dispense design down from on high against the wishes of the client', a model he sees as over-simplified (Till, 1998:69–70). He cites geographer Gillian Rose, who argues against a simplistic characterisation of power as good or bad (Rose, 1992:303), and argues that through a rejection of influence, community architecture risks losing the ability to drive through projects in face of conditions outside architectural control[17]. Success leading to wider social change, it could be argued, is more likely to result from a strategy of negotiation and contention with (or subversion from within) structures of power, utilising the designer's professional status. Till reaffirms the value of architectural knowledge, and writes that utopianism in both modernist and community architecture '. . . results in a will to create pure forms for pure occupation. . .' (Till, 1998:65).

This brings the argument back to the main difficulty in the case for community architecture: its assumption that the idea of a community is transparent, that communities already exist and are simply waiting for nicer places in which to live their coherent and well-directed, meaningful lives. This overlooks the complexities of informal spatial organisation in traditional inner city streets, their gradual development and accommodation of tensions; instant neighbourliness does not follow, either, when dwellers from a range of previous housing areas are mixed in new estates however well-designed, though some community architecture schemes concerned the preservation of streets in which long-term patterns of sociation existed. But the generation of community spirit, rather than conservation of streets occupied by communities, is a mythicised form of a loss of social cohesion due not so much to design as to the fragmentation of a post-modern urban environment. Metropolitan patterns of sociation, and the overlapping construction of publics according to shared interests (which cut through strata of class, race, gender and place), means that the relation to neighbours of pre-industrial society is replaced by something less definable. As sociologist John Eade writes from a study of south London: 'People could imagine themselves as members of communities which spanned the globe . . .' (Eade, 1997:140). Rootedness in place is less important in post-industrial cities, and where it retains currency the notion of community may exhibit a negative aspect. Sennett argues that it is used as an exclusionary device against the non-white and non-affluent, seen as intruders in white suburbia (Sennett, 1996, referenced in Till, 1998:63–4), and sees racial prejudice as a product of a lack of community: '. . . a cover for their fear of having to be social beings, to deal with each other in order to cope' (Sennett, 1996:42). Till, too, sees the term community as alluding to but not delivering mutuality, adding that whilst a reappropriation of the environment by a community might lead to spatial reorganisation, much community architecture resembles suburbia and carries on the utopianism which undermines modernism (Till, 1998:65).

Till argues that a simplistic dissolution of architecture's autonomy is unhelpful; that architects have specialist knowledge which remains valuable but requires an appropriate political context to be socially (rather than solely aesthetically) effective (Till, 1998:73). But if community architecture, often depoliticised, appears a flawed response, are there alternative models, for instance in informal settlements in the non-affluent world? John Turner writes that 'it is easy to anticipate how wealthy observers feel when confronted with such overwhelming demonstrations of local actions' (Turner, 1976:23)[18], and comparison of his text with that of Wates and Knevitt suggests the latter, too, perceive disorder in the environments of the poor. But, as Till states, Wates and Knevitt are identified with the messianic, media face of community architecture. This is not to say that estates such as Broadwater Farm are not catastrophic design failures, but it is to say there are more complex levels of the problem, including those of political economy, and that local actions by non-professionals may offer insights alongside those of professionals.

The Architectural Everyday

The literature of the architectural everyday is recent. As a category it is broader than community architecture, covering informal settlements in non-affluent countries (discussed in Chapter 9), appropriations of the built environment by dwellers in affluent countries, and the ephemeral, from the building of small or incidental structures such as huts to the temporary uses of space which constitute a transient architecture of occupation. Whilst the literature includes references to projects by professionals[19], much of what it covers is produced by anonymous non-professionals; it is thus free of the advocacy which attends community architecture whilst constituting, as a whole, a critical challenge to the hierarchies of conventional architecture. To include glossy images of houses in informal settlements (Ray, 1997), or caravans (Horn, 1998), in an architectural publication is itself a comment on signature architecture. This literature reflects the diversity of post-modern cultural frameworks; a (deconstructive) critical pluralism allows the attachment of value to a shack as much as to an architect-designed villa, and an emphasis on settlements, habitations and sustainability denotes a (reconstructive) concern for post-industrial urban futures. A concern for the overlooked and imaginary does not constitute a rejection of architectural expertise, but a move of architectural practice into a critical, documentary and conceptual arena. This is not new[20], but the publication of what begins to be a body of literature, since 1997, suggests a coalescence of interest, and recognition that social change is not produced by the models of consultation or empowerment proposed by community architects (any more than by modernism), but is taking place all around in the everyday.

Amongst the publications which have defined the territory are *Architecture of the Everyday* (Harris and Berke, 1997); 'The Everyday and Architecture', an *Architectural Design* Profile (Wigglesworth and Till, 1998); Ann Cline's *A Hut of One's Own* (Cline, 1997); and *Occupying Architecture* (Hill, 1998), which includes Till's critique of community architecture discussed above, Paul Davies on Las Vegas, a narrative of skateboarding by Iain Borden, and Jane Rendell's story of the deconstruction of a house in which she once lived (discussed in Chapter 2). A complementary literature of citizen engagement in, and radical critiques of, planning practice has emerged parallel to that of the architectural everyday – examples include *Cities for Citizens*, edited by Mike Douglass and John Friedmann (1998); Leonie Sandercock's *Towards Cosmopolis* (Sandercock 1998a) and (edited) *Making the Invisible Visible* (1998c); *Images of the Street* edited by Nicholas Fyfe (1998); and, more contextually, *Giving Ground: The Politics of Propinquity* edited by Joan Copjec and Michael Sorkin (1999). Whilst the scope of the last title includes issues of globalisation and difference which are part of a wider discourse, all these titles share a concern for critical frameworks which are multi-disciplinary in derivation, culturally diverse in range, and democratic in intention. Many of the texts engage with the theories of Henri Lefebvre, particularly the translation into English of his *Critique of Everyday Life* (1992).

Wigglesworth and Till use the image of an island to introduce what the architectural everyday is not. There, architects explore notions of style and form in a self-referential discourse which feeds sporadically on imported luxuries: 'Occasionally boats arrive . . . bringing with them fresh supplies of theory, geometry and technique which inject the flagging body . . . with new life.' (Wigglesworth and Till, 1998:7). The isolation of architectural discourse supports a concern for signature buildings and unique design solutions, and privileges product over process, completion over occupation. They write:

> But of course we didn't really come to the everyday from the furthest shores of architecture. The everyday was always there, and we, like everyone else, were always immersed in it. To some extent it is this immersion which prevents us from seeing the everyday . . . But it is also from this immersion that specialised disciplines . . . attempt to escape. (Wigglesworth and Till, 1998:7)

They aim to recognise what high architecture suppresses, refuse the possibility of definition of the everyday, and cite Lefebvre as the philosopher of the everyday. In contrast to Wates and Knevitt, they reject binary and oppositional thinking, seeing the everyday as a pervasive condition for, rather than an alternative to, architecture[21], as well as the visual and performing arts.

A more detailed but not, in content, dissimilar introduction to the architectural everyday is given by Steven Harris (Harris and Berke, 1997); he notes the influence of Structuralism and post-Structuralism in architectural education, coinciding with an 'abandonment of architecture's social and political ambitions' in favour of commodification and consumption (Harris and Berke, 1997:2)[22]. The everyday becomes an alternative political construct to an architecture of elitism, informed by Lefebvre and Situationism, and resistant to consumerism. Whilst Wigglesworth and Till cite Lefebvre as a writer on a residual, almost post-architectural world, and Harris writes similarly that 'The everyday is that which remains after one has eliminated all specialised activities', Harris extends the argument by saying that Lefebvre's work theorises resistance to 'the forces of late capitalist economy and their complicit governmental authority' (Harris, 1997:3) through its focus on the repetitive and ordinary, the anonymous and incidental[23]. The ordinary, whilst producing a repetitive daily routine, can paradoxically be festive and celebratory. Lefebvre writes: 'When the world the sun shines on is always new, how could everyday life be forever unchangeable, unchangeable in its boredom, its greyness, its repetition of the same actions?' and introduces, as a way beyond the binary model of decline and progress, the more elusive but integrated concept of possibility: '. . . we must demonstrate the breadth and magnificence of the *possibilities* which are opening out for man [sic]; and which are so really possible, so near, so rationally achievable (once the *political* obstacles are shattered . . .' (Lefebvre, 1992:228–9). For Lefebvre, signs of possibility, as much as political realities, are found in everyday places.

To give an example of what he might mean: in a public lavatory on the waterfront in Hull, the men's section has been turned by the attendant into a conservatory for plants, including exotic species such as papyrus (Figure 7.1). Every available space is used, and the skylights provide excellent growing conditions. The cultivation of plants requires a regular and seasonal routine of watering and care,

Figure 7.1 *Hull: public lavatory – men's side (photo M Miles)*

and in this case has a decorative function which co-exists with the regulated use of the space and its keeping clean, which it does not inhibit. Perhaps this is a case of that possibility of which Lefebvre writes, a local and imaginative realisation of a world which is more than that prescribed by the necessities of industrial production: 'Through . . . labour, man [sic] has made himself real by realising a human world. . . . The totality of objects and human products . . . form an integral part of human reality' (Lefebvre, 1992:169). All this might be a surprise to the attendant, but the public lavatory is an everyday space recoded by its dual use (and a landmark, to which visitors to the city are taken).

Harris writes that the material collected in *Architecture of the Everyday* shares a distrust of the heroic and fashionable, and that potential sites of the everyday begin with the body[24]. The first essay in this anthology is by Mary McLeod, who sees Lefebvre's work as central to the events of 1968[25], and increasingly important in North America following the translation of his work[26]. Lefebvre's own essay 'The Everyday and Everydayness' follows. Why is Lefebvre so central to the discourse of the architectural everyday, when his concept of the everyday is so elusive? Firstly, Lefebvre reconstructs elements of Marxist theory, allowing certain tensions to remain rather than being resolved in a neat model of Progress. McLeod writes:

> Lefebvre stressed that contradiction is intrinsic to its [the everyday's] very nature. While it is the object of philosophy, it is inherently nonphilosophical; while conveying an image of stability and immutability, it is transitory and uncertain; while governed by the repetitive march of linear time, it is redeemed by the renewal of nature's cyclical time; while unbearable in its monotony, it is festive and playful; and while controlled by technocratic rationalism and capitalism, it stands outside of them. (McLeod, 1997:13–14)

This positive ambivalence enables Lefebvre to see further than class struggle and economics, perhaps, rather as Herbert Marcuse drew from the theories of Freud to enlarge a Marxist analysis of culture and social relations in *Eros and Civilisation* (1956), to reconstruct Marxism for metropolitan society in late capitalism[27]. Lefebvre's work constructs a non-hierarchic position between the Marxist notions of base (economy) and superstructure (culture), which is more effective, in McLeod's reading, than the organisation of labour in determining social change (McLeod, 1997:14). Lefebvre himself writes that the everyday, as much as great art, offers access to meaning, and McLeod maintains that Lefebvre sees everyday life as impossible to contain, always harbouring a desire for transformation (McLeod, 1997:15)[28]; but, also, Lefebvre writes that in the industrial era, the everyday is '. . . the platform upon which the bureaucratic society of controlled consumerism is erected', where modern techniques of production impose uniformity. (Lefebvre, 1997:34–6). The question, then, is how repetition can be transformed into liberation.

Secondly, Lefebvre retains a commitment to political action, in contrast to Barthes and the Structuralists, with whom he took issue from the 1960s onwards (McLeod, 1997:17). This includes a (sometimes equivocal) interest in women's roles in society[29], and relates to his link to Situationism and the events of 1968. His interest in the alternative strategies of the Situationists, such as the *dérive* of Guy Debord (which reconstructed the rambling of the *flâneur* into a semi-directed series of urban encounters), is matched by a concern to invert the conventional relation of high thought to the mundane:

> Practical activities were always the basis and the foundation for 'pure' thought, and even for its most extreme form, pure contemplation. What does the contemplator contemplate, if not – from afar – the everyday, the crowd, the masses . . . ? And yet the situation is eventually reversed. The day dawns when everyday life also emerges as a critique, a critique of the superior activities in question . . . (Lefebvre, 1992:87)

Lefebvre saw social change as a gradual process, not the immediate event for which Debord searched. The display in public places by the Situationists of Lefebvre's maxim 'under the pavement a beach', denoting a world of play beneath the surfaces of alienated reality rather than literally the sand under the cobbles torn up to hurl at police lines in 1968, served only to demonstrate the ineffectiveness of street protest[30]. What remains, then, is the activity of a professional and academic intelligentsia working within the dominant culture.

If there is a third reason for Lefebvre's importance for the architectural everyday, it is the attraction for architects, planners and urbanists of his emphasis on the production of space. McLeod argues that his concern for cities 'distinguishes his notion of the quotidian from many English and American discussions of daily life' (McLeod, 1997:24). To Lefebvre, the city is where capitalism acts out its operations and where its contradictions are most evident, hence where the conditions for change are most likely to occur. Lefebvre's rejection of nostalgia in *Writing on Cities* (1996:63–181), and proposal for 'multifunctional' and 'transfunctional' spaces (McLeod, 1997:25) attunes well with calls for multi-use zoning and a multi-layered streetlife. Much of the material in works on the architectural everyday not only references Lefebvre's writing, but illustrates the everyday in contemporary forms, such as mass-produced housing, street signage, minor architectural detail and temporary shelters.

Whilst the literature depicts the everyday, in some cases as an equivalent to the anonymous found object of early modernist art, Wigglesworth and Till also offer a professional strategy for design; this refuses seduction by the most advanced technical possibilities, proposing the use of easily available materials such as the by-products of industry:

> Technology transfer is alright as long as it is a transfer to architecture from industries like aeronautical engineering, boat building or nano-technology: cutting-edge manufacturing to which earthbound architecture aspires. (Wigglesworth and Till, 1998:34)

They respond with a notion of reverse technology transfer which can be done without specialist skills (using materials such as sandbags and straw bales) and might be fun. This kind of transfer has been taking place for some time in the non-affluent world, where, for instance, old tin cans are cut, flattened and transformed into toys, oil lamps and briefcases[31]. Similarly, in the affluent world, as Ann Cline narrates (noted in Chapter 9), ordinary technologies and materials are used in the building of *casitas* in the Bronx (Cline, 1997:19). But if the architectural everyday refuses the consumption and high technology associated with conventional architecture, how, apart from that it is theorised, does it differ from community architecture, and what insights does this literature offer which that of community architecture does not?

By considering architectural forms which are in many cases not designed but simply produced, just as space is produced in society at all times, writers on the architectural everyday have no vested interest in the subject-matter of their texts. But if architectural authorship is relinquished in favour of a more eclectic practice, expertise is retained as a critical tool. Social criticism thus takes the place of modernism's social engineering and of social work in community architecture; this critical activity, in text or design, is informed by critical perspectives from feminism and theories of difference largely ignored by community architecture. Additionally, writers on the architectural everyday, and contemporary critics of planning such as Sandercock, take a more experiential approach to what constitutes the glue of society than is evident in the literature of community architecture. The insistence in community architecture on received notions of community excludes more ephemeral categorisations of common interest amongst the publics of metropolitan cities. Gillian Horn, on the other hand, takes caravan parks as a case in which publics are constituted through temporary association. Such parks are not open year-round, and residents are assumed to have permanent homes elsewhere. Horn sees this as critical to the shared values of the caravan park: 'The presence of an absent double . . . allows the necessary freedom . . . to detach from the stringent assessments which we use to form our "real", but in effect mythical, communities outside' (Horn, 1998:30). Horn sees caravans as bypassing the criteria of wealth and status denoted by real estate, coming closer than suburban enclaves to community, in that membership is voluntary, association is not permanent and social performances are suspended. Lisa Peattie, contributing to *Cities for Citizens* (Douglass and Friedmann, 1998) and also refusing trite notions of togetherness, differentiates conviviality from community. Referencing Ivan Illich (1990), she proposes that the autonomous and creative interactions which Illich saw as the opposite to the regime of industrial production, that is, the element of social pleasure in purposeful acts he terms 'conviviality', become a way to rise above problems 'by celebration' (Peattie, 1998:253)[32]. She contrasts the permanence, stability and desire for roots implied by the notion community with conviviality's energy of dissent and desire for the creation of a sense of something which is, for a moment at least, special – 'whether it is a dinner party or a piece of political theatre . . .' (Peattie, 1998:247)[33]. For Peattie, conviviality has the advantage of being applicable to bounded and unbounded domains, manifest in temporary associations such as street theatre and carnival as in the long-term commitment of participants in struggle.

A third factor which differentiates the architectural everyday from community architecture is the understanding that radical social change is possible through both professional intervention and non-professional appropriation, and that these are complementary rather than contradictory processes, contextualised by a pragmatism which does not deny hope but sees the failure of utopianism as a caution against idealism and its associations with nostalgia. Perhaps the role of professionals then becomes to legitimate change (on the assumption that power can only be taken, that what is called empowerment might be a liberal form of retention of power in the hands of those who empower, but that taking power is not itself a violent or divisive act)[34]. And a fourth difference, finally, is that the agendas of the built environment have shifted since the 1980s, giving greater emphasis to sustainability, and to the encroachment of privatisation on the spaces of the public realm, and the fictionalisation of space produced in malls and theme parks. One of the points of departure for the architectural everyday, contextualised by Lefebvre's reconstructive Marxism, is its objection to the commodification and depoliticisation of life in the world of Disney. Diane Ghirardo writes of idealisation in Disney's Main Street USA, a seven-eighths size replica of a nineteenth-century street with trolley cars and Victorian-style lamp posts which is neither conservation nor museum, and of its one-dimensionality:

> Pure consumerism drives Main Street, for the only activities possible entail spending money on food or trinkets. Main Street lacks industry, poverty, and, most of all, political life. It does have private police and laws . . . (Ghirardo, 1996:48)

A more extreme and extensive form than, say, Sony Plaza in Manhattan (where only Sony products are on sale in an atrium called Public Space[35]), Disney's entertainment parks, in which political activity is forbidden, constitute a new totalitarianism. Their streets offer a pretence of public space, attended by the forms of democracy but lacking their content, purveying only a freedom to consume inside a world within the world (which seeks to render the world outside redundant). The emphasis on control is extended in Celebration, Disney's model town in Florida, where every design detail is co-opted to a prescription of civic order (MacCannell, 1999). Whilst globalisation and mass entertainment colonise life, then, a redirection of attention to what people can do by themselves and for each other is a radical act.

Appropriations of Space in Affluent Countries

People do many things for themselves and others. This includes reappropriating public space, as much as occupying the domestic sphere. The mass placing of flowers along the Mall in London after the death of Princess Diana in 1997 can be seen as an act of reclaiming public space from its monumental function. Beneath the inscription VICTORIA REGINA IMPERATRIX, on the Victoria Monument in the Mall, another, hand-made notice reads 'Let the message that lived in Diana's heart flourish in yours forever' (Figure 7.2). Amongst the trees were shrines and candles, iconic images and countless bunches of (mostly unwrapped) flowers (Figure 7.3). The sentiments and the means through which they were expressed may have been drawn from a restricted vocabulary, sometimes trashy, just as Diana was sometimes trashy, but for a week or so spaces within London's monumental zone were occupied by ordinary citizens creating a ritual of public mourning, often becoming starkly aware of deficiencies in their own lives.

For the most part, the daily lives of urban dwellers take place with little drama in suburbs and ordinary streets. Sometimes, when empty buildings are squatted, or open spaces occupied, lives become transgressive[36]. It seems that appropriations of space are allowed or disallowed according to the extent to which property rights (particularly those of property developers) are involved. Taste is another matter; whilst the application of stone cladding to brick, terraced houses might be regarded as in bad taste (a judgement which implies there is good taste), it is not discouraged, either as a commercial activity for suppliers or sign of ownership for dwellers. In fact, the whole point about stone cladding is that it, like *hajj* painting, denotes status, in this case of ownership. Only when someone owns rather than rents a house are they allowed to make major changes to its appearance, and the location of stone cladding on the street facade is a sign, with Georgian-style doors and double glazing, of identity. At the same time, it has become a mark to some commentators of incompetence in constructing an identity, as with the notorious stone cladding accentuated by bright blue paint of the Duckworth's house in *Coronation Street*[37]. From a different perspective, a sociological report (on domestic violence) takes the presence of stone cladding as a sign of suburban (but deceptive) stability: 'The estate . . . is litter free and there is more evidence of the neo-georgian door and the stone clad walls of the privatised house than of graffiti' (Hood-Williams and Bush, 1995).

The reading of stone cladding here is dependent on its site. In other circumstances, stone cladding denotes luxury – there are many advertisements and web sites for property developers which specify various kinds of stone cladding as an upmarket material. It is not ridiculed when it is part of the original design of a suburban executive house or office tower[38]. Stone cladding, then, is a case of the architectural everyday which has complex meanings; it may denote approved or disapproved taste, according to its location, and when used to mark the ownership of a previously rented house, in context of a government-led drive to increase home ownership in the UK during the 1980s, it draws from a restricted vocabulary (of what is available from builders or the DIY store) as a means to state membership of a community of home-owners. However, unlike *hajj* painting, it is based on possession rather than participation – the cladding is simply there, just as the house and the

Figure 7.2 *Victoria Monument, London: flowers for Princess Diana (photo M Miles)*

Figure 7.3 *The Mall, London: flowers for Princess Diana (photo M Miles)*

car outside are there, or the cola in the refrigerator and the lifestyle magazines on the coffee table; the *hajji* or *hajja*, in contrast, engages in the pilgrimage through a shared journey, and in the feast which welcomes him or her home, as well as in the everyday life of the village. Whilst it is easy to romanticise village life, which has many privations especially for women, it has a coherence which is quite different from the lack of ability to relate in a mature way seen by Sennett as characteristic of white suburbia. Sennet's explanation could be extended by linking that lack to a reliance on possession of things to mark identity. MacCannell writes:

> A fiction of deep subjective unity at the neighbourhood level cannot be based on possessions, whether these are material, mental or biological. Whenever assignment to a group is made on the basis of possessions, the group is designed to fall apart. . . . Deep unity at the group level can only be based on shared *lack*. (MacCannell, 1999:125)

This fits well with the conviviality of protest marches and campaigns, and the perceived solidarity of working-class neighbourhoods in a previous era[39].

Other, more anarchic practices have dual readings, again related to site. Graffiti can be a criminal offence, or art. On the sides of subway trains it is regarded by Sennett as evidence, to a range of publics, of the existence of an underclass. Sennett writes that in a city which '. . . belongs to no one, people are constantly seeking to leave a trace of themselves', but that this writing also obliterates the (property-based) values of that society from which the taggers are excluded – '. . . we write all over you.' (Sennett, 1990:205–7). But, in a small plaza with white garden furniture near the Museum of Modern Art in Manhattan is another work of graffiti: a section of the Berlin Wall which was transported to New York following its demolition in 1989. The wall's western face was continuously covered with graffiti, some of it as part of an officially sanctioned project by graffiti artist Keith Haring[40], as a sign for the supposed freedoms of the capitalist world. This is in the context of the use of abstract art during the cold-war years to promote American values, in opposition to the perceived limitations of Socialist Realism. So, graffiti denotes freedom, but also raises fears of a mythicised underclass who might rise up to destroy the city. But graffiti also became a commodity in the art market, as artists such as Keith Haring and Jean-Michel Basquiat were signed up by SoHo dealers such as Annina Nosei (Cresswell, 1996:36–7)[41]. Tim Cresswell sees a third aspect in it – that it dissolves the boundary of public and private space:

> It interrupts the familiar boundaries of the public and the private by declaring the public private and the private public. Graffiti appears on the streets, the facades, the exteriors, and the interiors that construct and articulate the meanings of the city. To the graffiti writer everywhere is free space . . . (Cresswell, 1996:47)

and cites Susan Stewart's interpretation that it reflects a Latin use of the street as a 'room by agreement' (Stewart, 1987:168, cited in Cresswell, 1996:47). Yet this affirmation of fluidity in coding urban spaces, that is, in producing space ephemerally through traces of its use, is neutralised when graffiti becomes art, added as another chapter in a tradition beginning with pop art in the 1960s, or perhaps with early modernism's incorporation of the primitive (Cresswell, 1996:51), and celebrated in a range of picture books[42].

If graffiti is open to a kind of institutionalisation, subsumed by the art market, or when graffiti artists are commissioned by arts organisations to work with youths from ethnic minority backgrounds to produce cosmetic solutions to urban problems, other appropriations of space which leave no visual traces are less so. Skateboarding, seen frequently, for instance, in the concrete spaces around London's South Bank arts complex, recodes public space as belonging to its temporary users in a way uninviting to outsiders, but makes little physical change to the site. Iain Borden gives a history of skateboarding from the 1960s, when it was an alternative to surfing in times of calm weather, notes that *Skateboarder* magazine has 165 000 readers, and dates the first purpose-built skateboarding park to 1977 in Los Angeles (Borden, 1998:201). Borden sees skateboarding as a dialectical interaction with architecture in which resistance and recreation takes place; referencing Lefebvre (1991) he argues that it refuses intellectualisation and visualisation in favour of touch, hearing and agility, being body-centric and mobile (Borden, 1998:206). From a different viewpoint, amidst suburban streets and allotments, David Crouch suggests that in many everyday situations, visual readings of (and conditioning by) architecture are supplemented by tactile experience. Crouch sees allotments as agencies for empowerment as well as providing space for bodily enactments within a shared culture; whilst some observers may see an anachronism, others '. . . identify with an image . . . [of] human labour, a creative landscape and a direct engagement with the land . . . intense human activity . . . inscribed on the edges of the street' (Crouch, 1998:167). He sees the reinscription of vacant sites by children through play as a similar kind of activity, a transformation of public (in the sense of open and empty) space into the equivalent of a room for conversation and escape. In the case he notes (from north-west London), children take into the site detritus such as old prams, furniture, clothes '. . . to imprint identity in a place they feel is their own' (Crouch, 1998:168).

In Rotterdam, outside a new art gallery designed by Rem Koolhaas, local male youths appropriate a railing dividing the centre of a flight of concrete steps for an inventive and skilful form of roller-skating (Figure 7.4). The society they form in their temporary occupation of the site does not exclude the gaze of outsiders (such as foreign academics on their way to see pictures by Picasso), but it does not invite it either. The aim is to slide all the way down without falling off, achieved in about a third of the attempts. The practice is highly regulated, everyone taking their turn, the rules obvious and success resulting from poise, balance and split-second reactions. Like skateboarding, this is a process in which the built environment is an arena for the projection of space by the body, not one in which the body is, as it were, constructed by the environment. The one key element of the site, without

Figure 7.4 Rotterdam: roller-skate riders (photo M Miles)

which the practice would be impossible, is the slightly bent railing; this divides a notional up direction on the stairs from a notional down, negated by the lack of need for any such division in steps where pedestrian use is slight, and by the ambiguity as to which side is which and which is the other.

NOTES

1. See Habermas, 1991.
2. See Crouch, 1998:166–9 on allotments and the embodied street.
3. Turner relates contrasting perceptions of the informal settlement of Arequipa: '. . . Beltran [a newspaper editor] saw a vast shanty town, instead of a huge construction site. Bedoya [director of a regional branch of the national planning authority in Peru] was speechless when Beltran went on to speak of his determination to rid these poor people of their dreadful slums which were in fact their pride and joy' (Turner, 1976:22–3).
4. Denise Scott Brown, in a lecture at the Tate Gallery in 1988, argued that '. . . housing the poor isn't primarily a design, or even a technical, problem; it is first an economic and political problem' (Scott Brown, 1990:31), but nevertheless supported the role of specialist architectural knowledge, informed by and using material from other disciplines such as sociology: 'So architects will have to learn sociology, not the other way round. We at least get a verbal education in school. They don't get a visual one.' (ibid.:32).
5. Public art was used by developers to lend a cultural veneer to enclaved development schemes, such as Battery Park City. For advocacy for place-making see Fleming and Von Tscharner, 1987; for discussion of various cases of artist-designed places from the 1980s, see Beardsley, 1989:127–56; for brief critical comment on a specific case in Cincinnati, see Miles, 1997a:74–5; and for critical accounts of public art and its limitations, see Phillips, 1988 and Selwood, 1995.
6. The cases given by Scott Brown include Hennepin Avenue, Minneapolis and a 25-year plan for downtown Memphis.
7. Wilson notes that in a MORI poll in 1989, 87% of those polled supported traditional architecture as defined by the Prince of Wales, and his attacks on Modernism; 81% approved of his neo-Georgian taste. Wilson sees the Prince as speaking to both 'genuine anxieties and to a hardcore philistinism' (Wilson, 1991:141, citing Jencks, 1989).
8. Similarly, the causes of ill health are related through social research, for instance by Ashton and Seymour, to a range of indicators of social (and to a lesser extent cultural) well-being or its lack. The WHO Healthy Cities project seeks, for this reason, to address needs as an integrated matrix. (Ashton and Seymour, 1988:152–68).
9. See also NHSE, 1994:36–7. The Lambeth Community Care Centre project involved user groups extensively in discussion with the architect (Robin Nicholson of Edward Cullinan Architects) from the beginning of the scheme in 1981, and was perceived by the NHS research group, around eight years after opening, to be successful.
10. Towers makes only two references to Wates and Knevitt, one critical of their lack of concern for design theory: 'Where it is discussed it is quickly passed over. Nick Wates and Charles Knevitt state simply that community architecture is "Unselfconscious about style. Any style may be adopted as appropriate . . ." [which] begs the question of what styles are "appropriate". Some are more user friendly than others. The deepest and most fundamental division in the debates about architectural style are between "formal" and "informal"' (Towers, 1995:191).

11. Broadwater Farm won a design award (Towers, 1995:220). See also Roberts, 1991:145 on the development of the elevated walkway design used at Broadwater Farm by Alison and Peter Smithson.
12. See also Fausch, 1997:90–1 for reference to the Smithsons, in context of modernism's uses of vernacular forms.
13. In as much as they consider this, Wates and Knevitt seem to favour a conventional functionalisation of space. In a section headed 'Why Community Architecture Works: The Natural Laws Governing the Relationship between Human Beings and the Built Environment', they state: 'Locating shops together in one street or square is generally better than having them scattered all over the neighbourhood' (Wates and Knevitt, 1987:114). Within many nineteenth-century working-class areas, however, shops and pubs tended to be situated on street corners, throughout the neighbourhood, acting as focal points of a lattice of sociation.
14. Roberts points out, for instance, that only 7% of architects are women, and that they are habitually (and pejoratively) assumed by men to be able to design kitchens (Roberts, 1991:1). Interestingly, she does not include Wates and Knevitt in her bibliography.
15. Wates and Knevitt subscribe to the safety approach to women's interaction with the built environment: 'There is increasing understanding that the quality of life is immeasurably improved by neighbourhoods which function properly – where the streets are safe for women and children to walk alone . . .' (Wates and Knevitt, 1987:109).
16. For a note on model villages in context of the Garden City Movement, see Hall and Ward, 1998:12–15. See also Wilson, 1991:100–120.
17. Till is influenced by Rose (1992), in particular her formulation of the notion of a 'holy' middle way where tensions are concealed rather than allowed creative play. Till ends: 'My alternative occupies the less defined place of the broken middle in which both architects and users relinquish the impossible purity of their communities and open up to a critical engagement with the forces beyond. Together they create and recreate architectures of the impure community.' (Till, 1998:75).
18. Turner's earlier work, with Fichter, is cited by Wates and Knevitt: 'When dwellers control the major decisions and are free to make their own contribution to the design . . . both the process and the environment produced stimulate individual and social well-being.' (Turner, 1972, cited in Wates and Knevitt, 1987:112).
19. Two examples are the scheme for two blocks in El Raval, Barcelona by Le K Architects, and the design of artifacts in recycled cast iron by Michael Marriott, both featured in Wigglesworth and Till, 1998:85–7 and 40–1 respectively.
20. Deborah Fausch outlines a history of the architectural everyday beginning with the entry by Venturi and Scott Brown for the Brighton Beach Housing Competition of 1967. This was called 'ugly and ordinary' by critics, a label adopted by these architects as 'a code phrase for their attempts to incorporate the forms, data, and communication structures of postwar America into their architectural theory and practice' (Fausch, 1997:75). Fausch adds references to the show *Signs of Life, Symbols in the American City* (Smithsonian, 1976) and the critical debate which followed it. Fausch also notes modernism's interest in vernacular forms, from the 1950s, and Venturi's attempt to integrate high and low forms in his work, and recognition that the everyday is a source of 'the complex and contradictory order that is vital and valid for our architecture as an urbanistic whole' (Venturi 1966:54, cited in Fausch, 1997:91).
21. Till's argument, published the same year (Till, 1998), for a retention of architectural knowledge, is consistent with the joint statement he makes with Wigglesworth: ' . . . this unequivocal disavowal leads to a disempowerment of user and architect alike. Instead,

we suggest that the real productive potential for architects lies in an endless movement between engagement and retreat' (Wigglesworth and Till, 1998:7).

22. Harris also notes alternative approaches around the work of Herbert Marcuse and Norman O. Brown, but sees the triumph of Structuralism as an outcome of the failure of radical movements in the USA and France after 1968.
23. Harris links Lefebvre's interest in the everyday to the Annales school of historiography, with its detailed research into the conditions and human interactions of daily life in small towns and villages; and to critiques of popular culture, theories of abjection and feminist theory, amongst other discourses.
24. See also Deamer (1997) on the relation of the body as a site of the everyday to the work of Herbert Marcuse; Borden (1998) on skateboarding; and Crouch (1998) on embodied knowledge of the street. The latter two are noted below.
25. In a footnote, McLeod cites a claim by Michel Trebitsch that Lefebvre's most effective influence was on German thought in the 1970s, particularly on Habermas (McLeod, 1997:9). See Lefebvre, 1992:ix–xxviii.
26. McLeod cites the first translation of Lefebvre – *Everyday Life in the Modern World*, translated by Rabinovitch and published in New York by Harper and Row (1971) with a second edition (1984); the translation of *The Production of Space* by Nicholson-Smith (1991) and the first volume of *Critique of Everyday Life* by Moore (1992) have drawn more attention to Lefebvre, in part because the critical climate of the 1990s and increased interest in urbanism have created a demand for a radical theory of space.
27. Marcuse sees art as an articulation of a return of material repressed into the (individual or social) unconscious. But he writes that, in the time of late capitalism, 'Art survives only where it cancels itself, where it saves its substance by denying its traditional form and thereby denying reconciliation; where it becomes surrealistic and atonal.' (Marcuse, 1956:145).
28. This idea is close to that proposed by Ernst Bloch in *The Principle of Hope* (1986), that the desire for a world which is better never dies; Bloch sees cultural production as giving form to this desire, thus enabling it to be more possibly grasped.
29. McLeod notes Lefebvre's view of consumption as both oppressive and liberating for women in post-war France, and argues (despite citing one case of a blatantly sexist remark) that he '. . .conveyed a deep interest in and empathy for women', discussing women's magazines as early as the 1950s, and citing Irigaray within wider support for feminist reconstructions of psycho-analytic thought (McLeod, 1997:18).
30. See Shields, 1999:107–8. Shields argues that the failure of the 1968 revolt turned radical opinion away from Lefebvre (and the Situationists) and towards a more orthodox communism. He notes Lefebvre's formulation (in 1971) of the concept of an 'impossible-possible' revolution which celebrates difference and constitutes a utopianism aimed at questioning, or negating, the dominant reality. McLeod notes personal differences between Debord and Lefebvre – 'charges of plagiarism and relations with women' – and his link to another group around this time, the Utopie group, whose members included Baudrillard. (McLeod, 1997:21–3).
31. See http://www.artsnet.getty.edu/ArtsEdNet/Images/Ecology/Seriff/nescafe.html for illustration of a briefcase made in Senegal from misprinted factory-milled metal sheeting, and other recycled materials. The writer has seen a similar use of this technology in Mali and Yemen.
32. Illich had already begun to suggest the concept of conviviality in his earlier *Deschooling Society*, at the end of which he writes: 'We now need a name for those who value hope above expectation. We need a name for those who love people more than products . . . We need a name for those who love the earth on which we each can meet the other . . . (Illich, 1971:116). Towards the end of *Tools for Conviviality* he writes that, faced with

a 'crisis of the industrial mode of production itself', a necessity arises for social reconstruction in which conventional political structures – he sees the nation-state as a 'holding corporation for a multiplicity of self-serving tools' – are rethought: '. . . only the word in its weakness can associate the majority of people in the revolutionary inversion of inevitable violence into convivial reconstruction' (Illich, 1990:109–10).

33. Peattie writes: 'Commensalism has always been central to group membership. We establish social groupings by eating together convivially and by particular forms and settings of conviviality – think of the tea party, the seder, the communion.' She notes Simmel's identification of 'pure sociability' with assembly for the purpose only of joy (Peattie, 1998:248–9). Lefebvre mentions communal eating in *The Critique of Everyday Life*: 'In Greece countryfolk had their festivals and religious ceremonies . . . These country festivals consisted essentially of a large meal . . . Everyone brought a contribution to the communal meal.' (Lefebvre, 1992:207). This point is taken up again in Chapter 9.
34. An example of taking power is the setting up of settlements by groups of people who relinquish the conventional and normalised structures of society, as in alternative settlements such as Tinkers Bubble (UK) and Crystal Waters (Australia) – see Schwartz and Schwartz, 1998:44–54 and 124–41 respectively). Another kind of example, in an urban situation, is the growth of self-build housing schemes, in which architects, notably Walter Segal, have a clear but unconventional role. These are discussed in Chapter 9.
35. See Zukin, 1995:259–62. Zukin also notes Disney's nostalgic utopianism combined with an identification of corporations with an optimistic control of the future (1995:55–7).
36. See Schwartz and Schwartz, 1998:54–65 on Pure Genius, the resettlement of a disused brewery site in South London in 1996; and Smith 1996:3–12 on the occupation of Tompkins Square Park, New York in 1988. Another form of occupation is the use of empty properties for raves. In Luton, the Exodus Collective have organised free parties since 1992, squatting an empty warehouse in the same year; later they moved to Long Meadow Farm, an empty property purchased for a road-building scheme. Another property, an empty hotel, was squatted in 1993 and subsequently attacked by police with sledgehammers, though charges against members of the Collective were later dropped. By 1994, after restoring various derelict buildings and continuing to organise raves, a licence was granted by the local authority (with support from councillors) to hold festivals. The story of the Collective is told in the magazine *Squall*.
37. A visitor to Coronation Street, deconstructing the boundaries of fact and fiction in her account, states: '. . . suddenly I saw the worst house I'd seen in my life, it was covered in the most tasteless coloured stone cladding imaginable. I had to pause and blink several times in case my eyes were deceiving me.' (http://website.lineone.net/~bob.r/kayepisode.html)
38. For instances: Maple Homes Canada advertise two kinds of stone cladding – Castle Stone Grey and Cobblefeld Brown – under the heading 'Maple Homes has a great variety of cladding options and colours' (http://www.maplehomes.com/products/cladding.html). And the Terminal City Club Tower in Vancouver has limestone cladding on its first four levels – 'The Tyndall stone cladding evokes the 100–year old heritage . . .' (http://www.architectural-library.com/19980002).
39. MacCannell sees the new urbanism of Celebration as a site of shared lack, in the homogeneity of house design which denies privacy (the hiding of things others might not have but desire, or the not having of things desired which others have), where a gap between ego and ideal is filled in 'with the same fantasy of lack transformed into the appearance of a generosity of pure space painted white, a pure absence of being' (MacCannell, 1999:126).

40. See Cresswell, 1996:36 on Haring's co-option by the artworld.
41. Cresswell sees an influence from graffiti in the text-works of Jenny Holtzer, initially fly-posted in New York, and notes the association of graffiti with dirt and disease in the rhetoric of press reactions to it. He links its description as an 'epidemic' and associations of plague with its roots in ethnic minority publics regarded as polluting outsiders (Cresswell, 1996:36 and 38–42). In a later passage he comments: 'Again crime becomes creativity, madness becomes insight, dirt becomes something to hang over the fireplace. Just as the reactions of the press to graffiti tell us about the role of place in the construction of order and thus of deviance, so does the more positive reaction of the art establishment' (Cresswell, 1996:50).
42. For an international survey of graffiti see Chalfont and Prigoff, 1987.

Chapter 8
Art and Intervention in Post-industrial Cities

Introduction

This chapter considers new practices in art at the opening of the twenty-first century, contextualised by discussion of the uses of culture in post-industrial cities[1]. The reuse of redundant industrial buildings for arts purposes, or recoding of districts as cultural quarters tends to denote affluence; just as public art lent a veneer of cultural value to developments such as Battery Park City and Broadgate in the 1980s, so cultural quarters mask equally divisive extensions of a strategy of enclaved development in the 1990s, when new museums act as flagships for an aestheticisation of the city. Interventionist art, in contrast, works in the same situation to question dominant narratives and imagine alternative futures. But whilst previous avant-garde strategies, from Realism in France after 1848 to Constructivism in Russia after 1917 and protest art in the USA in the late 1960s[2], saw a choice between resistance and complicity, emerging practices today investigate ways of working in the crevices of the dominant society, researching, documenting, creating transparency in urban or cultural processes and subverting them from within. Much of this work takes place outside conventional sites for art in the gallery or the plaza, though cultural spaces, too, are an arena in which to question the values of an art market itself part of the dominant social order.

The chapter does not seek to be comprehensive, nor to make judgements on aesthetic quality; neither does it constitute a new theory of the avant-garde. Its aim is to consider a small number of cases from a growing range of new, interventionist practices, to learn something of the intentions and strategies involved. The artists are not all widely known outside their milieu, but are included because their work constitutes a critical practice, retaining an aesthetic dimension whilst demonstrating a commitment to agendas of social justice and cultural difference. Discussion of these examples complements that of the Nine Mile Run Greenway project (discussed in Chapter 6) by demonstrating a diversity in terms of media, relation to site and definition of community, and the *Parish Maps* project included in Chapter 9. Many emerging practices use ephemeral forms to address generic issues of belonging, control and change, sometimes appropriating monumental, mass media or art spaces for new meanings, sometimes working in new media such as digital imaging and cyberspace, and sometimes intervening in patterns of sociation which take place, and mutate, in the spaces of the architectural everyday[3].

For many of these cases, the site of intervention is not so much a physical space as a narrative.

Post-industrial Cities

But, first, what makes a post-industrial city? One, obvious factor is a shift from a manufacturing to a service-based economy; the services may be financial, cultural (including tourism, leisure and the arts), or knowledge-based; they are accommodated in enclaves of new development, either the result of clearances as in Canary Wharf, or in redundant industrial buildings like the Tate Gallery at Albert Dock in Liverpool or the Warhol Museum in Pittsburgh. In some cases, whole districts are given a new class identity – as in the redevelopment of SoHo in New York in the 1970s and 1980s (Zukin, 1989), or more recently Temple Bar in Dublin, El Raval in Barcelona and the district around the Tate Gallery at Bankside in London[4]. Recoding as a cultural district means aestheticisation and gentrification. Rosalyn Deutsche (1991b) has shown that, contemporary with the development of Battery Park City, the City of New York sought to exclude homeless people, many evicted due to gentrification, from the streets of the downtown area. This extends the Enlightenment pattern of exclusion and confinement which began with the founding of the first general hospital in Paris in 1656 as a place for the containment of the vagrant and insane (Foucault, 1967), and extends to the exclusion of odours from the city (Illich, 1986) and, now, the poor and the recently immigrant from visibility.

In El Raval, Barcelona's red light district, there is a new Museum of Contemporary Art, and adjacent Centre for Contemporary Culture. Like the Tate at Bankside, the museum acts as a flagship development, linked on the tourist map to historic sites such as the fifteenth-century Hospital de la Santa Creu, and Gaudi's Palau Güell[5]. The gentrification of El Raval follows the model used to re-present Barcelona for the 1992 Olympics, when its port area was transformed into a fashionable corniche, and new public spaces with commissioned sculptures by international and Catalan artists integrated the city's reconstruction of its image with most of its neighbourhoods, rich and poor. El Raval is the site, in 1999, of a further reconstruction in which demolition of nineteenth-century buildings in its core provides for another, larger public space to be planted with trees and furnished with seats. The official promotion of the scheme makes no mention of where residual publics will go when their apartments are demolished, but the experience of SoHo suggests that the poor move ever further out. Public space, rather than art, is the signifier of space for the habitat of a new middle class.

Monica Degen observes[6] that new apartment buildings in El Raval are designed in pale shades of grey and stone, and have no (or shallow) balconies (Figure 8.1). In these narrow streets, the balconies of older buildings project as threshold spaces between public and private, where dwellers hang washing, place bird-cages and

Figure 8.1 *Barcelona: old and new buildings in El Raval, 1999 (photo M Miles)*

plants, and watch the life of the street pass by. Conversations are held from balcony to balcony, but people also observe silently, making the balcony an extension of both the room and the street. Degen notes changing patterns of street use in this area of ethnic diversity and a high proportion of elderly residents, as old shops which supplied local needs close and new bars, boutiques and hairdressers appeal to outsiders. But at night, when the museums and shops are closed, the old El Raval is reasserted as North African men meet on street corners, youths race cars over the new Plaza dels Angels, and a mix of drinkers, substance abusers and street people reappear. Degen writes that '. . . every morning new graffiti appear . . . sometimes only paintings, at other times more political statements' (Degen, 1999 – see note 6). The clean, light and balcony-free walls of new buildings in El Raval, however, correspond to the image and hard spatial boundaries of a northern city, and are statements of a visual aesthetics rather than of a multi-sensory engagement. Sennett laments the lack of interface between the publics of contiguous neighbourhoods in New York, and in El Raval two equally distanced lattices are superimposed – one of residual publics, itself complex and involving certain tensions; the other of day visitors, and the more intrepid who seek out characteristic bars at night. Planning consultants working for Barcelona's city authorities claim that the balance of publics in the city is not affected by its redevelopment, that, for example, people from all social classes use the city's new public beaches; and perhaps Mediterranean cities do not conform to the myth of purification which drives urban development in the northern, post-Enlightenment city. But the pattern of redevelopment in Barcelona still adheres to a global and homogenising model.

This is not to say El Raval is part of the global city defined by Saskia Sassen (1991). There seem to be two phases in the pattern of urban renewal: during the 1980s, enclaved developments of office towers in New York, London, Frankfurt, Tokyo and elsewhere constituted a global city of financial and advertising services, of which Battery Park City and Canary Wharf are parts, linked by information superhighways, 24-hour dealing in shares, currencies and futures, and by the language of consumption. The enclaves of the global city are linked more closely to each other than to geographically adjacent neighbourhoods of the residual city, which they cast as margins. The second phase, from the 1990s, is the construction of post-industrial cities through a reuse of redundant industrial buildings, or recoding of districts as cultural quarters. A post-industrial city, then, contains zones which reconstruct the city's identity as a whole in their reproduction of space. Such zones can be normalised through postcard images and publicity brochures, but what is constituted is a new dominant conceptualisation of the city as clean, safe and attractive to the gaze. H V Savitch sees a capacity to foster '. . . new industry, new classes, and . . . new opportunities for those ready to enter a new economic order' (Savitch, 1988:11) as a pre-condition for a post-industrial city. This extends Louis Wirth's notion of the city as a place where everyone is on the move and on the make (Wirth, 1938, in Smith, 1980:9); but whilst Savitch sees an integration of political, financial and technological interests, those of residual publics, identified with old industries, classes and opportunities, appear to fall off the map[7]. Whilst the post-industrial city is not the global city, it is the market for globalisation: '. . . the world as a whole is articulated as the appropriate arena in which to pursue marketing, intellectual, environmental and other practices' (Albrow et al., 1997:27–8). And if public art embellishes the global city, cultural spaces characterise post-industrial cities, and a museum is a sign for affluence[8].

Waterfront development, as well as culture, has become a sign for the post-industrial city, as in Baltimore's Harbor District, Cardiff Bay, the casino area of Melbourne, Barcelona's Port Vell and current redevelopment of the harbour islands and western dock area in Amsterdam. Many new cultural institutions occupy waterfront sites, and developers favour waterfront images in their publicity material. But because affluence recodes only fragments of a city, advocacy for cultural reuse of redundant buildings, and for creative cities[9], tends to mean advocacy for enclaved development, to which the publics of a city do not have equal access. Jon Bird notes that nearby social housing was screened from new lofts in Docklands by rebuilt picturesque dock walls (Bird, 1993:125). In a post-modern culture, then, signs float free of given signifieds, being ideologically determined. A waterfront signifies abundance, the little gabled roofs, like hats, developers add to social housing blocks denote privatisation, and public art denotes that a city has bought its place on an international culture map.

The model of a division of signifiers from signifieds was elaborated by Roland Barthes in the early 1970s (Barthes, 1982), and absorbed by the creative staff of advertising agencies, as a separation of image from product enabling anything to be marketed through association with anything else. One example is the use of artificial scents in the commodification of space. In the travel section of *USA Today*, in May 1999, it was reported that stations on the Paris Metro are perfumed 'with a musk-citrus-floral scent called Madeleine'. In Las Vegas, the Mirage hotel uses coconut butter in the lobby, whilst at the Bellagio it is lavender-sage. Mark Peltier, co-founder of the company AromaSys which supplies the scents adds 'We don't do subliminal scents, you notice' (Grossman, 1999). The association between scent and place is a design choice: the coconut-citrus-spice-vanilla of the Mandalay in Las Vegas complements its Indonesian-style decor (itself a sign for an artificial world, explicitly not the geographical Indonesia[10]); but musk-citrus-floral has no direct association to the allegorical (or Proustian) Madeleine, and the column lists other selective affinities such as jasmine-rosemary in the furniture departments of large stores. These signs are disconnected from their sources – mediated, and combination scents rather than smells, their purpose is to conjure dreams of consumption. The scents, then, are signifiers of a lifestyle. In the post-modern surface-world of the post-industrial city, things are as they seem in a new totalitarianism of appearances, and the idea they might be not as they seem, or imagined as other, is exiled to a past of modernist naivety[11].

The disruption of an easy relation of signifier to signified upsets other certainties of modern thought, including the relation of (signifying) cause and (signified) effect. One application of this rupture is to question the assumption of modernist planning that a new society might be engineered through design. This realisation is a catalyst to a necessary reconstruction of the idea of agency. Sociologist David Byrne proposes a post-modern 'dual city', where modern, linear causality and post-modern chaos theory (an extended intricacy rather than lack of connection between event and aftermath) are integrated in what he terms a 'post-postmodern programme' (Byrne, 1997:51). In other words, layering Byrne's ideas on Barthes', cause does not lead to given effect any more than signifier denotes given signified, but may lead to contradictory effects, just as signs have multiple possibilities of meaning in systems of difference. Byrne adopts a model in which the outcome of any urban policy can take opposing forms affected by slight shifts within a matrix of conditions. His aim is to reclaim a possibility for intervention through a 'taxonomy of possible urban futures' which assists urban policy to modify the direction of development for the public good (Byrne, 1997:60). He summarises his position:

> What this means is agency. It is precisely the human capacity to imagine and seek to construct a future which is so crucial to understanding the potential of trajectories within a complex world. (Byrne, 1997:67)

He adds that this does not produce blueprints, but nor does it leave the market as the only determining factor in urban futures. This suggests, for artists in a repoliticised avant-garde, a strategy of intervention through, for instance, the creation of transparency in the urban process.

Art as Intervention

The art practices discussed below, in both gallery and non-gallery settings, engage with issues and publics outside the self-referential discourse which has characterised contemporary art in museums since the 1970s, and allowed art to be increasingly absorbed into the market economy. Some derive their languages from the varieties of conceptualism, whilst others interact with identified publics. Conceptualism itself, in the 1960s, represented a refusal of the market, by making work less open to commodification. Other new practices then included collage, or the design of street posters, to protest against the American war in Vietnam[12], and, in the 1980s, against the US administration's attitude to HIV[13]. The market, however, is adept at incorporating art's dematerialisation, marketing reputation in place of objects. Emerging practices at the end of the twentieth century, then, contend with the failure of previous avant-gardes, from 1848 to 1968, to realise the kinds of social change once envisaged. And as the architectural everyday is not a matter of signature buildings, so artists working in these emerging areas avoid individualist notions of the artist as lonely frontiersman and revealer of primordial truths[14]. But if the artist does not carry a Promethean fire, what specialist knowledge or skills does he or she have? Or is everyone, as Joseph Beuys asserted, an artist?

Joseph Beuys was contained in a specific historical moment which briefly promised liberation – the same moment (in the 1960s and 1970s) in which Marcuse foresaw 'society as a work of art'[15]. The opening of the twenty-first century offers different conditions and agendas for art, less given to millenarianism and more concerned with incremental and negotiated, whilst sustainable, degrees of change. The complexities of urban society are addressed now in ways which defuse the categories of art and not-art, using new technologies of digital imaging and cyberspace as well as performance and public interaction; the specialist role of the artist now becomes that of informed critic and tactician. If, for Beuys, the question was how everyone's creative potential might be realised, today it is how everyone might contribute to, and take power over, the determination of dominant narratives such as the conceptualisation of the city. Artists, then, retain a role of agency in the process by questioning (or negating) the present, as members of a society of intelligence (or reconstruction of the European idea of an intelligentsia), working through culture. Whilst protest marches and demonstrations disrupt specific geographical sites, the site of intervention for new art practices is in the narratives which condition the parts people play in society.

Two examples demonstrate the aim of intervention in social and historical narratives in different ways: the *Anti-monument to Fascism* by Jochen and Esther Shalev Gerz, and *Les Must de Rembrandt* by Hans Haacke, both begun in 1986. The *Anti-monument* is sited in a public space (in Harburg, a suburb of Hamburg) and interrogates a history largely buried in Germany through a monument which is also buried. A lead column was sunk in stages into a pit, and people invited by a notice accompanying the work to inscribe the column's surface – some signing their names, others adding comments, each layer becoming invisible as the column sank. Some of the inscriptions were racist in content, revealing the continued presence of an abjection which was a condition historically for the Holocaust. Now, the monument is invisible, under an empty place, its interaction with the city one of negation and its site recoded by absence, not only of the monument but of the city's Jewish population (Young, 1992). Hans Haacke, on the other hand, makes work which is exhibited in major museums and art fairs, but which mirrors back to the art world its closeness to the world of global capital, intervening in a rhetoric of artistic freedom of expression which since the cold war has been a cover for art's co-option to capital. *Les Must de Rembrandt* was an installation at the Pompidou Centre which unpicked the use of holding companies to mask the interests of the Rembrandt Group of South Africa, a corporation investing in mines, tobacco, petrochemicals, financial services, timber, alcohol, and with a 25% stake in a company which, in 1985, used firearms and tear gas to break a strike of its black workers. The work juxtaposes the actualities of exploitation with the labyrinths of corporate finance which erase accountability, framing an image of protesting workers with lists of Rembrandt's holdings (Bourdieu and Haacke, 1995:32–5). In its re-presentation of current events and contexts, it follows the precedent of, say, Géricault's *Raft of the Medusa*, which depicts an incident within contemporary narratives around the slave trade. Whilst Géricault relied on contemporary reports in the press to inform his audience, Haacke, in the face of the invisibility of many facets of corporate finance, produces the documentation himself. Both cases – by Haacke and Jochen and Esther Shalev Gertz – renegotiate art's conventional condition of the object, one in being a monument which is not a monument, the other a combination of image and text which has a temporary existence in the gallery but a longer term presence through publication.

Art, in media coverage as much as in non-gallery settings, competes for attention with other vocabularies of signs, including advertising, just as posters advertising art exhibitions compete with those for popular culture in urban spaces (Figure 8.2). Sometimes the boundaries between art and advertising are blurred: in 1999, an image of a naked Gail Porter, seen from behind, her face coyly turned to the spectator, was projected on to the Houses of Parliament in London. The work mimicked the projections of Krzysztof Wodiczko, but promoted *FHM* magazine, and in the process recoding a site standing for constitutional democracy through advertising and the masculine gaze[16]. In the reverse direction, artists such as Les Levine and Barbara Kruger have made work for billboard sites, using the codes of mass media to subvert their normalising messages[17]. Wodiczko's own projections, for instance in Trafalgar Square in 1985 – placing a cruise missile on Nelson's Column, and, without official sanction, a swastika on South Africa House – and at the Whitney Museum in New York – two open hands bearing the message GLASNOST IN USA – recode monuments with overtly political readings. Wodiczko writes:

> The aim . . . is not to 'bring to life' . . . the memorial nor support the happy, uncritical, bureaucratic 'socialization' of its site, but to reveal and expose to the public the contemporary deadly life of the memorial . . . to attack the memorial by surprise, using slide warfare, or to take part in and infiltrate the official cultural programs taking place on its site. (Wodiczko (1986) cited in Freshman, 1993:115)

Whilst monuments construct a dominant narrative of national identity and military power disguised as virtue and civilisation, and normalise that content by being subsumed in urban streetscapes, Wodiczko's nocturnal projections, which might last an hour, make an incision in the narrative which, for the spectator, changes the reading of the monument for longer than the time of the performance. The technology is, as the projection of a nude on to the Houses of Parliament shows, open to co-option by the market, but Wodiczko's work infiltrates the dominant culture to expose structures of power through unanticipated nuances of meaning; it constitutes a repoliticisation of the public realm, offering readings of difference in face of homogenisation.

Figure 8.2 *Aachen: posters for art and entertainment mixed in public space (photo M Miles)*

Other cases of shock tactics include the work of the Guerrilla Girls in New York, an anonymous group of women artists whose fly-posted messages expose the absence of women and people of colour from museums and galleries, that of another anonymous group, The Institute for Applied Autonomy, and the multi-part work 90% Crude, by Platform, a London-based group of artists for democracy and ecology. The relation between artists' groups engaged in agitation and cultural institutions is not always easy. In 1989, for instance, the Guerrilla Girls were commissioned by Public Art Fund in New York to design a billboard poster, as part of the agency's continuing programme of art in public spaces[18]. The poster included an image of a naked woman derived from Ingres, and the text 'Do women have to be naked to get into the Met. Museum?' – referencing the preponderance of female nudes in art and male artists in collections. The design was rejected by Public Art Fund as unclear; the Guerrilla Girls then rented space on New York's buses to exhibit the design on a smaller scale. Public Art Fund is a non-profit organisation, and perhaps its trustees enjoy the same circles of cultural influence as members of museum boards; perhaps it also has a wary eye on its funding from a range of public and private sources, given the intricacies of finance interrogated by Haacke[19]. Whatever, the case demonstrates that institutionalisation inhibits critical practice.

Is it possible, then, for art to liberate? Is it always compromised if it operates through established (funded) channels? Or is the concept of Art itself an inhibition? Does the weight of its history and, above all, its aestheticisation of content, prevent the articulation of ideas which are dangerous to the dominant society? Peter Bürger argues that 'Art as an institution prevents the contents of works that press for radical change in society (i.e. the abolition of alienation) from having any practical effect' (Bürger, 1984:95–6). And Rosalyn Deutsche contends that art history reduces the reading of art in relation to the city to one of aestheticisation: 'All connections between art and the city . . . are . . . articulated as a single relationship: timeless and spaceless works of art ultimately transcend the very urban conditions that purportedly "influenced" them . . .' (Deutsche, 1991a:46–7). But the definition of art is increasingly open, and art practice overlaps with political agitation, just as direct action (as in road protest) has a characteristic culture[20]. And, artists, New Age travellers, campaigners in single-issue and extra-parliamentary politics, and those who dig their allotments or place election posters in the windows of their houses, are all involved in culture, if culture is taken as the superstructure of values in society. These values are expressed in narratives, for the dominant society through war memorials, ceremonies and civic architecture; for the dominated but insurgent society in graffiti, alternative music and radical art. Some of that art, as noted above, is sited in public, urban spaces. Other cases have little physical presence but circulate conceptually within the art world.

The Institute for Applied Autonomy, for example, publishes (in collaboration with Critical Arts Ensemble) a booklet called *Contestational Robotics: Theory and Practice*[21]. This outlines the possibility to make a robotic graffiti writer, a small machine using standard components costing around £1250. Its purpose is, by surprise and manoeuvrability (with a maximum speed of 15 kph), to avoid immediate detection and arrest whilst reinscribing pavements with anti-capitalist texts. Essentially, the graffiti writer is a remote-control model car with an encoder, a micro-controller, and five industrial spray cans as used for road markings, which it operates like a dot matrix printer. The graffiti writer can be (and has been) built, but the booklet is also a counter-narrative. It begins:

> Since the notion of the public sphere has been increasingly recognized as a bourgeois fantasy that was dead on arrival at its inception in the 19th century, an urgent need has emerged for continuous development of tactics to reestablish a means of expression and a space of temporary autonomy within the terrain of the social. (*Contestational Robotics*, p 3)

Projects such as this are developed by artists using their own resources, rather than through the arts funding system. This allows autonomy on the margins of legality. The work retains critical distance, and the idea of the graffiti writer is at one level a trope to draw attention to the machinery of control and the possibilities of dissent, like Wodiczko's call for glasnost.

Platform's project 90% Crude, working in a more public way, addresses the impact of transnational corporations on ecology and social justice. The first phase focused on oil and included a performance work 'Carbon Generations' by James Marriott, networking through a series of seminars on 'Funding for Change', construction of an 'Agitpod', and distribution of a spoof newspaper, *Ignite* in 1997. Platform was formed in 1983, its members coming from backgrounds which include literature, theatre and anti-nuclear campaigning as well as art; they contribute between them a concern for political instrumentality, a rejection of conventional art education and practice in favour of extending the legacy of Joseph Beuys, and an involvement in pedagogy and the study of alienation in art. This has enabled the group to use its own internal differences as a creative basis, defining projects through investigation of the tensions between, say, art and activism, or observation and confrontation. One factor in the group's thinking is to ask what artists can do that larger campaigning organisations, such as Greenpeace, cannot; another is an understanding of the questions of critical theory and its method of questioning its own assumptions, and critique of utopianism which leads to engagement with realities rather than refusal to face them – a strategy of working in the crevices of the dominant society to develop art as a critical practice.

The elements of 90% Crude are linked through interactions with other narratives. The performance 'Carbon Generations', for instance, interweaves Marriott's family history with a history of oil as used in domestic central heating and the family car, and the history of global warming. Photographs, as if from a family album, are used to emphasise the aspect of personal experience, as are an old school book and a piece of wood impregnated with oil. Global warming, then, is associated with the burning of fossil fuels, but also with ordinary and seemingly innocent acts of everyday life. Yet oil is, simultaneously, associated with the destruction of the lands of the Ogoni in Nigeria, and whilst the oil industry presents one of the least acceptable faces of global capital, it plays, at the same time, a part in a story of domestic ordinariness. Marriott speaks of the value of intimate knowledges, such as those within families, as a counter to the surface knowledges of large industries and organisations.

A spoof newspaper produced in three editions, in April, November and December 1997, took the strategy into another domain of the everyday, mimicking the popular papers which commuters read on trains going home. The first issue, titled *Evading Standards*, produced with the help of a former press officer for an environmental campaigning organisation, was intended to be distributed shortly before the 1997 general election, to coincide with a march by sacked Liverpool dockers and a direct action by the group Reclaim the Streets. Its headline reads: 'GENERAL ELECTION CANCELLED', under an invitation to win a dream home (superimposed on a picture of the door of 10 Downing Street) and an image of the Spice Girls (whose offer of national leadership is stated as being on page 9[22]). The front page reveals that the findings of recent opinion polls have shown such high levels of voter cynicism that party leaders have felt no choice but to abandon the election, looking instead to the possibility of national government, if matters have not already gone beyond control. The stock market, of course, has collapsed. On a more positive note, the paper reports that 'With London Underground under staff control and all travel now free . . . London's transport problems have been solved' (*Evading Standards*, 11 April 1997, p 1). Inside are further revelations, such as an image of Tony Blair handing out junk food to entice young voters, but also advice on DIY economics and DIY communities, and an account of the Direct Democracy movement in Germany.

The first issue was never distributed due to police action, and the second and third issues, titled *Ignite* were less provocative in content, combining campaigning information with stories of exploitation and repression associated with the oil industry in Nigeria. Issue two included the names of sponsors, such as the Arts Council of England, London Arts Board, Friends of the Earth and Greenpeace. There is still humour on an edge of aridity, as in Stella Spliff's recipe for stuffed lungs in issue three, or a competition to win 'an exotic developing country' (open only to multinational companies). All this might suggest that Platform are implacably opposed to the operations of companies such as Shell, which in a way they are; but in the seminars on Funding for Change, representatives of arts organisations met those of companies including Shell (who are also known for their Better Britain campaign and wildlife posters), around the question of how new kinds of mutually educative relations can be formed between groups seeking to retain the critical as well as aesthetic autonomy of art, and sponsors who see the arts as lending them a positive public image. The next part of 90% Crude will investigate structures of global trade in London's financial district, making new relationships with workers in the financial services industry whose ethical compartmentalism enables the industry to run on while it depletes the planet's natural resources.

Whilst artists use the vocabulary and materials of mass culture, as in a spoof newspaper, so radical campaigns appropriate the language of art; the web-site presentation, for instance, of June 18 – a coalition of environmental activists and others – resembles an image-text work in which the word 'IMAGINE' is repeated at intervals down the page[23]. Electronic communication and the creative design of web-sites underpins such campaigns, constructing an area of practice between art and activism, which could equally be said of Platform, whilst in another deconstruction of the categories of art, media and radical praxis, the group People for the Ethical Treatment of Animals has commissioned an advertising agency to produce billboard posters with cartoon and photographic images resembling those of a transnational burger company, juxtaposed with texts such as 'Cruelty to go'[24] (Armstrong, 1999).

If cyberspace and the mass media constitute new spaces for public intervention, so, too, does fashion. In fashion magazines and fashion shows, as much as in television programmes and film, stereotypes are replicated as norms to which women conform in order to gain the promises of consumerism, to be beautiful, to desire that which men desire them to desire (that is, the gaze of men). The history of the masculine gaze has been well rehearsed by John Berger and Laura Mulvey; and Craig Owens (1983) and Doreen Massey (1994) note the privileging of the visual sense in modern culture as another form of patriarchy. Owens sees the work of Cindy Sherman as playing with this condition of always being the object of a gaze and representation of masculine constructions of desire; he writes that '. . . Sherman's photographs themselves function as mirror-masks that reflect back at the viewer his own desire . . .', adding that this desire is 'to fix the woman in a stable and stabilizing identity' (Owens, 1983:75). Sherman, by taking back and subverting the process – scripting and dressing herself in a long series of *Untitled Film Stills* – destabilises representation, renders identity no longer a possession. And Alba d'Urbano, in *Il Sarto Immortale*, for the Natural Reality exhibition at the Ludwig Forum in Aachen in 1999, intervenes in the gaze in another, almost complementary way. A set of garments – d'Urbano Couture – use the vocabulary of fashion to examine a dialectic of exposure and concealment in clothes (Figure 8.3). The work was presented as a fashion show, in boxes like those of the couture industry, and through wall-posters. Whilst Sherman conceals herself under make-up and costume, d'Urbano exposes herself, literally by being naked, and literally again as a photographic image. A fabric imprinted with a real-size image of the artist's body is used for a dress, a skirt, a trouser suit, and so forth; this second skin of fabric, to which fashion lends high value, becomes ambiguously like the first skin it covers. The styling of the second skin in fashion-shoots for glossy magazines dictates stereotypes of beauty and conformity as it covers, clings to or selectively reveals the first skin, but these idealised forms are refused by d'Urbano

Figure 8.3 *Alba d'Urbano,* Il Sarto Immortale, *1999, Natural Reality Exhibition, Ludwig Forum, Aachen (photo M Miles)*

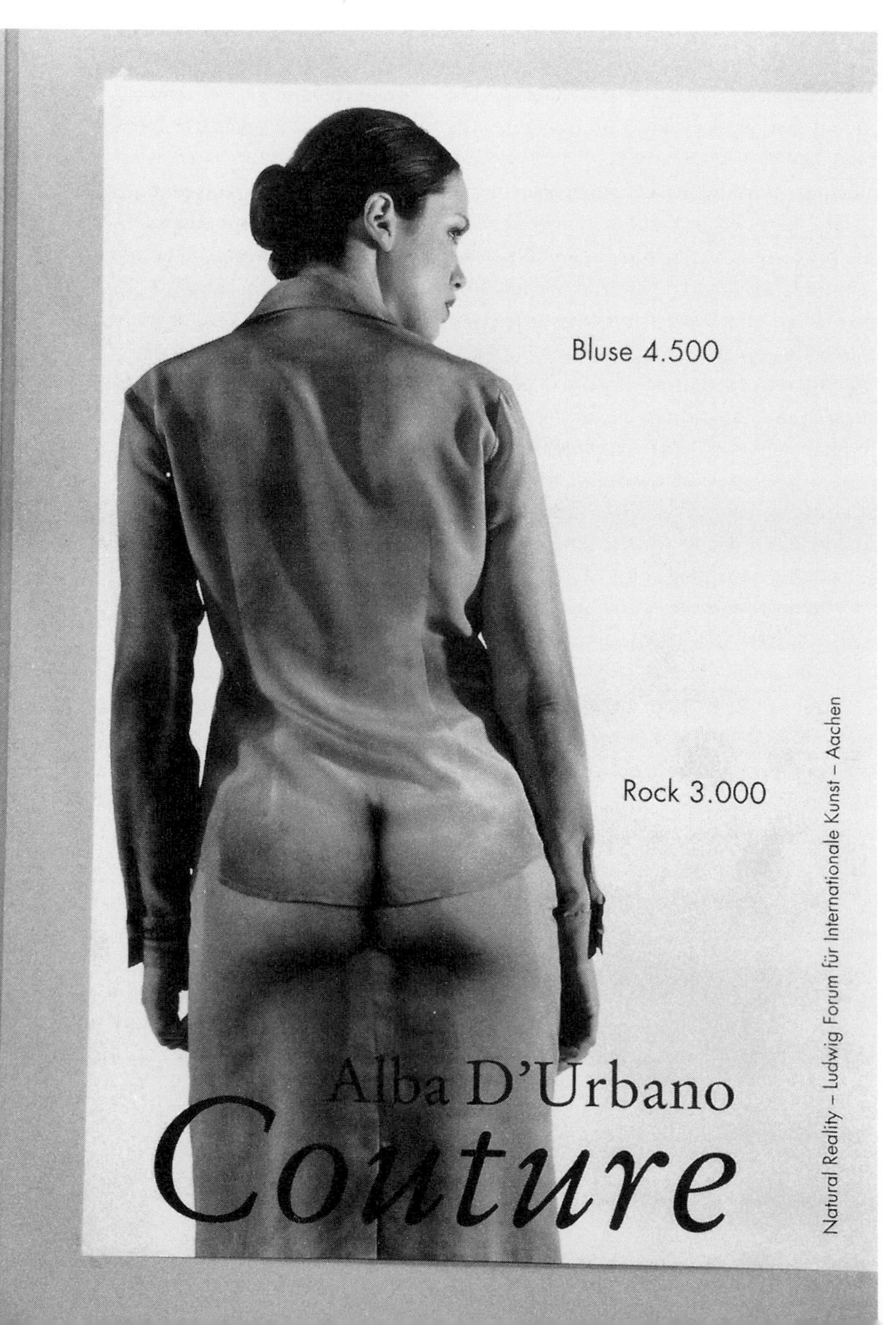

in using the specific image of her own body, reflecting back, as Sherman does through concealment, the distanced, manipulated relation to their bodies allowed women in a patriarchal society. This is like short-circuiting the gaze.

Working with Communities and Places

The above discussion, then, concerns artists whose interventions are in narratives which construct social values. Lucy Lippard, however, writes in the opening sentence of *The Lure of the Local* that 'Place for me is the locus of desire' (Lippard, 1997:4). She writes later that few people know the place in which they live as a location of belonging[25], and that for many it is displacement which defines a colonised place. The book includes illustrations of a large number of artworks which in some sense are about or rely on an identification with place. Lippard's criteria for inclusion are broad, and she is not always supportive; Edward Barney's *Star Axis, looking south, 1/7/83* documents a piece of land art in the making, exposing its 'devastation of the land . . . in service of an artist's vision' (Lippard, 1997:188–9). Other cases include the non-professional artist, and the artist known mainly within a local context or tradition of Outsider Art[26]. The *African-American Heritage Cultural Centre*, for instance, is a sculptural installation and museum in his yard made by Charles Smith, a social sciences graduate, Vietnam veteran and ordained minister of religion. Smith began the work during a period of post-traumatic stress; the museum, with its figures of slaves (from the 'African Holocaust'), and references to Vietnam, Somalia and Rodney King, is intended as a healing place, perhaps much as Maya Lin's *Vietnam Veterans Memorial* is a site for healing the rift in American society caused by the war, as much as a commemoration of the dead[27]. Lippard quotes Smith: '. . . it is designed to tell the raw truth. Nor will we have anyone telling us these pieces are too graphic . . . All of it is history' (Charles Smith cited in Lippard, 1997:109).

But professionals, too, work with history. In Los Angeles, The Power of Place is a multi-disciplinary team led by architecture professor Dolores Hayden and graphic designer Sheila Levrant de Bretteville[28]. The team works with women members of minority communities to elucidate and then give form to their memories of place, seeing the construction and visibility of cultural identities as a means to empowerment. This may entail both the conservation of parts of the built environment, and prevention of redevelopment, and the making of local monuments which speak of histories other than the dominant. Hayden writes:

> To reverse the neglect of physical resources important to women's history and ethnic history is not a simple process, especially if preservationists are to be true to the insights of a broad, inclusive social history encompassing gender, race, and class. Restoring significant shared meanings . . . involves claiming the entire urban cultural landscape as an important part of American history, not just its architectural monuments. (Hayden, 1995:11)

The spaces of the everyday, then, in which people's memories and associations lend meaning to ordinary forms, are sites in which alternative narratives are made, and to focus on these is to challenge the hegemony of monuments and grand facades.

The Power of Place has completed two projects which have resulted in additions to the streetscape of their neighbourhoods: one on the site of the former home of black midwife Biddy Mason (331 Spring Street), the other referencing the experiences of Japanese Americans in Little Tokyo. In 1986, Spring Street was a declining area, as businesses relocated out of the downtown area or to more up-market (and culturally signed) Bunker Hill; following a fire which stopped plans for restoration of an old fire station (used by the Los Angeles Community Design Centre), The Power of Place switched its interest to the recovery of memories of Biddy Mason, using local history workshops and assembling a team of artists including de Bretteville, letterpress book artist Susan King and sculptor Betye Saar. Each artist produced a work the content of which was derived from memories and associations accessed through the workshop and subsequent contact with local people. King's book *HOME/stead* (in an edition of 35) was donated to the Los Angeles Public Library and the City Archives, and sold to other archives (Hayden, 1995:176–8); Betye Saar's installation (in the lobby of a new building on the site) *House of the Open Hand* consisted of a photo-mural showing Mason on the porch of her home, and an assemblage inside a window including artifacts excavated on the site (Hayden, 1995:179–80); and de Bretteville produced images and text for a wall framing a pedestrian area behind a commercial arcade. The wall charted the history of the city from its Mexican origins, as well as the narrative of Mason's arrival in Los Angeles and suit for freedom (Hayden, 1995:181–5; Lippard, 1997:100). Little Tokyo presents a more complex and contended past. In 1930 it housed 35 000 Japanese Americans; but after Pearl Harbour and the entry of the USA into the war against Germany and Japan, this whole community was forcibly relocated, first to the Santa Anita Racetrack, then, from 1942 to 1945, to 10 prison camps specially erected in the desert; meanwhile, black jazz clubs took over Japanese shops, and, after 1945, the community identity of the neighbourhood remained fragmented. By the 1980s, partial redevelopment had changed the physical face of Little Tokyo, whilst some of its inhabitants began to look to conservation of what remained as a site of memories and associations. In 1986, the north side of First Street was nominated as a National Historical Register District, and in 1988–89, Susan Sztaray, working with The Power of Place (and a speaker of Japanese), formulated a public art plan for the site. This proposed a decorative pavement, unifying the block and representing the histories of small businesses which had occupied the site, illustrated by images such as kimonos and Japanese sweets (Hayden, 1995:220–3). The proposal was used by de Bretteville, with two Japanese American assistants, to generate a final design.

Both projects make evident histories which might otherwise be lost, and the project in Little Tokyo contributes to the conservation of local, small-scale architecture in face of development; but other questions remain. If constructing a cultural identity from memories of place is a means to empowerment, what do people do once empowered? And if projects derived from local narratives are directed by professionals based elsewhere, to what extent are standard solutions applied in ways similar to the demarkation of space in modern planning? Less charitably, it could also be asked why people should want to put their histories in a sidewalk where others will walk all over them. But perhaps the biggest question is the extent to which projects can, in a post-modern culture and a post-industrial city, work with mono-ethnic communities whose identities are seen only in terms of links to a geographical site. Urban neighbourhoods are increasingly multi-ethnic, layers of different histories, and histories of difference, superimposed and superinscribed on them – as in El Raval. And alongside the processes of globalisation, through which transnational economic interests diversify production and marketing on a global scale, are those of migration, and an increasing mobility of people in response to opportunities for work. This operates in more than one direction, as people, mainly the poor, move into cities, but others, mainly disenchanted professionals in affluent countries, downshift or use telecommunications to live and work in rural areas. At the same time, large numbers of people are immigrants, who may retain links (or rediscover them) to other places. Sociologist Martin Albrow argues that the modern notion that community and place are linked by culture is strained by the emergence of multi-cultural publics, and that assimilation into a dominant (pre-existing) community is no longer the obvious solution for immigration (Albrow, 1997:37–8). He summarises the problem:

> In the last thirty years transformations of industrial organization in the advanced societies, accompanied by the acceptance of the ideas of post-industrialism and post-modernity, mean that the problem-setting for community analysis has shifted. In the last decade globalization theory has brought issues of time, space and territorial organization into the centre of the frame of argument. We have to look again at the way social relations are tied to place and re-examine issues of locality and culture. (1997:43)

In a world of flows rather than static formations, where only relative stability is possible[29], art which seeks to fix community cultural identities in alternative but semi-permanent monuments may be nostalgic.

Working with Networks and Flows

Four further projects linked to local narratives are taken to suggest ways out of the difficulty. The first two relate to networks of people rather than place-rooted communities; the second two derive from specific locations, but in one the site is contested, whilst in the other group identity is a result of temporary incarceration.

Awakenings (1995–96) is a digitally produced reworking of Stanley Spencer's *Resurrection, Cookham* in the Tate Gallery, which resulted from a collaboration between the Tate's Education Department, the Art of Change, a London-based artists' group, previously known as the Docklands Community Poster Project[30] (Figure 8.4), and George Green's School on the Isle of Dogs. Lorraine Leeson and Peter Dunn write that the project brought together elements central to their practice, including '. . . the use of the creative process as a vehicle to allow people to move from present circumstances to future possibilities', and the use of participatory processes for making images through which '. . . participants . . . see and have confirmed that they have contributed something concrete that they can feel proud of'[31]. Students from the School, which has a high level of ethnic diversity[32], visited the gallery and worked individually and in groups to express intuitive reactions to works; Spencer's painting was then deconstructed as a large set of specific images (each allowing adaptation by a participant), relocated (by replacing Cookham with the Isle of Dogs as the setting) and retitled (to remove its Christian associations). The resulting cibachrome print (60% of the size of the original, with adapted proportions) included photographic images of every participant bearing a gift for a new life from her/his own experience and culture (Figure 8.5), and was exhibited in 1995–96 at the Tate. Although *Awakenings* uses specific place images, such as a view of Canary Wharf, what it makes most visible is the participation of a diverse group in making the image, rather than local histories or mono-ethnic narratives. The links to other places, and diverse ways of thinking about birth, death and regeneration, which inform the imagery suggest those flows and socio-scapes of which Albrow writes.

Digital imaging is used, too, in *End of the Line* (1996–97), a project by Lisa Link, Carolyn Speranza and Debra Tomson, based at the Studio for Creative Inquiry at Carnegie Mellon University, Pittsburgh. This project uses narratives derived from local memories, but of people rather than place, while the imagery of biography intersects that of current redevelopment, which it problematises. Six branches of the Carnegie Library were sites for workshops in which local people contributed memories, associations and images which were selectively incorporated, with a line of text from the words of the person celebrated, into five posters displayed on the backs of Pittsburgh buses[33]. The network of bus routes carried each image outside the locality in which it was generated, again emphasising the fluidity of a post-industrial city's patterns of cultural reception. In addition, a web-site was maintained as a location for discussion and interaction. For Speranza, Link and Tomson, the role of librarians, eager to draw attention to community services based in local libraries, was crucial in bringing people together; this network continues, it is hoped strengthened by the project. The artists write that 'art is leaving the salon for more publicly accessible electronic networks, community operated cable TV, billboards, neighbourhood gardens and subway systems . . .'[34].

Two further projects address specific but in different ways contended and mutable sites: one an informal settlement, the other a juvenile detention centre.

Figure 8.4 ***Figure 8.4*** *Docklands Community Poster Project,* The Changing Picture of Docklands, *1981–85 (reproduced by permission of The Art of Change)*

Figure 8.5 Awakenings, *after Stanley Spencer's* The Resurrection, Cookham, *The The Art of Change, digital montage displayed as 13ft × 17ft photo-mural, Tate Gallery, London, 1995–96 (reproduced by permission of The Art of Change)*

The question of social work obviously arises in such situations, but the role of artists may be more appropriately defined in terms of communication and the articulation or facilitation of dialogues. These may be socially healing or not – acceptance of cultural diversity means acceptance also that there are tensions within society, and that these might not be resolved through art projects. What can be done is to make narratives visible, thereby aiding a political process; or to open a space for conversation where such possibilities are generally closed, in a society in which social institutions and market forces tend towards various forms of repression. In Maclovio Rojas, an informal settlement in Mexico first occupied in 1986, plans to expand a nearby Hyundai container plant threatened the eviction of the inhabitants and demolition of the settlement, which included a school and community centre. Border Arts Workshop, whose members had worked since 1984 on issues around the US–Mexico border and deportation of immigrants across it, met Hortensia Mendoza, the leader of Maclovio's resistance, in 1996, and filmed a protest march to the state capital, Mexicali. The project *Twin Plant: Forms of Resistance, Corridors of Power* involved the importation of wooden garage doors[35] from which to construct buildings – which could be used for other purposes after the project – and art works. A group of young people from the settlement worked with Border Arts Workshop, in exchange for being granted plots on which to build houses by the settlement's elected leaders. The project included installations, photography, video work and mural painting using the garage doors as a support. David Harding, who spent five weeks at Maclovio in 1997, comments on the continuing currency of a mural tradition in Mexico, and on the 'direct political action' which characterises the project; he sees intervention by an international group of artists (who have no claim to a link to the locality) as potentially tipping the political balance in the settlement's favour. In more general terms, Harding argues that 'The very engagement of people in collaborative art practice changes the perception of individuals to such an extent that their life can become transformed' (Harding, 1997:7).

Mauricio Dias and Walter Riedweg, contributing to *Conversations at the Castle*, an arts project curated by Mary Jane Jacob to coincide with the 1996 Olympic Games in Atlanta, worked with offenders at the Fulton County Child Treatment Centre School and Atlanta Federal Penitentiary, using video to construct dialogues between the two groups. The artists state:

> We consider interaction to be a form of artistic expression. We base our work in the philosophy that art, as a creative experience, has enormous potential as a communication vehicle among people. We work exclusively through interactive processes in which the representation of themes and issues directly involves concerned people or groups. (Dias and Riedweg, 1998:88)

Noting publicity material for a boot camp which advertised 'How to de-construct and re-construct a person in ninety days', Dias and Riedweg liken the notion to

Nazi methods of exclusion, both irrational and dangerous to society. Like Border Arts Workshop, the artists were foreign to the site, a factor they see as enabling communication in a way not available to those conditioned by or perceived as part of an institution. Over a period of eight weeks, workshops were held in which offenders took part in perception exercises, and drew floor plans from memory of places in their lives. The drawings became a foundation for video-taped conversations on intimacy, childhood, crime, sentence and family. The youth group extended the workshops into the creation of a nest, based on that of the weaver bird, which has multiple entrances and cells; also into the use of car licence plates (manufactured by prisoners) to carry questions, such as 'Did you put me in to leave me out?' and 'Who should I fear?'. Is this social work? The artists maintain it is not: they argue that by not controlling or directing the conversations (outside a role of agency in setting up the project and making available the necessary resources), their work differs from social service, education and other state-operated functions – 'because it is not conceived to control or produce a certain outcome'. Dias and Riedweg state that they do not see art as changing things with which they disagree as such, but having 'a place in that change' by demonstrating alternative possibilities. This seems quite close to Ernesto Laclau's position, in his essay on 'Emancipation(s)', that '. . . a democratic society which has become a viable social order will not be a totally free society, but one which has negotiated in a specific way the duality freedom/unfreedom' (Laclau, 1996:19). Perhaps the work of artists such as Dias and Riedweg aims to bring closer that society.

Notes

1. The section of the chapter dealing with post-industrial cities is developed from a paper to the workshop on Waterfronts of Art, organised by the University of Barcelona for the European League of Institutes of Art thematic network The Public Art Observatory, September, 1999.
2. See, for examples: on Realism, Nochlin (1967) and Clark (1973a and b); on art in Russia after 1917, Cullerne-Brown and Taylor (1993); on art in the USA after 1945, Crane (1987). For critical and theoretical discussion of the avant-garde, see Bürger (1984) and Foster (1983 and 1987). For recent feminist art criticism, see Deepwell (1995). For discussion of participatory art practices, see Gablik (1991), Felshin (1995) and Lacy (1995).
3. Wigglesworth and Till include two cases of art practice in 'The Everyday and Architecture' (1998): 'The Uses of Gravity: The Everyday Sublime in the Work of Station House Opera', by Nicholas Till (1998:12–15); and 'Turning the Commonplace, Sure . . . A Poetic Appreciation of Jessica Stockholder's Art' by Åsmund Thorkildsen (1998:52–56).
4. An economic study for the London Borough of Southwark saw the proposed Tate in a disused power station as 'the power house for Bankside's other visitor attractions', without which the development of a cultural quarter would be impracticable (MCA, 1995:7, cited by Paul Teedon in an unpublished paper to the British Sociology Association's working group on public space, University of Westminster, June 1999. Teedon concludes: 'What we have seen, then, in Bankside is a complex exercise in identity

creation, in which a cultural landscape has resulted that is design rich and architecturally significant with particular bourgeois appeal. In turn, this has been based upon the production of a landscape, in which the past is being aestheticised . . .'.

5. One popular guidebook describes El Raval as '. . . a neighbourhood in the process of gentrification with whole blocks being pulled down, previous no-go areas transformed into broad boulevards and inevitably . . . house prices going through the roof.' (Jules Brown, *Barcelona – The Rough Guide*, London, Rough Guides, p 71.)
6. Monica Degen (1999), 'Regenerating Public Life? A sensuous comparison of regenerated public space in El Raval (Barcelona) and Castlefield (Manchester)', unpublished paper to the working group on public space of the British Sociological Association, University of Westminster, June 1999.
7. For a critical account of the new relation of economic, political and cultural factors in the post-industrial city, see Byrne, 1997. Byrne, who draws evidence from Cleveland and Leicester, begins from an idea of a 'dual city'. He writes, for instance, about '. . . the nature of urban space, and in particular about its potential for becoming divided into two quite distinctive socio-spatial forms, characterised by different economic and cultural relations, and equally distinctive relationships with both political activity and governmental management through policy regimes' (p 51).
8. See Zukin, 1995:118–22 on the role of museums in gentrification in New York.
9. Landry and Bianchini argue that 'A creative city requires land and buildings at affordable prices, preferably close to other cultural amenities. These are likely to be available in . . . areas where uses are changing, such as former port and industrial zones.' They cite Barcelona and Melbourne as cases of regeneration through '. . . a synthesising creativity, which brings together unexpected elements' (Landry and Bianchini, 1995:28–31).
10. At the time of writing, many thousands of people are known to have died during Indonesian repression, and hundreds of thousands continue to be displaced following UN intervention in East Timor. No doubt (but the author does not know) the Mandalay still sells coconut rice in its coffee shop, trading on another Indonesia fantasised by its promotional staff.
11. Hal Foster comments on the tendency of one kind of post-modernism, associated with neo-conservatives, to repudiate modernism but sever its cultural and social aspects to propose a new affirmative culture. Foster supports another kind of post-modernism which resists the status quo. (Foster, 1983:xi–xii).
12. For example the collages of Martha Rosler – see Rosler, 1994.
13. See Crimp and Rolston, 1990; and Gott, 1994.
14. The notion of the artist as carrier and revealer of the primordial is discussed critically in Kuspit, 1993:1–27.
15. This phrase is used in Marcuse's paper to the Dialectics of Liberation Congress at the Roundhouse, London in July 1967. More fully: 'this means one of the oldest dreams of all radical theory and practice. It means that the human imagination . . . would become a productive force applied to the transformation of the social and natural universe. . . . And now I throw in the terrible concept: it would mean an "aesthetic" reality – society as a work of art. This is the most Utopian, the most radical possibility of liberation today' (Marcuse, 1968:185).
16. See Chris Cleverly, 'Life's a pitch – and then you buy', *Guardian*, 14 June 1999 Media section, pp 8–9.
17. See Owens, 1983, for discussion of work by Kruger, Rosler, Holzer and other artists working in feminist and radical territories.
18. See Miles, 1997b, for discussion of public art and issues of women's place in culture and the city.

19. Haacke writes: 'Private patronage is in fashion. Some public relations firms, for example, are hired to help businesses choose the best place for their symbolic investments and to assist them in establishing contacts in the world of art.' He adds: 'In face of this, critical awareness is nil' (Bourdieu and Haacke, 1995:15).
20. See McKay, 1996 for an account of the culture of road protest campaigns at Twyford Down and elsewhere.
21. No bibliographic reference can be given because the booklet is published anonymously and states neither place nor date of publication. The technology it describes is real, but its aim is to provoke (and amuse) rather than be a practical handbook.
22. *Evading Standards* has eight pages.
23. http://www.gn.apc.org/june18/home.html – referenced by the author in May 1999.
24. See web-site: www.MeatStinks.com.
25. 'When I asked twenty university students to name a place where they felt they belonged, most could not' (Lippard, 1997:9).
26. For material on a range of Outsider Artists working in the spaces of everyday life, see *Public Art Review*, vol. 4, no. 1, Summer/Fall 1992 – an issue dedicated to 'Spontaneous Construction – Environments By Self-Taught Artists.' Included are articles on Eddie Williamson, Tyree Guyton, Howard Finster, Ferdinand Cheval, James Hampton and Kea Tawana and others.
27. See Griswold, 1992.
28. Both Hayden and de Bretteville hold academic positions at Yale.
29. Albrow lists four characteristics of post-modern/post-industrial social movement – to paraphrase more briefly, these are: 1. global information which affects values and behaviour; 2. immediacy of global news and impact of global change on local lives; 3. time-space compression through which social relationships are maintained over any distance through new technologies; 4. mobility which means lifestyles and routines can be maintained almost anywhere (Albrow, 1997:44).
30. See Dunn and Leeson (1993) for an illustrated commentary by the artists on this project. See also Rosler, 1987:14: 'It may be only with the relatively circumscribed . . . agitational works which emerge from a specific community and are staged within it that we can speak about the building of a public in art. I am thinking about Loraine Leeson and Peter Dunn's billboards in London's East End.' Rosler goes on to contrast these with artists' billboards which use languages closer to advertising and act in the art world despite their public sites.
31. From explanatory material circulated as a folder with illustrations by The Art of Change, 1998.
32. The main groups are Bengali, Chinese, Irish, Greek and English.
33. The images were produced in PhotoShop and printed electrostatically on vinyl, then coated with a protective layer to reduce fading in sunlight. This project continues the process of *It Makes My Bread Sweeter* (1994), a celebration of self-appointed street-sweeper Mario Ezzo (1876–1939) – see Lippard, 1997:284–5.
34. 'End of the Line', project notes issued as press release and through the Internet (1997).
35. In the USA, these are being replaced for security reasons by metal doors, and are available at little cost beyond transport from scrap yards. The doors (each 16 by 8 feet), with other recycled materials, were taken to Mexico as art materials to avoid customs interest. (Harding, 1997:6)

Chapter 9
The View from Here: Sustainability

Introduction

This last chapter concerns the concept and practices of sustainability: in particular, how cities can be sustained as the primary form of human settlement. It supposes a future in which the majority of the planet's human inhabitants continue to dwell in cities; but also that alternatives to current approaches to urban planning, design and housing are necessary if cities are to be places of joy rather than dis-ease. This means seeing beyond the war stories, interrogating notions of community and development, recognising social and cultural diversity as positive characteristics of city life, and addressing problems of environmental destruction and social deprivation. The gulf between the rich and the poor, and zoning of cities into enclaves of abundance amidst margins of disenfranchisement, is no more sustainable than the devastation of rainforests. Since both result from processes of globalisation, the creation of sustainable cities requires alternative models of political economy which utilise local initiatives and invest in local knowledges.

An understanding of the architectural everyday contributes to sustainability by emphasising the specifics of locality. Informal settlements in the non-affluent world show that dwellers can order their own lives, whilst interventions by professionals which focus on design rather than process and occupation may be disordering[1]. Similarly, vernacular architectures tend to employ appropriate technologies in human-scale constructions, having a low environmental impact. These factors suggest that understandings from the non-affluent world can be applied in the affluent world, and that sustainable solutions to urban problems will be found outside the dominant structures of development. And, in refuting the model of globalisation, the architectural everyday has implications beyond design, in terms, for instance, of local economies and trading systems[2].

The chapter begins by questioning the model of productivity which underpins the global economy, seeing an alternative basis for social and economic relations in the concept of conviviality proposed by Ivan Illich (mentioned briefly in Chapter 7). This shifts attention from economic outputs to processes of sociation and exchange, and from the abstraction of a global free market to the immediacies of everyday lives. Common Ground's *Parish Maps* project is discussed as an example of how local narratives can be shaped, and cases of informal and experimental architecture are noted as, respectively, expressions of local identities, and potential models for alternative forms of settlement. The chapter next considers the use of the methods of action planning in non-affluent countries; and, finally, discusses self-build housing in the UK based on a design by Walter Segal, suggesting that sustainability follows from a reclamation by dwellers of the production of space.

CULTURE AND SUSTAINABILITY

Sustainability has several competing definitions[3]. Amongst the most frequently cited is that of the Brundtland Report of 1987 from the World Commission on Environment and Development (WCED): 'a process of change in which the exploitation of resources, the direction of investments, the orientation of technological development and institutional changes are made consistent with future as well as present needs' (WCED, 1987, cited in Nijkamp and Perrels, 1994:4). Later, the report defines sustainable development as: '. . . development that meets the needs of the present without compromising the ability of future generations to meet their own needs' (WCED, 1987:43, cited in Elliott, 1999:7 and Meadowcroft, 1999:13), which it explains in terms of recognition of the essential needs of the poor of the world, whilst also seeing technological and social limitations to development. But if reports of this kind, or the principles of Agenda 21 agreed at the United Nations Conference on Environment and Development (UNCED) in Rio de Janeiro in 1992[4], are to inform a radical shift of attitudes towards the sustainable use of the planet's natural resources, and the socially just distribution of benefits from these resources, then there are two main difficulties: the limited effectiveness of governments in directing the distribution of wealth in a world characterised as a market increasingly free of regulation; and that although the Brundtland Report recognises that past exploitation has produced effects which are unacceptable in democratic societies, its terminology reflects the economic model of productivity, making its programme potentially self-defeating.

Other, conventional definitions of sustainable development also affirm the current economic system and its insistence on growth – for instance: 'The net productivity of biomass . . . maintained over decades to centuries' (Conway, 1987:96 cited in Elliott, 1999:7); and, '. . . an optimal (sustainable growth) policy would seek to maintain an "acceptable" rate of growth . . . without depleting . . . the natural environment asset stock' (Turner, 1988:12, cited in Elliott, 1999:7). Nijkamp and Perrels argue that the long-term continuity of an urban system depends on structural changes which may be stable or unstable, linear or non-linear, and conclude that sustainable cities are sites of co-evolution of socio-economic interests, environmental concern and energy efficiency (Nijkamp and Perrels, 1994:4). Their main concern is with energy, but the difficulty in their position, like others, is that the socio-economic interests of which they write may be incompatible with environmental needs, and the parameters remain economic rather than social in determination[5].

These definitions and approaches, reformist rather than radical, mask certain complexities which critics of development (and development aid) have sought to reveal. James Meadowcroft, for instance, argues that sustainable development is a matter of more than economic change, and 'implies a positive process of social change . . .' which avoids the kinds of contradiction '. . . which would undermine the possibility for future advance' (Meadowcroft, 1999:15); and William Rees argues that the provisions of Agenda 21 for an improvement in the living standards of the poor reflect contradictions. He asks: 'how can we produce the growth deemed necessary . . . when historic patterns of material growth seem responsible for present unsustainable levels of ecological disintegration?' (Rees, 1999:23). Wendy Harcourt, editor of *Development*, the journal of the Society for International Development, sums up some of the issues by arguing that whilst 'Development = economic growth is at the centre of development discourse', for many commentators it equally concerns issues which are social, political, cultural, environmental and gender-based (Harcourt, 1994:11). She draws attention to the marginalisation of women in conventional development strategies, and worsening of their social and economic position through western modernisation. Jennifer Elliott, similarly, observes that societies construct needs for some social groups '. . . without satisfying even the basic needs of others' (Elliott, 1999:7), and that, after three decades of development on the model supported by the economic and financial institutions of the affluent world, many countries in the non-affluent world have debt burdens several times the size of their Gross National Products (Elliott, 1999:13). In the late 1990s, many of these nations are able to enter the world economy only on the terms of the neo-liberal policies of the World Bank and International Monetary Fund, whose prescriptions include reducing state expenditure and liberalising trade (Elliott, 1999:31–2). So the rich become richer by taking from the poor the little they once had. Alternative definitions of sustainability, then, require initiatives which question the concept of development itself, whilst a shift from an accounting culture to one based on the values of sustainability might use a term other than 'asset stock' to describe the complex ecologies of living organisms.

Taking a more radical view, can the term 'sustainability' be separated from the term 'development' to produce a new concept of sustainable sociation? This has three implications, which will be addressed here as a prelude to discussion of practices for sustainable urban societies: firstly, if development is based in productivity, an alternative model of political economy is necessary if the contradiction between development and sustainability is to be resolved; secondly, an emphasis on sociation – the ways in which people in societies associate with each other and construct or receive narratives to rationalise this – shifts attention from the outcome of economic growth towards the process of economic exchange; and, thirdly, given the limitations of action by governments and an emphasis on sociation, much of what happens is likely to be local, accepting that local networks may no longer be described only in terms of a geographical neighbourhood but may be far-reaching whilst still identifiable in terms of individual experience[6]. What happens in ordinary life is affected by global mechanisms which determine, for instance, the price of oil and the range of films distributed at local cinemas; but it may be also at the local level that change, through consumer resistance or the setting up of non-money economies and local exchange trading systems, can begin – as recognised by the artist-activists discussed in the previous chapter.

To take first the need for an alternative to the model of productivity. The concept of productivity assumes that the global economy has no limits to growth, that new markets can always be found and that increased production, through new technologies and construction of new wants, will continue to generate increased profits for the owners of the means of production. This concept is central to capitalism, and is derived from histories of European colonial expansion since the sixteenth century, and reflected in a myth of an expanding universe; it is given increased licence by free-market economics which decrease the role of nation-states in the regulation of economic exchange[7]. Productivity has undergone historical change, in that development in a post-industrial world is a question of transnational flows of capital and consumption in sectors such as financial services and mass communications media, rather than of discrete urban economies based in manufacturing (Nijkamp and Perrels, 1994:4), but remains the dominant model of economic thought which conditions social organisation. The outcomes of productivity are alienation and the consumerism of affluence. The former is a key concept, not outworn, in Marxist theory[8]; and the manufacture of wants and their marketing by the culture industries as needs[9], and promotion through mass communications of lifestyles which require increasing levels of consumption whilst remaining unsatisfying, thus requiring further consumption leading to further expansion of markets and profits, are the means by which the interests of capital today prevent an ending of alienation. Through the false liberty of consumer choice, and fusion of real life and entertainment, Janis Joplin could be said to have needed a Mercedes Benz; and through built-in obsolescence and rapid cycles of fashion she might have needed a new one a year later.

Ivan Illich writes that '[An] increasing demand for products has come to define society's process' (Illich, 1990:11). His argument, like that of Victor Papanek in *Design for the Real World* (1984), draws attention to the manufacture of wants which is the condition of affluence. Yet, as Marcuse argued in 1968, the affluent society is obscene in the uneven distribution of its wealth[10], while productivity displaces imagination to the fantasy worlds of entertainment and fashion, leading to repression of the desire for liberation through social change (Marcuse, 1968:183–5)[11]. The concept of conviviality, on the other hand, defined by Illich (1990) and referenced by Lisa Peattie (1998), suggests a new equilibrium of the planet's biological, social and cultural ecologies, and a relational rather than objectifying attitude to people and environment. It means the replacement of the ends-directed values of productivity with the means-led values of appropriate technologies and economies of need. Illich writes:

> . . . I propose the vision of a convivial society. A convivial society would be the result of social arrangements that guarantee for each member the most ample and free access to the tools of the community and limit this freedom only in favour of another member's equal freedom. (Illich, 1990:12)

In a convivial society, satisfaction is no longer defined as maximum consumption, and futures are shaped according to the needs of survival, social justice and self-defined work – 'Rationally designed convivial tools have become the basis for participatory justice' (Illich, 1990:13). Illich does not pretend a transition to conviviality will be easy or smooth, nor that affluent publics will not be disadvantaged in the process; he aspires to a world in which a joyful sobriety and liberating austerity are discovered in a renewal of mutual dependence. The argument advanced by Illich in *Tools for Conviviality* (1990) could be compared to Kropotkin's in *Mutual Aid* (1902)[12], which traces mutuality to biological roots in animals and humans, and sees survival as a product of co-operation rather than competition; this reclaims Darwin's idea of survival of the fittest in terms of the most appropriate to conditions, rather than the most aggressive. Illich foresees, like Kropotkin, an ending of the economic problem of scarcity through technological advances; but he shares, equally, an emphasis on creativity which characterised the liberationist cultures of the late 1960s, seen in the work of Marcuse, Papanek and Brown[13]. Illich writes that 'People feel joy, as opposed to mere pleasure, to the extent that their activities are creative' (Illich, 1990:20), adding that the growth of tools beyond a certain point increases regimentation, dependence and exploitation. Tools, here, include any means of production, and the institutions of society – in other words, all agencies, from machines to communication systems and school curricula. Convivial tools are those which, in contrast to industrial productivity under capitalism, '. . . give each person who uses them the greatest opportunity to enrich the environment with the fruits of his or her vision' (Illich, 1990:21).

It might seem that Illich is arguing for an adoption of Ghandi's embrace of hand tools[14]; and he does say that industrial tools deny conviviality. But his argument is not a call for a return to a pre-industrial society, more a reconsideration of structures of control in society, including localised control over technologies and prioritisation of those which can be easily used by anyone autonomously and without obligation, allowing the user an expression of meaning through such action (Illich, 1990:22). So, whilst productivity manipulates human labour for profit, and sets targets for growth unrelated to human need, conviviality reclaims economic organisation for creativity, and replaces it in the hands of those who use and make goods rather than those who own the means of production. For Illich, then, conviviality is a reassertion of people's right to the creative and autonomous use of their energy. But, he writes that it '. . . will remain a pious dream unless the ideals of social justice prevail' (Illich, 1990:12). The difficulty here is that social justice, which is not in the minds of global entrepreneurs, may take a long time to build, whilst environmental destruction is rapid.

But is it necessary for social change to be accomplished first? For Marcuse (1978), the aesthetic dimension is a space in which the surfaces of the dominant reality are ruptured, so that social change follows, rather than is a pre-condition for, changes in culture. And if biology, society and culture, concerning the totality of life forms, the political and economic organisation of human life, and the articulation of human values, respectively, are seen as mutually informative and conditioning, it is in culture that meaning and value are given form. Cultural values are contingent not absolute, and frame complex perspectives, so that biodiversity has margins of acceptability and possibility determined by human agency. Whilst, for instance, the Nine Mile Run Greenway project (discussed in Chapter 6) seeks to reclaim the biodiversity of a brownfield site, it accepts this can be done only by human intervention, and will not restore the site to a wilderness state. Indeed, the desire for wilderness is itself a cultural construct with limitations; few citizens of the affluent world would seek to reintroduce smallpox, nor to return to the life of the hunter-gatherer[15]. The eradication of a virus alters the ecology of the planet irreversibly, as does the loss of species caused by industrial-scale timber felling, but the point is that cultural value is a means of differentiation between these interventions, and once one form of differentiation is understood, all history and all narratives become open to discourse.

Perhaps, to move to the second implication of sustainability outlined above, in place of the Marxist orthodoxy of a base of economic organisation which determines models of sociation and produces a cultural superstructure, culture can be seen as conditioning as well as being conditioned by social and economic organisation, so that base and superstructure merge in a new mutability. This, which is not dissimilar to Lefebvre's reconstruction of this aspect of Marxism (McLeod, 1997:14, noted in Chapter 7), implies that a move from productivity to conviviality entails new narratives to replace those which normalise exploitation. If conviviality questions more than economics, then a narrative of conviviality might state an alternative to the Cartesian separation of observer from observed, which Brown links to political passivity in representation[16], whilst Peattie links conviviality to the activities of everyday life, such as drinking coffee (presumably distributed by a fair-trade company)[17]. Peattie's example of the communal meal brings together the biological need to eat in order to sustain life, the social need for co-operation, and the cultural process of cooking, through which identity and difference are manifest, in a model of sociability (Peattie, 1998:248).

If, then, productivity is a dominant narrative which inhibits free association, it is also a site into which interventions can be made, just as Krzysztof Wodiczko's projections question conventional or normalising readings of monuments. When the monument is recoded, making, for instance, its association with militarism transparent, the narrative is redirected in a way which retains currency in the consciousness of the spectator. Narratives, then, are not immutable objects, but processes which are influential in how individuals are constituted as subjects and hence how they relate with others, so that to shift the narrative is to shift the course of social formation. Narratives operate at the levels of myths and stories, and of language itself, since in the conditions imposed by a given language are implicit the narratives which can be constructed in it. Looking to the former, Arran Gare writes that '. . . we only know what to do when we know what story or stories we are in' (Gare, 1995:139), and argues that in order to bring about a change in attitudes to the environment, new narratives are required which have the force and complexity to induce action. He adds that environmental problems are global in scale, and that the stories derived from local conditions and lives are most likely to orient people towards action when integrated in a global narrative, and '. . . ultimately with a grand narrative revealing the relationship between the lives of individuals and the dynamics of the global political and economic order' (Gare, 1995:140)[18]. Illich, looking to a more fundamental operation of narrative, writes that 'Language reflects the monopoly of the industrial mode of production over perception and motivation' (Illich, 1990:89), and that the 'mythical majority paralyses political action' when a mythicised 'they' are invoked as guardians of vested interests (Illich, 1990:102)[19]. Luce Irigaray draws attention to the dominance of masculinity through the gendering of verbal language, and the normalisation of the mother-son relation and erasure of the mother-daughter couple in visual imagery (Irigaray, 1994:26–30 and 8–14). And Raff Carmen notes a terminology of '. . . strategic planning, campaigning, combating, extermination . . .' which linguistically links development to martial arts (Carmen, 1994:61). The power of dominant narratives is seen by Charles Lindblom as the only viable explanation for the absence in history of attempts to establish non-market economies[20]. He writes that '. . . our minds are systematically shaped' and non-market systems '. . . excluded from the thinking of most people' through thought control, adding that whilst '. . . we are taught the benefits of the market, we are systematically taught the alleged virtues of hierarchy, inequality, deference, respect for authority, and so on' (Lindblom, 1999:52).

What is to counter this? Gare proposes a new grand narrative lending meaning to local and individual narratives, but perhaps this suffers from the same deficiency as existing grand narratives, and from the same condition as dominant forms of language – that what speaks through a grand narrative is dominance itself. To subordinate the local to the global even in a counter-narrative is to replicate that which the counter-narrative seeks to replace. If the power of the market economy is to be diminished, it is more likely to happen in the everyday lives of people who reject its illusions in favour of the liberating austerity proposed by Illich. Similarly, development aid is unlikely to solve the problems of the poor, who are more likely to find local solutions for themselves[21]. Leaving aside the problem of rebuilding grand narratives when even polyphonic ones may become instruments of dominance, the arguments proposed by Gare and Lindblom suggest that cultural interventions are more influential in creating the conditions for radical change than the various programmes and policies which emerge from intergovernmental conferences and institutions. The WCED report, for example, contained a six point agenda for change, which can be sketched as: a political system based on participation; an economic system addressing uneven distribution; a production system which preserves the ecological base; technology which fosters sustainable trade and finance; an international system which does the same; and an administrative system which can correct its own failings (Elliott, 1999:9). But although some states or cities have adopted policies which incorporate some of these points[22], mainly under Agenda 21, this is not in itself a guarantee of change. Meanwhile, despite the liberal agendas of conferences and commissions, the energies of international financial institutions such as the World Bank and International Monetary Fund are directed towards extending capitalism. At the same time, the activities and distinctive local cultures of various kinds of alternative society have gained increasing attention. Road protest in the UK during the 1990s, for instance, has produced identifiable cultural forms (of dress and body decoration, song and adoption of non-given personal or group names) through which participants feel a sense of belonging (McKay, 1996); and it has probably lessened government's commitment to road building. Similarly, the increasing popularity of non-GM food suggests an exercise of democratic aspiration, but here directly on the market. New narratives, then, are emerging, linked not by assimilation in a grand strategy, but through informal communication and open networks (including cyberspace).

Perhaps a new sensuality will begin to characterise social and environmental relations in place of the coldness of productivity[23]; and perhaps, in response to the third implication of sustainability noted above, the limits to state effectiveness, this will emphasise the limits to power and the potential for local autonomy. Peattie cites Dumont's term 'Socialist carnival' to describe the mobilisation of voluntary labour in Cuba in 1968, and uses the term 'purposive conviviality' for political protest (Peattie, 1998:249, citing Dumont, 1970:87)[24]. Chaia Heller goes further in proposing a socio-erotic narrative in which the form of society itself takes on an erotic quality. This was proposed by utopian socialist Charles Fourier in the nineteenth century, though Heller draws on the work of eco-feminists[25]. Referencing Audre Lorde (1984), she writes:

> If we were to demand from our everyday lives the same pleasure and passion that we hope to find in sexuality, then we would have to make some pretty profound institutional changes. If such institutions as racism, sexism, capitalism, and the state make misery out of our work and political engagement, in turn making a misery out of our social, familial, and sexual relationships, if hierarchy and authority inhibit the cultivation of creativity, participation, and pleasure, then surely, fighting to restore the erotic means nothing short of a social and political revolution. (Heller, 1999:85)

Since power is never given, it can only be taken, whilst the manner of its taking determines the ends to which it is later put. From this it follows that alternative models of social organisation, and the narratives through which they are rationalised, will remain local, thus deconstructing rather than reforming power. Besides, as Elliott concludes: '. . . it is the immediate adverse effects on survival for the urban poor of such basic procedures as cooking, washing and working . . .' which mean that local environmental questions matter as much as, and constitute, global warming (Elliott, 1999:173). Local projects, then, such as the creation of a wetland to cleanse water sources polluted by mining residues at Quaking Houses in County Durham, provide local solutions to global threats (Griffiths and Kemp, 1999).

Parish Maps

One point of departure for new narratives is a sense of locality, as gained from the kind of direct and incremental experiences offered by, for instance, walking through a landscape. This is repressed by conventional cartography which reduces all occurrences to the signs of a universal and objectifying set of categories and signs. That a diversity of features should be seen as a scape at all, of course, is an act of cultural mediation; but it does not necessarily lead to a universal system of representation when carried out according to the memories and associations of the mental life of individuals. The *Parish Maps* project initiated by the ecological charity Common Ground in 1986 involved the creation of maps in which such personal recollections, rather than impersonal information, were inscribed using any appropriate visual language. Professional artists[26] and non-professional local groups were invited to make maps of the places in which they lived, or to which they had particular attachment. Parish boundaries in the UK are often the oldest recorded and frequently follow features in the landscape, and the parish is the smallest, most local unit of administration. The artists' maps were exhibited to draw attention to the project, offering a range of departures from conventional cartography. Simon Lewty, making a map of Old Milverton in Warwickshire (Figure 9.1), wrote:

> My map relates to the experience of this landscape, to its genius loci, and to layers of memory and association that are for me an integral part of it. The actual landscape – itself already a multi-layered palimpsest – merges in the imagination with a fragmentary mental landscape, whose paths are like fissures in the earth, constantly opening on to new levels of interpretation. (Common Ground, 1986)

The map develops a personal language of signs for this experience, and retains a sense of terrain and contour without using the vocabulary of conventional maps. Viewing the *Parish Maps* project as geographers, David Crouch and David Matless set Common Ground's work in a context of reconstructions of the map, seeing the use of 'older or non-western mapping traditions', and of media including photography, ceramics and textiles, as unsettling the perceived authority of cartography[27]; but they also observe a tension '. . . between Common Ground's fostering of consciously artistic experiment and a tendency, strong in many community maps, to hold to a

Figure 9.1 *Simon Lewty,* Parish Map of Old Milverton near Leamington Spa, *1986–87 (detail; reproduced by permission of Common Ground)*

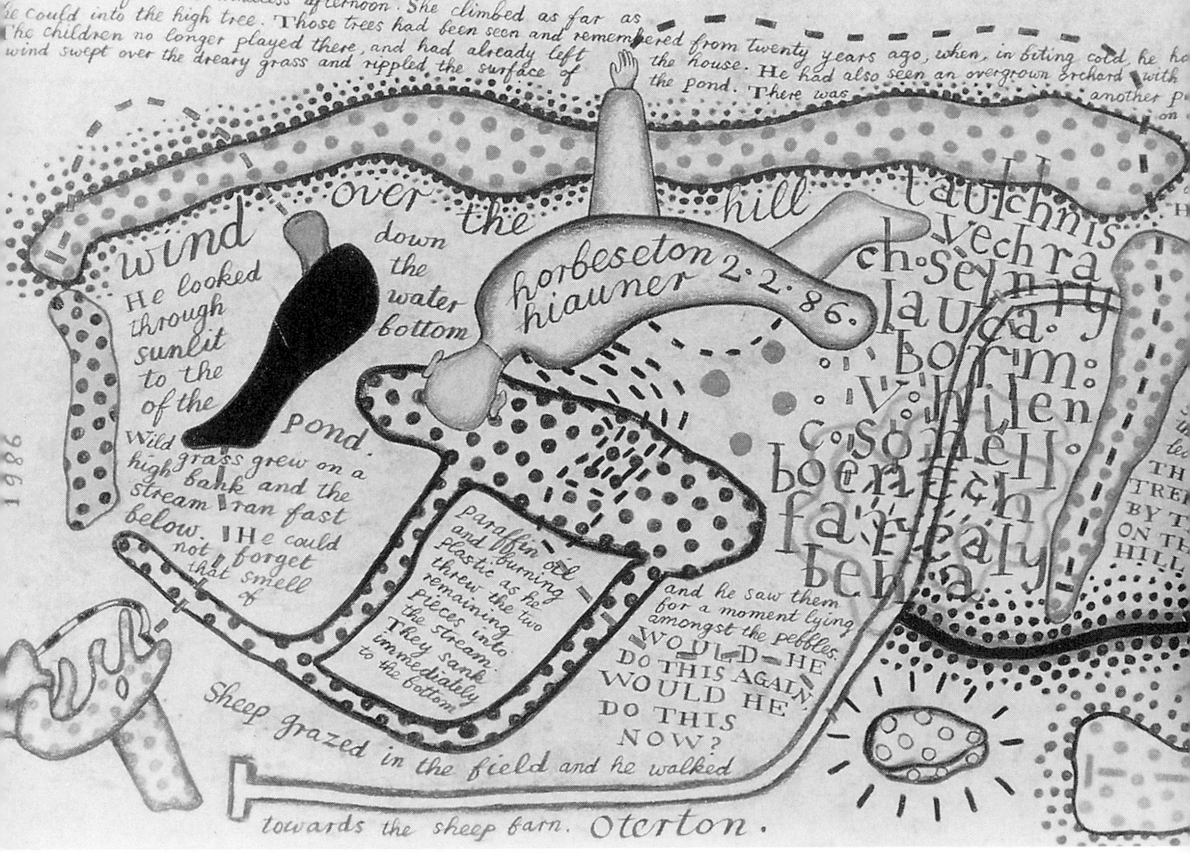

tracing of the real' (Crouch and Matless, 1996:237)[28]. They define mapping as '. . . a process of self-alerting, putting people on their toes against unwanted change and producing an active sense of community' (Crouch and Matless, 1996:236), and write on Lewty's map that it '. . . acts as a permit of entry to a geographical art of memory' (Crouch and Matless, 1996:241). By 1996, more than 1500 maps were completed, suggesting that the project has entered the consciousness of many thousands of people.

Perhaps the art of memory as exhibited in these maps has wider implications, is a reverie which questions by its introspection the universalised map of productivity. Any space which has been inhabited is a location of the complex meanings which overlay the spaces of plans and conventional cartography, constituting the representational spaces which, for Lefebvre, persist alongside dominant representations of space (Lefebvre, 1991:78–9). To visualise these associations challenges the dominance of the conceptual space in which urban and economic futures are constructed, and since planned futures tend to reflect global and national priorities, to draw attention to the local is a form of negation of the dominant order, whilst local knowledges may be, in practical terms, crucial to the conservation of local ecologies. Part of the project's aim was to legitimate these personal geographies:

> by emphasising that everyone is an expert in their own place, Common Ground hopes that increasing confidence will lead people towards involvement in active caring for the wild life, landscape, buildings and historic features of their own surroundings. (Common Ground, 1986)

If dwellers are experts in their own place, this expertise may lead to involvement in the determination of economic and political futures beyond, though conditioning, the preservation of landscapes for future generations.

HUTS

Mapping gives form to personal awareness of place; but another level of the production of space is its physical making, as in the building of informal settlements, or erection of huts in marginal spaces within the built environment of the affluent world. Huts translate the practices of rural areas to urban situations, yet also have a specific urban quality as places of sociation rather than dwelling. Huts may be spaces of social gathering for minority groups, or places of private retreat. Recently, some architects have turned to the description or construction of huts as an antidote to signature architecture. Three cases are noted here, one of informal constructions in New York, one of a building, part domestic shelter and part artwork, by an artist in Newark, and one of a hut made by an architect as a place of retreat from the world.

Dolores Hayden and Ann Cline both illustrate the *casitas* built by Puerto Rican dwellers in East Harlem and the Bronx (Hayden, 1995:36; Cline, 1997:19). The yards of huts built in front of tenement blocks are semi-public, semi-private spaces, like the balconies of El Raval. Hayden writes of shared meanings and rituals, and the specificity of spatial patterns to ethnic groups[29]. The *casita*, she explains, is a rural dwelling type (a small, wooden house with porch and front yard) transposed to an urban environment as a public space within the territory of a defined community, where '. . . rural vernacular architecture was chosen to serve a polemical function, emphasising the importance of the "enacted environment" as a bridge between built and natural worlds' (Hayden, 1995:35)[30]. The buildings, painted yellow, turquoise or pink, are used for political meetings, musical events, inter-family gatherings and education. Cline writes of the same *casitas* in San Juan as objects of the tourist gaze, but also sites of 'independent initiative' and 'democratic impulse', contrasting the planner's view of 'shantytowns' with their liveliness, and notes, like Hayden, that when Puerto Ricans move to New York, they build these small dwellings, some with signs saying 'Villa Puerto Rico', as expressions of '. . . longing engendered by absence' (Cline, 1997:21–2).

Building a shelter is a basic act of settlement, and, because no two shelters made by their occupants are identical, an expression of identity, hence they are both functional and aesthetic. John Turner sees a grass-roots ordering of space in informal settlements, arguing that 'The complexity and variability of individual household priorities and consequent housing behaviour are beyond the practical grasp of any central institution or organisation', adding that 'If general rules . . . were developed into proven laws . . ., then it would be theoretically possible for a Big Brother central intelligence . . . to programme the provision of suitable housing for all (Turner, 1976:100), and using this trope to make explicit the failure of mass-housing solutions, and to affirm the authority of people over their own settlements, which he sees as outweighing that of design or the state (an argument close to Illich's). Hayden, more concerned with the politics than the reveries of *casitas*, like Turner, sees them as setting up an opposition to the dominant architecture of abandoned blocks of project housing – 'an alternative kind of social reproduction within their space' and a case of Lefebvre's formulation of 'counter-space' (Hayden, 1995:36). As counter-spaces, these brightly painted huts constitute statements of group and family identity in face of the dehumanisation of the dreary spaces imposed by social administration. In a quieter reclamation of space, a wooden garden shed stands on one of the concrete balconies at Thamesmead (Figure 9.2).

A feeling of resistance permeates the (now destroyed) work of Kea Tawana – a Japanese American whose mother was killed in the American bombing of Tokyo and father died in an internment camp in San Diego – in Newark[31]. In 1987, when parts of Newark were burnt in civil unrest, reporters came to visit Tawana's *Ark*, 80 foot long, three floors high and built by hand. The materials were recycled from demolition sites and empty buildings, and the process of construction begun in 1982 (the first drawings dating to 1973), using nineteenth-century methods learned

Figure 9.2 Thamesmead: garden shed on concrete balcony (photo M Miles)

from old technical manuals found in empty houses. But the concept is contemporary, a statement of displacement, of the lack of safety offered by a built environment of dispossession: 'There's no place safe on land', as Tawana told reporters (Metz, 1992:22). The first site of the Ark was a vacant lot subsequently acquired by the New Community Corporation, a state-funded developer of prefabricated condominiums. Using rollers, Tawana moved the *Ark* to adjacent church property and became the church caretaker; it was then condemned as unsafe by the Newark Department of Engineering, subject to widely divergent views from officials, professionals and local residents – one calling it garbage, another seeing it as amazing. Holly Metz cites a curator from the Smithsonian Museums who described it as '. . . reflecting the city's critical history of opulence, decay and renewal' (Metz, 1992:23). The spread of opinion reflects conflicting attitudes to development, between those seeking to upgrade the area in line with mass-produced housing schemes representing a conservative new urbanism, and those seeking to retain the autonomy of the neighbourhood and highlight its long-term neglect by city authorities. The city won, and the *Ark* was taken down by Tawana to avoid its destruction by others. She no longer lives in Newark.

Tawana sought shelter and safety in her *Ark*, with the immediacy of a displaced person. From a privileged position, Ann Cline seeks in the building of huts a space of withdrawal. Referencing huts in which Zen monks and Confucian officials sought seclusion, and in which the tea ceremony is conducted in Japan, she recounts the building of her own hut in her backyard. She writes that 'Survival wasn't the issue, of course, but retirement was', and that 'Like a Chinese civil servant, I could imagine living part of my life in my backyard' (Cline, 1997:27). Such a practice (which is a necessity for the poor) might seem dilettante for the privileged, yet one of the possibilities open to professionals is to subvert their practice from within, just as artists in the 1960s dematerialised the art object as a way to confound the art market.

Beginning with a simple platform six by eight feet, Cline added corner columns and a pitched roof; sheets of plywood and windows from demolition sites produced a complete enclosure, with opening at ground and eye levels. Then, a kettle, bowls and books were introduced, composed as aids to contemplation (in what reads in her account like the composition of a still life[32]). Cline writes:

> As my dwelling took shape it began to shape my life as well. And when I sat inside reading the recluse poets, the terse simplicity of their record framed my own perception, one I likened to a camera recording a world of pure experience. (Cline, 1997:32)

As she admits, the notion of pure experience is problematic in the days of deconstruction; there are questions, too, about the appropriation of cultures. But Cline recognises, parallel to her borrowings from East Asian models, a set of classical categories, including delight. A reference to Vitruvius (Cline, 1997:36) might seem commonplace in an architectural text, yet the world in which Vitruvius wrote is a long way from North America (and the narrative of the log cabin, which Cline does not reference) and constitutes an appropriation only marginally less problematic than that of the tea ceremony. Perhaps the value of a notion of pure experience for Cline, as in the contemplation of a bowl in a certain, momentary light, is that it enables a stripping away of the layers of architectural culture, of the distancing which constitutes the architect's ensconcement, as Lefebvre puts it, in Cartesian space (Lefebvre, 1991:361). The question, then, is whether this space of retreat allows insights to be gained which are both embedded in the world of everyday life and conducive to the imagination of its futures.

Social groups, as well as individual architects, have withdrawn from the dominant society to make their own models of settlement and collaboration. Whilst they are outside the scope of this chapter, and might be the material for another book, alternative settlements – from self-sufficient communities such as Tinker's Bubble in the UK or Crystal Waters in Australia (Schwartz and Schwartz, 1998:44–54 and 124–46), to cities such as the Open City at Ritoque (Pendleton-Jullian, 1996), Auroville in India (Schwartz and Schwartz, 1998:315–30), and Arcosanti in Arizona (McLaughlin and Davidson, 1985:251–5; Roelofs, 1999:240) – are part of its context, acting as an avant-garde of settlement. Noted here, however, is a group of experimental houses at Almere in the Netherlands, on the grounds that it offers a set of models for future low-cost, possibly self-build, housing. Just as Fathy calls for a no-cost solution to the housing needs of non-affluent countries, so equivalent solutions are required in the affluent world, setting aside luxury in favour of that liberating austerity proposed by Illich.

The street called *Realiteit* at Almere resulted from the second of two competitions, in 1982 and 1985, to design alternative housing using environmentally friendly and low-cost materials and technologies[33]. Although only two of the houses are today used as permanent homes, others being either studios or weekend cottages, they represent a prototype solution of potentially broad application. Almere is a new town in Flevoland, an area of reclaimed land north-east of Amsterdam, and several of its housing areas are of innovative design, extending the Dutch tradition of social housing begun in the early 1900s by the Amsterdam School (Casciato, 1996)[34]. The Film village, for instance, a grid of streets to the east of the town centre (named for some reason after Hollywood stars) consists of terraces each designed by a different architect in a different modern or post-modern style, giving high density and variety, with small gardens and patios rather than the large public spaces of high-rise developments[35]. Innovation, however, is confined to the design of buildings and the zoning of housing separate from work, leisure and other aspects of urban living, remains conventional. *Realiteit* is an enclave of about a dozen buildings, in a residential area on the edge of Almere, surrounded by fields and lagoons. The area is rich in wildlife, particularly seabirds, but remote from shops, cafés (of which there are few in Almere) and public transport. Questions might also be asked about the desirability of living in a street inhabited entirely by architects. However, it is the design of structures which is interesting, those built being selected from 182 competition entries[36]. Materials were mainly provided by sponsors, and include both the recycled and new, and in some cases energy-saving devices such as solar panels[37].

Campus, by Hans Slawik, uses five red shipping containers, three up-ended and linked by a glass atrium to form the main structure (Figure 9.3). *Sailtower*, by Thijs Gerretsen, is a small, blue house surrounded by trees, with one room on each of two floors, the upper having a glass dome over the bed space (Figure 9.4). Awnings shelter a wide wooden deck on each side. These are, in one way, architectural fantasies enabled by a sponsored competition; some of them, used as second homes, are spaces of retreat like Cline's hut. But in another way, as new models, they suggest points of departure for housing which is low-cost, and need not be regimented in straight rows, nor built (as these were) by contractors. Jos Abbo, designer of *Golfhuis* and one of the permanent residents of the site, has moved his office to the town centre, but is extending the house to create additional spaces for a family which has grown by two more children since 1985. This demonstrates the flexibility of the design, and simplicity of construction in standard industrial materials[38]. Each house offers adequate living space on a small plot, without foundations, and could be built in (or transported to) any comparable location; the houses are all in good condition after more than 10 years, and some, such as *Campus*, suggest a widely applicable reutilisation of materials in what could be, literally, a post-industrial city.

Building in the Non-affluent World

Cline, of course, can choose to build a hut and when to sit in it. Her meditative space is a retreat from the affluent society, but also a privileged withdrawal made possible by her inclusion as a professional in that affluence. Similarly, the architects of *Realiteit* enjoyed a freedom to design according to their own ideas, within a cosmopolitan and affluent culture. Whilst their designs are possible prototypes for mass housing, they remain, in the absence of a political will and economic reorganisation to facilitate such a scheme, utopian. In the informal settlements which surround many large cities, particularly in the southern hemisphere, there are few choices, and the construction of shelters from industry's waste material is a necessity rather than a matter of design innovation or fun. In many cases, the landowner complies with squatting, thinking that services such as water and electricity will be extended to the land by city authorities, increasing its value, while the poor hook up lines to whatever sources they can. At the same time, solutions imposed by external authorities, often as a form of crisis management when the housing of the poor is seen as an instrument of social stability, tend to be inflexible and to worsen living conditions (Hamdi, 1995:12). Aerial photographs show the stark difference between the urban textures of a built environment which

Figure 9.3 *Almere:* Campus, *Han Slawick, 1986 (photo M Miles)*

Figure 9.4 *Almere:* Sailtower, *Thijs Gerretsen, 1986 (photo M Miles)*

has grown over time and that inscribed by planners for recent social housing. In non-affluent countries, the housing needs of the migrant poor are met by such regimentation of space, which tends to rapid dereliction and may use expensive imported technologies which are inappropriate to local conditions, or offer too little flexibility to support the mix of uses which the poor need to make of their shelters. Turner contrasts the cases of a self-build factory worker's home on a plot purchased illegally on the outskirts of Mexico city, and that of a government employee in a housing project. Whilst the government employee's family spend a lower part of their (higher) income on housing, they have less space, little equity and are secure only through the surplus income allowed by the fact that the house is part of a heavily subsidised show-case project. The factory worker, on the other hand, sees a substantial return on his labour and outlay through increased property value, and intends to add a shop and second unit either for rental or to accommodate a larger family. Turner, from these and other cases, contrasts the production of homes of high construction standard but doubtful value, at high cost, with the low-cost production of homes of variable standard but high use-value through informal settlement (Turner, 1976:74–82). His examples, of course, are in non-affluent countries and resistance may be encountered in mapping observations from such cases on to the housing economies of affluent countries. But what might he say of El Raval? (Figure 9.5)[39].

In both affluent and non-affluent countries, housing may be an instrument of social control; as Nabeel Hamdi writes: 'Providing housing enables reformers to control and direct the impact of what is provided . . .' (Hamdi, 1995:13). His position is similar to that of Robbins – that regulated social housing, even when progressive in intention and design, enforces a divide between the poor and the rest of society, and seldom addresses 'the realities of community life' (Hamdi, 1995:13). Such a divide can be seen, also, at Chandigarh, designed by Le Corbusier in 1949; it has been described as an 'oasis' for the rich, whilst 100 000 poor are 'banished to distant slums' devoid of industry (or employment) and not served by public transport (Goldenberg, 1999). The poor, of course, practise their own fragile economies in all cities, and huts and stalls appear spontaneously, often without licence, in the midst of structures the very scale of which is an imposition (Figure 9.6).

Hamdi cites several criticisms of conventional development aid, such as its contribution to poverty, and its promotion of a spiral of violence when industrialised agriculture displaces subsistence farming, or new roads, dams and power stations degrade the environment and cause migration to cities. He notes that 38% of US aid and 45.6% of UK aid is tied to purchases by the recipients of what are frequently inappropriate technologies from the donor country (Hamdi, 1995:5). Citing the terminology of productivity, Hamdi and Goethert argue that most development aid is driven by management frames of reference – 'with indicators of performance designed to ensure good ratings for the next round of grant awards and to impress visiting evaluation committees' (Hamdi and Goethert, 1996:8–10). In place of the orthodoxies of development planning, they offer three assumptions to underpin an alternative approach: that the complexities of urban change cannot be addressed through reductionist, top-down schemes[40]; that the routine of planning first and acting later is not appropriate, because good practice is not produced by good policy in isolation from actuality and participation, but has its own momentum within practical situations; and that project monitoring and evaluation seldom filter through as a means to adapt practices, ending instead in '. . . extensive reports which no one knows quite how to use' (Hamdi and Goethert, 1996:20).

What, then, is the alternative to the orthodoxies of development planning, and how is an alternative set of assumptions translated into practice? Hamdi works mainly (though not exclusively) in non-affluent countries[41], using methods derived from action planning, beginning from direct observation of local conditions. These do not reveal themselves immediately to the outsider's eye, and require local knowledge to be decoded. The stall, for instance, in Figure 9.6, which is in Cairo, may be a viable means of economic survival for its owner, yet seem to an outsider a residual element of the kind of messy urban scape replaced by the gleaming (or dehumanising) tower block behind it. As well as observation, action planning entails semi-structured interviews with local people, for example asking what single addition to their environment would make their lives better. Answers frequently include the provision of clean drinking water, and separation of drinking water from drains; but Hamdi also tells of a barber in India who asked for a chair so that his clients could sit on it rather than the floor whilst he cut their hair standing up, relieving pressure on his back[42]. Simple interventions using local provision, such as the chair, may ensure the viability of local economies, and items, such as water pumps, needed in one non-affluent country may be manufactured in another. After looking and listening, come technical processes such as measurement and resource surveys, which provide information used in brainstorming, diagramming and modelling, which in turn inform workshops using techniques such as role playing (Hamdi and Goethert, 1996:34–5). Direct interaction between a planning team and local people can reveal problems not initially stated[43], and both draw on local sources of knowledge. The charettes used in the Nine Mile Run Greenway project represent a similar process used in an affluent country.

Hamdi notes the changes which occurred in the practice of action planning in non-affluent countries between the 1960s and 1980s[44], concluding that:

> . . . most development in Third World cities followed lines of least resistance, not plans drawn up by architects and planners, and that most major cities were planned according to self-help principles. More importantly, what emerged was a willingness to accept that the vast majority of slums, squatter settlements and land invasions were a sign of healthy cities which were working and which were, in any case, unstoppable. (Hamdi, 1997:25)

He cites an alternative paradigm for planning in non-affluent countries which includes the promotion of self-sufficiency, key input of NGOs rather than

Figure 9.5 *Barcelona: El Raval, demolition site (photo M Miles)*

Figure 9.6 *Cairo: a stall in front of a high-rise block (photo reproduced by permission of Nabeel Hamdi)*

governments, a role for professionals as catalysts rather than authorities, decentralisation of decision making, and growth which is incremental rather than instant. In keeping, industry is based on small and informal enterprises of the kind local people can start and manage themselves. This is not a position likely to be popular amongst professionals, for whom it offers little scope for intervention or control, and less for glamour (Hamdi and Goethert, 1996:33); nor for local or national authorities seeking to raise their own prestige through high-budget development projects. But the participatory process of action planning, adapted to local conditions rather than being seen as a static model solution, is the most likely to produce the conditions for conviviality, and, in its rejection of global solutions and import of high-cost technologies, to resist the dominance of productivity. Perhaps it could be argued that these practices are up-dated forms, informed by deeper knowledge, of Fathy's facilitation of the project at New Gourna. And when local people are able to shape their own futures using local knowledges, with the assistance of experts who are facilitators rather than providers of pre-determined designs, and to build those futures with their own hands, an extraordinary degree of autonomy is produced. Its implications may lead to alternative attitudes to more than architecture and the provision of housing. But can this alternative vision which has begun to grow in the non-affluent world, largely through a critique of development aid, be reapplied in the affluent world?

Self-build Housing

There are cases of user participation in the design process of large and small buildings in the affluent world, one being that of the NMB bank in Amsterdam (Vale and Vale, 1991:156–68). This is a complex of offices and other spaces around a winding, central street. The design is organic, in being without straight lines or perpendicular edges, and the building is energy-efficient whilst maximising the use of daylight through glass vaulting. The site was selected by a vote amongst 2000 staff, beginning a series of participatory processes of decision making. Under Dutch law, Workers' Councils have a right to be consulted over changes in the working environment, and, as noted above, there is a tradition of decoration rather than purely functional design in Dutch urban architecture. But the NMB bank extends this (hitherto sometimes paternalistic) tradition in a way which offers a radical alternative to the impositional approaches (often involving signature architecture of a kind permitting no user interface) of most large corporations elsewhere; in the UK, it is mainly in the public sector, for example in the National Health Service, that user groups have been members of design teams (HMSO, 1994). A particular case of this is the Lambeth Community Care Centre (noted in Chapter 7) by Edward Cullinan Architects. In the field of housing, most new homes are mass produced by developers according to consumerist models of marketing; for the most part, only those of the very rich are individually designed. Yet self-build schemes demonstrate a potential for the participation of dwellers in the production of space, and perhaps a foundation for a society based more on connective aesthetics than the mechanisms of market exchange. One of the first, modern self-build projects was initiated by Christopher Alexander in Mexico in 1976, where self-build was simply an adaptation, introducing external design skills, of normal practice in informal settlements. Self-build is the norm in the non-affluent world, generally carried out co-operatively, whilst in the affluent world it reduces the cost of house purchase for those in marginal economic categories, enables unemployed people to use their time as a means to gain capital under their own control, unites the processes of design and construction to offer degrees of flexibility in the building process, and gives an emotional ownership unavailable in mass-produced housing even when its design is innovative.

In part, the roots of this approach are in the alternative movements which embraced communal self-sufficiency in the late 1960s (Roelofs, 1999:240); and one model of self-build housing, which can offer high-density in urban situations, is co-housing, either as new-build or as a reutilisation of existing housing (or ex-industrial) stock. An example is N Street in Davis, California, where 12 houses in a suburban street have been renovated, with communal gardens and certain facilities, including a sauna, for a largely professional group of residents who participate, as they please, in common meals whilst retaining the privacy of their own homes. As Walter and Dorothy Schwartz point out, Davis was a centre of protest against the American war in Vietnam, the city authority follows green policies, and students run the bus system (Schwartz and Schwartz, 1998:29). Whilst many alternative settlements, and elements of alternative culture such as the Travellers who adopt a nomadic lifestyle, tend to rural living, N Street is a model for a new conviviality in cities. In the UK, as in many other countries, there is a network of such initiatives, called 'eco-villages', which seeks to '. . . model sustainable, low-impact, human settlements' in both rural and urban settings. Here, according to the network's web-site, settlement is designed '. . . in harmony with its bio-region', and '. . . projects use the principles of permaculture for creating integrated, interactive and efficient systems for structural planning, food production and social needs . . .'[45]. Co-housing has been pioneered in Denmark, but two other examples are Het Groene Dak (the Green Roof), a project at Utrecht, and MW2, at Maasport near 'S Hertogenbosch, both in the Netherlands. At the Green Roof, there are 66 houses, and a mix of families, couples and single people, who retain their own cooking and eating facilities and arrangements but share gardens, play areas and a common house with a grassed roof used for ecological education, meetings and parties, and festive events (Roelofs, 1999:240–1). MW2, which includes small business premises as well as houses, offers an economic as well as domestic environment of autonomy, uses a Finnish system of pre-cut timbers and a design by Renz Pijnenborgh (one of the residents); the group worked collectively for the first 18 months, to produce the shells of each house, then individually on their own homes. Broome and Richardson, comparing MW2 with UK self-build schemes, note its attention to ecological aspects such as underground water sources and the need for non-toxicity in materials such as paints (Broome and Richardson, 1995:113–6).

In the UK, the best-known method for self-build is probably that using a timber-frame designed by Walter Segal, first used for a group of houses in Lewisham, south London in the 1970s (Broome and Richardson, 1995:73–86; Vale and Vale, 1991:135)[46], and then in the 1990s for a scheme in Brighton (Broome and Richardson, 1995:107–12)[47]. Patrick Keiller writes that housing '. . . has been an unfashionable subject for architects and theorists' in the UK, and that Segal was one of few professionals interested in it, apart from architects who design their own (high-cost) houses. Instead, attention, since the Futurists, has attached to sites of transit and movement (Keiller, 1998:37), or, it could be added, to non-places (Augé, 1995), whilst the highest level of investment in the built environment is in corporate space. Keiller cites Heidegger's description of a farmhouse in the Black Forest as an antidote to this neglect: 'Here the self-sufficiency of the power to let earth and heaven, divinities and mortals enter *in simple oneness* into things, ordered the house' (Heidegger, 1975:160, cited in Keiller, 1998:26 [emphasis as in the original]). Setting aside questions around the relation of Heidegger's hut in the Black Forest to the doctrine of blood and soil, Keiller's reference is useful in reminding the reader of vernacular traditions in which order is an articulation of appropriateness in use, over time, rather than the inscription of power – and the Black Forest house is certainly an antithesis of the new Chancellery (Dovey, 1999:58–67).

At Lewisham, each household was responsible for the construction of its own home (apart from drains and roads), though some group working took place. Whilst, in some other schemes a more collaborative method is used to construct the frame and shell, the Segal method requires little specialist knowledge, and, as Broome and Richardson state: 'The essential point is that they [collaborated] . . . out of choice, not necessity', adding that the balance of individual and shared effort contributed to good relations on the site (Broome and Richardson, 1995:79). Following the success of the first scheme, after lengthy planning delays, a second group of houses was built, bringing the total to 27. Half the occupants were ex-council tenants, the others having been on the waiting list, making the whole project a response to housing need[48]. Further projects in Lewisham in the 1990s maintained the original social basis, working through housing associations such as Fusion Jameen, Greenstreet Housing Cooperative and South London Family Housing Association (Broome and Richardson, 1995:86); and the Brighton scheme, begun in 1992, includes ex-tenants of the private rental sector.

Although not a self-build project, Coin Street in east London is also a model of local control by the tenants of social housing, which in another way suggests a future for cities in which space is produced according to the needs of dwellers rather than the interests of developers. Similarly, the Nieuwmarkt neighbourhood contrasts in the diversity and multi-use of its high-density spaces with a more regulatory approach in other recent housing developments in Amsterdam, reflecting the engagement with the development process there of local activist groups. A narrative of the area's redevelopment and the conflicts which arose is depicted in photographic murals by Jan Sirhuis on the platforms of the metro station. What emerges from this range of cases is that: firstly, it is possible for dwellers to drive a process of urban renewal in a way which refutes and subverts the dominant ideology of productivity; secondly, the growth of cities can include projects which (not confined to retreats of rural self-sufficiency) act as models for alternative futures, in many cases deriving understanding from experiences in non-affluent countries; and thirdly, these futures are sustainable through the integration of biological, social and cultural needs. The last factor might be interpreted as including cultural and bio-diversity, but has wider implications. It suggests that, just as productivity leads to environmental destruction through an economic mechanism of profit and globalisation, so conviviality, in deconstructing the Cartesian position of an isolated observer for whom the world is reduced to its representation in signs, leads to a creativity which is localised and self-sustaining, and a basis for sustainability in forms of habitation which reclaim the production of space. In such a creative project, the knowledge of dwellers on dwelling is as valuable as that of designers on designing in the imagination and shaping of futures no longer threatened by the unsustainable illusions and obscenities of affluence, but which give form to a hope for a world which is better – a hope founded on the erotic quality of sociation, and the memories of joy which, even if repressed into the unconscious, never die.

NOTES

1. Turner contrasts formal and informal buildings in Mexico (noted in Chapter 3): from a study in depth of 25 buildings, he concludes: 'Some of the poorest dwellings, materially speaking, were clearly the best, socially speaking . . .' (Turner, 1976:52).
2. See Schwartz and Schwartz, 1998:209–13 on local exchange trading systems.
3. Elliott suggests there are over 70 definitions of sustainable development in current use (Elliott, 1999:6). See also Meadowcroft, 1999:15–18.
4. See Satterthwaite, 1999:13–14 for more information on local Agenda 21 aims; and Lafferty and Eckerberg, 1998, for cases of Agenda 21 initiatives in Finland, Sweden, Norway, Germany, Austria, the Netherlands, the UK and Ireland.
5. They accept that '. . . urban sustainable development is a process riddled with conflict and incompatibilities' and that commitment to environmental policy is necessary. But they add that 'Economic (market-based) incentives are necessary also . . .' and that failure to adopt a policy which balances these interests will lead to urban sprawl (Nijkamp and Perrels, 1994:6).
6. See discussion of the post-industrial city in Chapter 8, in particular references to Eade, 1997.
7. See Lindblom 1999:44–8 on the non-regulatory influence of governments, for example through the link between industrial policy and planning, or support for science and technology.

8. See Fischer, 1973:45–51: 'In a world of advanced division of labour . . . alienation is generalised: not only the worker who sells his labour but also the employer who appropriates the product of another man's [sic] work and the merchant who takes the commodity to market . . . are alienated from their work, from others and from themselves.' (p 46).
9. Adorno and Horkheimer see the culture industries as maintaining and intensifying the operations of capital: 'Real life is becoming indistinguishable from the movies', continuing that 'The entertainments manufacturers know that their products will be consumed with alertness . . . for each of them is a model of the huge economic machinery which has always sustained the masses, whether at work or leisure – which is akin to work. . . . The culture industry as a whole has moulded men [sic] as a type unfailingly reproduced in every product.' (Adorno and Horkheimer, 1997:126–7).
10. 'This society is obscene in producing and indecently exposing a stifling abundance of wares while depriving its victims abroad of the necessities of life; obscene in stuffing itself and its garbage cans while poisoning and burning the scarce foodstuffs in the fields of its aggression; obscene in the words and smiles of its politicians and entertainers; in its prayers, in its ignorance, and in the wisdom of its kept intellectuals' (Marcuse, 1969:17).
11. Gare notes Marcuse's beginning of an effort to formulate, but failure to develop in depth, a critique of environmentalism (Gare, 1995:82 and 175, note 29), citing Eckersley 1992:Ch.5). However, Marcuse was writing in the aftermath of 1968, when issues of social justice and militarism were more prominent.
12. The first publication of sections of this work took place in 1890–96 – see Kropotkin, 1902:10); the reference is to the first complete publication of the work in English.
13. See in particular Brown, 1966.
14. See Shirer, 1981:36–7 on Ghandi's rejection of industrialisation in India. See also Harcourt, 1994:18–20 on the differentiation of instrumental (or disembodied) knowledge from the embodied knowledges of craft production.
15. An exception is the case of artists Rachel Dutton and Rob Olds, interviewed by Suzi Gablik (1995). Inspired by the writing of Tom Brown Jr, Dutton and Olds sold their homestead and studio in New Mexico to raise money for courses taught by Brown in wilderness living, intending to leave civilisation permanently. Brown claims to have learned his wilderness skills from an Apache warrior called Grandfather, whose vision (received in the 1920s) has, if genuine, extraordinary foresight. Grandfather foresees four warnings of an end of humanity: famine, a disease born of monkeys, holes in the sky that cannot be healed, and a sky which turns to blood: 'During this time, the earth will heal itself and man will die' (Gablik, 1995:59). Dutton and Olds see art as no longer having a role, in face of imminent apocalypse, and see daily life as '. . . a prayer that is holy' (Gablik, 1995:68). For them, the point of survival skills is the experience of a life coming directly from the earth. Olds concludes the conversation with Gablik: 'Hunter-gatherers are the apex of human civilisation. We need to go back to that point. All else is a bastardisation and a plague . . .' (Gablik, 1995:83).
16. 'The detached observer, who participates without action, is the passive spectator. The division of citizens into politically active and passive is the major premise of modern political (party) organisation.' (Brown, 1966:120).
17. 'Conviviality can take place with few props: the corner out of the wind where friends drink coffee together, the vacant lot which will become a garden' (Peattie, 1998:249).
18. To avoid the repressive quality of previous grand narratives, Gare cites Mikhail Bakhtin's idea of polyphonic narratives able to include diverse voices, and in which dialogue offers a dimension of criticism within the narrative (Gare, 1995:141).
19. Illich goes on to note the role of elites in providing interpretive frameworks for new alignments of interest at times of crisis (Illich, 1990:102).

20. Lindblom defines a non-market economy as '. . .using money and prices but, like the Soviet model, using administrative fiat rather than the market for directing production and allocation of resources' (Lindblom, 1999:41–2; see also 51–2).
21. Carmen states: 'The poor have no interest in being reached, being intervened in, being fitted (to projects), being appraised . . . As organic intellectuals . . . they are quite capable of doing all these things by themselves and for themselves' (Carmen, 1996:52). Fig. 3.3 shows a cartoon in which people in a desolate landscape say 'Thank God for that. A panel of experts', as an aircraft drops its aid cargo by parachute (1996:63).
22. The Netherlands, for example, has a National Environmental Policy Plan, which encourages the use of public transport, seeks to reduce pesticide use by 50% of 1985 levels by 2000, and establishes a sustainable building project (Elliott, 1999:90). Girardet notes, amongst others, the example of 'a particularly rational public transport system' in Curitiba, Brazil (Girardet, 1992:150), and the model of Combined Heat and Power (CHP) systems in Stockholm, Stuttgart and Helsinki (Girardet, 1992:142–3). See also Lafferty and Eckerberg, 1998.
23. This would suggest radical changes in the pattern of urban development, so that, for instance, thresholds of public-private space, such as balconies, became commonplace rather than being (as in El Raval) removed.
24. Peattie problematises, though retains, the concept of conviviality proposed by Illich, pointing out, for instance, that 'the "autonomous and creative intercourse among persons" of which Illich speaks is not so autonomous or creative as to constitute an exception to the rule against free lunch. There is a complex economics of conviviality' (Peattie, 1998:250).
25. Citing Nancy Chodorow and Jessica Benjamin, amongst others, Heller writes that 'Like the Situationists and social anarchists before them, these feminists looked beyond a reactionary "returnist" outlook toward a reconstructive possibility of creating a new kind of subject able to cooperate and live harmoniously with others' (Heller, 1999:83).
26. Amongst the professionals were Conrad Atkinson, Adrian Berg, Helen Chadwick, Hannah Collins, Stephen Farthing, Antony Gormley, David Nash and Stephen Willats.
27. Crouch and Matless link the authority of signs to power, citing Harley 1988 and 1992). They cite Deleuze and Guattari on the rhizomatic presence of maps in society: '. . . The map is open and connectable in all of its dimensions . . . It can be torn, reversed, adapted to any kind of mounting . . . it always has multiple entryways' (Deleuze and Guattari, 1988:12, in Crouch and Matless, 1996:237) which they liken to the 'multiple performativity' of mapping.
28. Crouch and Matless illustrate maps made by local groups of Charlbury and Standlake in West Oxfordshire, both of which have multiple images arranged around fairly conventional, if adapted, charts based on the aerial view. The map of Standlake, however, carries concerns for the expansion of nearby gravel extraction, whilst that of Charlbury remains a celebration and 'item of local cultural capital' (Crouch and Matless, 1996:246–7).
29. Hayden references Dubrow et al. (1993) on Asian-Pacific settlements in Washington State; Lai (1988) on Chinatowns in Canada; and Anderson (1991) on Vancouver's Chinatown.
30. The term 'enacted environment' is derived from a study by architect-planner James Rojas of threshold spaces between public and private space in east Los Angeles (Rojas, 1993).
31. This account is derived from Metz, 1992.
32. Cline cites Vermeer: 'Sitting inside felt a little like entering a Vermeer painting – but even more compressed – as if Vermeer's table had been pushed up against the windows with the walls drawn in around the table's edge' (Cline, 1997:29).

33. The first competition also produced a set of buildings, called *Fantasy*, sited by one of the lakes on the town's periphery. See Murphy, 1998 (though her account is not entirely accurate).
34. This history has two aspects, between which there is an interesting tension: whilst the design of social housing, for example by M de Klerk and P L Kramer at Takbuurt, Amsterdam (1919–23), offers working people houses and apartments of a high quality of design, with much attention to detailing and use of traditional materials, it also acts as a form of social control, eliminating balconies on street-facing facades, separating kitchens from living rooms, excluding bars from the street plan, and otherwise introducing a moral and behavioural sobriety. See Casciato, 1996:135–140; critical perspective derived from conversation with Joost Smiers, Takbuurt, September 1999.
35. A similar method of employing several architects to design buildings for parts of the site has been used in housing for Nieuw Sloten, a suburb of Amsterdam. Whilst some designs are innovative, unfortunately the general plan, with its straight lines, resembles that of a military camp (Kloos, 1997:118–125).
36. The designers include: Han Slawik, Jos Abbo, Mike Janga, Flip Holvast and Dan van Woerden, Hans and Roeland van Well, Thijs Gerretsen, Hans Hamminck, Eduard Böhtliningk, Peter Classens and Migiel van der Palew, Maarten Meijs, Bart Jan van der Brink, Marene van Gessel and Marc van Roosmalen, Leo van Bemmelen and Hoo Liem, Jan Wagenaar and Hans Wijsenfeld, Teun Koolhaas and Michel Koolen.
37. *Lakeview* by Bart Jan van der Brink uses a 40 000-litre tank to store water heated by solar panels on the roof. Another house has an earth roof to give high levels of insulation.
38. These are not as sustainable materials as, say brick, but insulation is used to give an even temperature throughout the year and minimise energy consumption (from a private generator). For comment on the embodied energy of buildings through their materials, see Brennan, 1995.
39. The photograph in Figure 9.5 is of demolition in El Raval to provide public space at the cost of homes in a multi-ethnic neighbourhood.
40. 'Practices based on prescriptive, reductionist thinking and management displace ordinary people including marginal entrepreneurs, the poor and most vulnerable, in favour of project officials, businessmen, contractors and development workers . . .' (Hamdi and Goethert, 1996:19).
41. Hamdi has also undertaken projects in the industrialised world, for instance in Belfast (Hamdi and Goethert, 1996:165–73).
42. Lecture by N Hamdi, Oxford Brookes University, November 1998.
43. Hamdi and Goethert cite a case in which a request for a clinic was seen to be, in effect, a statement of inhibition in using an existing clinic where formal procedures were bureaucratic and off-putting; a possible solution was identified as a training programme for paramedics to work within the neighbourhood to identify symptoms and help people administer their own treatments (Hamdi and Goethert, 1996:47).
44. See also Sandercock, 1998b:170–80.
45. The Ecovillage Network UK web-site: Http://www.ecovillages.org/uk/network/. (20 February 1999).
46. Armor and Snell assert that a timber house can be built more quickly than a brick house, and is as strong and long-lasting (Armor and Snell, 1999:153). Vale and Vale note that Segal used timber as a material which could be worked with basic skills, but add that such designs need to be adapted to climate conditions, but that '. . . systems of building based on machined timbers are still problematic in countries where most of the timber is imported'. They cite a scheme in Papua New Guinea as a solution (Vale and Vale, 1991:135).

47. Armor and Snell note a self-build scheme for ex-servicemen in Brighton in 1948, using land owned by the local authority (Armor and Snell, 1999:266). For another scheme in Bristol, called Zenzele, see Armor and Snell, 1999:268, and Broome and Richardson, 1995:87.
48. Broome and Richardson note that, after 14 years, only four of the Lewisham houses had been sold, the rest still being occupied by their builders, two having added extensions to accommodate larger families (Broome and Richardson, 1995:85).

Bibliography

Abdel-Messih M-T (1994) *Hassan El Shark* [catalogue], Fürth (Germany), Ursula Schernig Gallery [Arabic and German]

Adorno T W (1994) 'The Stars Down to Earth' in Crooks (ed) (1994)

Adorno T W and Horkheimer M [1944] (1997) *Dialectic of Enlightenment*, London, Verso

Albrow M (1997) 'Travelling Beyond Local Cultures: Socioscopes in a Global City', in Eade (ed) (1997) pp37–55

Albrow M, Eade J, Dürrschmidt J, and Washbourne N (1997) 'The Impact of Globalization on Sociological Concepts: Community, Culture and Milieu', in Eade (ed) (1997) pp20–36

Anderson K J (1991) *Vancouver's Chinatown: Racial Discourse in Canada, 1875–1980*, Montreal, McGill-Queens University Press

Angotti T (1993) *Metropolis 2000 – Planning, Poverty and Politics*, London, Routledge

Armor M and Snell D (1999) *Building Your Own Home*, London, Ebury Press

Armstrong S (1999) 'Bun Fight', *The Guardian*, 13 September 1999, Media 8–9.

Ashton J and Seymour H (1988) *The New Public Health*, Milton Keynes, Open University Press

Augé M (1995) *Non-Places: Introduction to an Anthropology of Supermodernity*, London, Verso

Ayse Ö and Weyland P (1997) *Space, Culture and Power*, London, Zed Books

Bachelard G (1969) *The Poetics of Space*, Boston (MA), Beacon Press

Barber S (1995) *Fragments of the European City*, London, Reaktion

Barthes R (1982) *Empire of Signs*, New York, Hill and Wang

Beall J (ed) (1997) *A City for All*, London, Zed Books

Beardsley J (1989) *Earthworks and Beyond*, New York, Abbeville Press

Becker C (1994) *The Subversive Imagination*, London, Routledge

Benjamin A (ed) (1989) *The Problems of Modernity*, London, Routledge

Benjamin W [1973] (1997a) *Charles Baudelaire*, London, Verso

Benjamin W [1977] (1997b) *One Way Street*, London, Verso

Berman M [1982] (1983) *All That Is Solid Melts Into Air*, London, Verso

Bird J (1993) 'Dystopia on the Thames' in Bird et al. (eds) (1993) pp120–135

Bird J, Curtis B, Putnam T, Robertson G, Tickner L (eds) (1993) *Mapping the Futures* London, Routledge

Blackman A M (1910) 'Some Egyptian and Nubian Notes', *Man*, vol X, II, p29

Blackman W S (1927) *The Fellahin of Upper Egypt*, London, Harrap

Bloch E [1959] (1986) *The Principle of Hope*, Cambridge (MA), MIT

Bloch E [1935] (1991) *Heritage of Our Times*, trans. Plaice N and Plaice S, Cambridge, Polity Press

Bookchin M (1992) *Urbanization Without Cities*, Montreal, Black Roof Books

Borden I (1998) 'Body Architecture – Skateboarding and the Creation of Super-architectural Space' in Hill (ed) (1998) pp195-216

Bourdieu P (1984) *Distinction*, London, Routledge

Bourdieu P and Haacke H (1995) *Free Exchange*, Cambridge, Polity Press

Brennan J (1995) 'Embodied Energy in Buildings', *Resurgence*, no. 169, March–April, pp40–42

Brettell R and Pissarro J (1992) *The Impressionist and the City*, London, Royal Academy of Arts

Brigham J (1985) 'Reclamation Artists: A Report from Boston', *Leonardo*, vol 26, no 5, pp379–385

Broom J and Richardson B (1995) *The Self-build Book*, 2nd edn, Totnes, Green Books

Brown N O (1966) *Love's Body*, New York, Random House

Buck-Morss S (1995) *The Dialectics of Seeing*, Cambridge (MA), MIT

Buie S (1998) 'Market as Mandala: The Erotic Space of Commerce', *Organization*, vol 312, pp225–232.

Bürger P (1984) *Theory of the Avant-Garde*, Minneapolis (MN), University of Minnesota Press

Byrne, D (1997) 'Chaotic Places or Complex Places? Cities in a Post-industrial Era', in Westwood and Williams (eds) (1987)

Carmen R (1994) 'The Logic of Economics vs. the Dynamics of Culture: Daring to (Re)Invent the Common Future', in Harcourt (ed) (1994), pp60–74

Carmen R (1996) *Autonomous Development*, London, Zed Books

Casciato M (1996) *The Amsterdam School*, Rotterdam, 010 Publishers

Chalfont H and Prigoff J (1987) *Spraycan Art*, London, Thames & Hudson

Clark T J (1973a) *The Absolute Bourgeois: Art and Politics in France 1848–1851*, London, Thames & Hudson

Clark T J (1973b) *Image of the People: Gustave Courbet and the 1848 Revolution*, London, Thames & Hudson

Cline A (1997) *A Hut of One's Own*, Cambridge (MA), MIT

Coleman A (1985) *Utopia on Trial*, London, Hilary Shipman

Collins T and Goto R (1996) 'Urban Reclamation', Pittsburgh, Carnegie Mellon University, research paper published on internet: http://slaggarden.cfa.cmu.edu

Colomina B (1996) *Privacy and Publicity – Modern Architecture and Mass Media*, Cambridge (MA), MIT

Comacho D (ed) (1998) *Environmental Injustices, Political Struggles – Race, Class and One Environment*, Durham (NC), Duke University Press

Common Ground (1986) 'Knowing Your Place: Artists' Parish Maps', press release, December

Conway G R (1987) 'The Properties of Agroecosystems' *Agricultural Systems*, vol 24, pp95–117

Coombes A (1994) *Reinventing Africa – Museums, Material Culture and Popular Imagination*, New Haven (CT), Yale University Press

Cooper D (ed) (1968) *The Dialectics of Liberation*, Harmondsworth, Penguin

Copjec J and Sorkin M (1999) *Giving Ground: The Politics of Propinquity*, London, Verso

Cosgrove D and Daniels S (1988) *The Iconography of Landscape*, Cambridge, Cambridge University Press

Courtney-Clarke M (1986) *Ndebele – the art of an African Tribe*, New York, Rizzoli

Crane D (1987) *The Transformation of the Avant-Garde*, Chicago (IL), University of Chicago Press

Crawford M (1992) 'The World in a Shopping Mall', in Sorkin (ed) (1992) pp3–30

Cresswell T (1996) *In Place, Out of Place: Geography, Ideology, and Transgression*, Minneapolis (MN), University of Minnesota Press

Crimp D and Rolston A (1990) *AIDS Demographics*, Seattle (WA), Bay Press

Crook S (1994) *Adorno - The Stars Down to Earth and Other Essays on the Irrational in Culture*, London, Routledge

Crouch D (1998) 'The Street in the Making of Popular Geographical Knowledge', in Fyfe (ed.) (1998) pp160–175

Crouch D and Matless D (1996) 'Refiguring Geography: Parish Maps of Common Ground', *Transactions of the Institute of British Geographers*, vol 21, pp236–255

Cullerne-Brown M and Taylor B (eds) (1993) *Art of the Soviets: Painting, Sculpture and Architecture in a One-party State*, Manchester, Manchester University Press

Davis M (1990) *City of Quartz*, London, Verso

Deamer P 'The Everyday and the Utopian' in Harris and Berke (eds) (1997) pp195–216

De Certeau M (1984) *The Practice of Everyday Life*, Berkeley (CA), University of California Press

Deepwell K (ed) (1995) *New Feminist Art Criticism*, Manchester, Manchester University Press

Deleuze G and Guattari F (1988) *A Thousand Plateaus: Capitalism and Schizophrenia*, London, Athlone

Denyer S (1978) *African Traditional Architecture*, New York, Africana Publishing

Deutsche R (1991a) 'Alternative Space' in Wallis (ed) (1991), pp45–66

Deutsche R (1991b) 'Uneven Development: public art in New York City', in Ghirardo (ed) (1991) pp157–219

Dias M and Riedweg W (1998) 'Question Marks', in Jacob and Brenson (eds) (1998) pp86–97

Dormer P (1994) *The Art of the Maker*, London, Thames & Hudson

Douglass M and Friedmann J (eds) (1998) *Cities for Citizens*, Chichester, Wiley

Dovey K (1999) *Framing Places – Mediating Power in Built Form*, London, Routledge

Dubrow G L, Nomura G, et al. (1993) *The Historic Context for the Protection of Asian/Pacific American Resources in Washington State*, Olympia (WA), Department of Community Development

Dumont R (1970) *Cuba: Socialism and Development*, New York, Grove Press

Dunn P and Leeson L (1993) 'The Art of Change in Docklands', in Bird et al. (eds) (1993) pp136–149

Eade J (ed) (1997) *Living the Global City*, London, Routledge

Eade J (1997) 'Reconstructing Places: Changing images of Locality in Docklands and Spitalfields', in Eade (ed) (1997), pp127–145

Earth Centre (1999) 'The Future Works', no 1, Doncaster, Earth Centre [publicity brochure and newsletter, not paginated]

Eckersley R (1992) *Environmentalism and Political Theory: Toward an Ecocentric Approach*, London, University College London Press

Eitner L (1971) *Neoclassicism and Romanticism, 1758–1850*, London, Prentice-Hall

Eliot T S (1954) *Selected Poems*, London, Faber and Faber

Elliott J A (1999) *An Introduction to Sustainable Development*, 2nd edition, London, Routledge

Elsen A (1985) *Rodin's Thinker*, New Haven (CT), Yale University Press

Engels F (n.d.) *Ludwig Feuerbach And the Outcome of Classical German Philosophy*, London, Martin Lawrence

Fanon F (1967) *The Wretched of the Earth*, Harmondsworth, Penguin

Faris J C (1972) *Nuba Personal Art*, London, Duckworth

Fathy H (1973) *Architecture for the Poor*, Chicago (IL), University of Chicago Press [text and pagination identical with Fathy (1989)]

Fathy H (1986) *Natural Energy and Vernacular Architecture*, Chicago (IL), University of Chicago Press

Fathy H (1988) 'Palaces of Mud' *Resurgence*, no 103 March/April 1984 pp16–17

Fathy H [1969] (1989) *Gourna – A Tale of Two Villages*, Cairo, Egyptian Ministry of Culture

Fausch D (1997) 'Ugly and Ordinary: The Representation of the Everyday', in Harris and Berke (eds) (1997) pp75–106

Felshin N (ed) (1995) *But Is It Art?*, Seattle (WA), Bay Press

Fekete J (ed) (1987) *Life After Postmodernism*, New York, St Martin's Press

Field P (1999) 'The Anti-Roads Movement: The Struggle of Memory Against Forgetting', in Jordan and Lent (eds) (1999) pp68–79

Finnegan R (1998) *Tales of the City: A Study of Narrative and Urban Life*, Cambridge, Cambridge University Press

Fischer E (1973) *Marx in His Own Words*, Harmondsworth, Penguin

Fleming R L and Von Tscharner R (1987) *Placemakers: Creating Public Art that Tells You Where You Are*, New York, Harcourt Brace Jovanovich

Flehr-Lobban C (1990) *Modern Egypt and its Heritage*, Pittsburgh (PA), Carnegie Museum of Natural History

Freshman P (1993) *Public Address – Krzysztof Wodiczko*, Minneapolis (MN), Walker Art Centre

Forester J (1989) *Planning in the Face of Power*, Berkeley (CA), University of California Press

Foster H (ed) (1983) *The Anti-Aesthetic – Essays on Postmodern Culture*, Seattle (WA), Bay Press

Foster H (ed) (1987) *Discussions in Contemporary Culture*, Seattle (WA), Bay Press

Foucault M (1967) *Madness and Civilisation: A History of Insanity in the Age of Reason*, London, Tavistock

Foucault M (1976) *The Birth of the Clinic*, London, Tavistock

Foucault M (1977) *Discipline and Punish: The Birth of the Prison*, London, Allen Lane

Frisby D and Featherstone M (eds) (1997) *Simmel on Culture*, London, Sage

Fuller P (1980) *Art & Psychoanalysis*, London, Readers and Writers Cooperative

Fyfe N R (ed) (1998) *Images of the Street*, London, Routledge

Gablik S (1991) *The Reenchantment of Art*, London, Thames & Hudson

Gablik S (1995) *Conversations Before the End of Time*, London, Thames & Hudson

Gare A E (1995) *Postmodernism and the Environmental Crisis*, London, Routledge

Ghannam F (1997) 'Re-imagining the Global: Relocation and Local Identities in Cairo, in Ayse and Weyland (eds) (1997) pp119–139

Ghirardo D (ed) (1991) *Out of Site*, Seattle (WA), Bay Press

Ghirardo D (1996) *Architecture After Modernism*, London, Thames & Hudson

Gilbert A and Gugler J (1992) *Cities, Poverty and Development: Urbanization in the Third World*, Oxford, Oxford University Press

Girardet H (1992) *The Gaia Atlas of Cities*, London, Gaia Books

Gittins R (1978) *Young Thomas Hardy*, Harmondsworth, Penguin

Goldenberg S (1999) 'Chaos Creeps Up on India's City of the Future', *The Guardian*, 13 January

Goldfinger M (1993) *Villages in the Sun*, New York, Rizzoli

Gordon L (1977) *Eliot's Early Years*, Oxford, Oxford University Press

Gott T (1994) *Don't Leave Me This Way: Art in the Age of AIDS*, Canberra, National Gallery of Australia

Greater London Council (GLC) (1969) *Thamesmead: a Riverside Development*, London, GLC

Greater London Council (GLC) (1971) *Architecture 1965/1970*, London, GLC

Griffiths J and Kemp P (1999) *Quaking Houses – Art, Science and the Community: A Collaborative Approach to Water Pollution*, Charlbury, Jon Carpenter

Griffiths J G and Ibrahim A I (1938) 'The Use of Plates and Saucers to Decorate Houses in Lower Nubia and Upper Egypt', *SNR*, vol xxi, pp217–20

Griswold C L (1992) 'The Vietnam Veterans Memorial and the Washington Mall: Philosophical Thoughts on Political Iconography', in Mitchell (ed) (1992) pp79–112

Grossman C L (1999) 'USA Turns Up Nose at Subway Scents', *USA Today*, 28 May, 1999, p9D

Grunenberg C (1994) 'The Politics of Presentation: The Museum of Modern Art, New York', in Pointon (1994) pp192–211

Gunn, J M et al. (1995) *Restoration and Recovery of an Industrial Region*, New York, Springer Verlag

Habermas J (1991) *The Structural Transformation of the Public Sphere*, Cambridge (MA), MIT

Hall P and Ward C (1998) *Sociable Cities: The Legacy of Ebenezer Howard*, Chichester, Wiley

Hall T and Hubbard P (eds) (1998) *The Entrepreneurial City*, Chichester, Wiley

Hamdi N (1995) *Housing without Houses*, London, Intermediate Technology Publications

Hamdi N and Goethert R (1996) *Action Planning for Cities*, Chichester, Wiley

Harcourt W (ed) (1994) *Feminist Perspectives on Sustainable Development*, London, Zed Books

Harcourt W (1994) 'Negotiating positions in the Sustainable Development Debate: Situating the Feminist Perspective', in Harcourt (ed) (1994) pp11–25

Harding D (1997) 'Maclovio Rojas: An Exercise in Social Sculpture', *Variant*, vol 2, no 4, Autumn, pp6–7

Hardy T [1895] (1998) *Jude the Obscure*, Taylor D (ed) (1994), London, Penguin

Harley J B (1988) 'Maps, Knowledge and Power' in Cosgrove and Daniels (1988) pp277–312

Harley J B (1992) 'Rereading the Maps of the Columbian Encounter', *Annals of the Association of American Geographers*, vol 83, pp522–542

Harris S (1997) 'Everyday Architecture', in Harris and Berke (eds) (1997) pp1–8

Harris S and Berke D (eds) (1997) *Architecture of the Everyday*, New York, Princeton Architectural Press

Harvey D (1989) *The Condition of Post-Modernism*, Oxford, Blackwell

Harvey D (1996) *Justice, Nature and the Geography of Difference*, Oxford, Blackwell

Hayden D (1995) *The Power of Place*, Cambridge (MA), MIT

Heidegger M (1975) *Poetry, Language, Thought*, New York, Harper & Row

Heller C (1999) *Ecology of Everyday Life: Rethinking the Desire for Nature*, Montreal, Black Rose Books

Henslowe P (1984) *Ninety Years On: An Account of the Bourneville Village Trust*, Birmingham, The Bourneville Village Trust

Heskin A D (1980) 'Crisis and Response: An Historical Perspective on Advocacy Planning', *Journal of the American Planning Association*, vol 46, no 1, pp50–63

Hess T B and Ashbery J (eds) (1967) *Avant-Garde Art*, New York, Macmillan

Hill J (ed) (1998) *Occupying Architecture*, London, Routledge

Hill R L and Feagin J R (1987) 'Detroit and Houston: two cities in Global Perspective', in Smith and Feagin (eds) (1987)

HMSO (1993) *Environments for Quality Care*, London, HMSO and NHS Estates

Holston J (1995) *The Modernist City: An Anthropological Critique of Brasilia*, Chicago (IL), Chicago University Press

Hopwood D (1982) *Egypt: Politics and Society 1945–1981*, London, Allen & Unwin

Hood-Williams J and Bush T (1995) 'An Ethnographic Study of Domestic Violence on a London Housing Estate', *Research & Statistics Bulletin*, no 37, London, Home Office

Hooks B (1990) *Yearning: Race, Gender, and Cultural Politics*, Boston (MA), South End Press

Horkheimer M (1991) *Between Philosophy and Social Science: Selected Early Writings*, Cambridge (MA), MIT

Horn G (1998) 'Everyday in the Life of a Caravan', in Wigglesworth and Till (eds) (1998) pp28–30

Howard P (1898) *To-morrow! A Peaceful Path to Real Reform*, London, Swan Sonnenschein

Hoy D C and McCarthy T (1994) *Critical Theory*, Oxford, Blackwell
Illich I (1971) *Deschooling Society*, New York, Harper & Row
Illich I (1986) *H_2O and the Waters of Forgetfulness*, London, Marion Boyars
Illich I [1975] (1990) *Tools for Conviviality*, New York, Harper & Row
Illich I (1990) *Tools for Conviviality*, London, Marion Boyars
Irigaray L (1994) *Thinking the Difference*, London, Athlone
Jacob M J and Brenson M (eds) (1998) *Conversations at the Castle*, Cambridge (MA), MIT
Jacobs J (1961) *The Death and Life of Great American Cities*, New York, Random House
Jacobs J M (1996) *Edge of Empire: Postcolonialism and the City*, London, Routledge
Jameson F (1984) 'Postmodernism, or, the Cultural Logic of Late Capitalism', *New Left Review*, vol 146, pp53–92.
Jencks C (1989) 'Public Opinion and Princely Intervention', *The Independent*, 22 November
Jordan T and Lent A (1999) *Storming the Millennium: the New Politics of Change*, London, Lawrence & Wishart
Karnouk L (1988) *Modern Egyptian Art: The Emergence of a National Style*, Cairo, American University in Cairo Press
Katz B (1982) *Herbert Marcuse: Art of Liberation*, London, Verso
Keiller P (1998) 'The Dilapidated Dwelling', in Wigglesworth and Till (eds) (1998) pp22–27
Kenny M and Meadowcroft J (eds) (1999) *Planning Sustainability*, London, Routledge
King A D (1990) *Urbanism, Colonialism and the World-Economy*, London, Routledge
King A (ed) (1996) *Re-Presenting the City: Ethnicity, Capital and Culture in the 21st Century Metropolis*, London, Macmillan
Kloos M (1997) *Amsterdam Architecture, 1994–96*, Amsterdam, Arcam
Kracauer S [1963] (1995) *The Mass Ornament*, Cambridge (MA), Harvard University Press
Krauss R (1983) 'Sculpture in the Expanded Field', in Foster (ed) (1983) pp31–42
Kropotkin P A (1902) *Mutual Aid*, London, Heinemann
Kuspit D (1993) *The Cult of the Avant-garde Artist*, Cambridge, Cambridge University Press
Laclau E (1990) *New Reflections on the Revolutions of Our Time*, London, Verso
Laclau E (1996) *Emancipation(s)*, London, Verso
Lacour C B (1996) *Lines of Thought*, Durham (NC), Duke University Press
Lacy S (ed) (1995) *Mapping the Terrain*, Seattle (WA), Bay Press
Lafferty W and Eckerberg K (1998) *From the Earth Summit to Local Agenda 21: Working Towards Sustainable Development*, London, Earthscan
Lai D C (1988) *Chinatowns: Towns Within Cities in Canada*, Vancouver, University of British Columbia Press
Landry C and Bianchini F (1995) *The Creative City*, London, Demos
Lang P (ed) (1995) *Mortal City*, New York, Princeton Architectural Press
Leavitt J (1994) 'Planning in an Age of Rebellion: Guidelines to Activist Research and Applied Planning', *Planning Theory*, Summer, vol 10/11, pp111–30
Lefebvre H (1962) *Fondements d'une Sociologie de la Quotidienneté*, Paris, Grasset
Lefebvre H [1974] (1991) *The Production of Space*, Oxford, Blackwell
Lefebvre H [1947] (1992) *Critique of Everyday Life*, vol 1, London, Verso
Lefebvre H (1996) *Writing on Cities*, Oxford, Blackwell
Lefebvre H (1997) 'The Everyday and Everydayness' in Harris and Berke (eds) (1997) pp32–7
LeGates R T and Stout F (eds) (1996) *The City Reader*, London, Routledge
Lindblom C E (1999) 'A Century of Planning' in Kenny and Meadowcroft (eds) (1999) pp39–65
Lippard L (1995) 'Looking Around: Where We Are. Where We Could Be' in Lacy (ed) (1995) pp114–130
Lippard L (1997) *The Lure of the Local*, New York, The New Press
Loftman P and Nevin B (1998) 'Pro-growth Local Economic Development Strategies: Civic

Promotion and Local Needs in Britain's Second City, 1981–96', in Hall and Hubbard (eds) (1998) pp129–148

Lorde A (1984) *Sister Outsider*, New York, The Crossing Press

Ludwig Forum (1999) *Natural Reality* (exhibition catalogue), Aachen, Ludwig Forum for International Art

Luxemburg R B (1997) *London – A Modern Project*, London, Black Dog Publishing

Lynch K (1960) *The Image of the City*, Cambridge (MA), MIT

Lynch K (1981) *Good City Form*, Cambridge (MA), MIT

MCA (Martin Caldwell Associates) (1995) 'Bankside Economic Study', London, Martin Caldwell Associates

MacCannell D (1999) 'New Urbanism and its Discontents', in Copjec and Sorkin (eds) (1999) pp106–128

MacIntyre A (1970) *Marcuse*, London, Fontana

McKay G (1996) *Senseless Acts of Beauty: Cultures of Resistance since the Sixties*, London, Verso

McLaughlin C and Davidson G (1985) *Builders of the Dawn*, Summertown (TN), Book Publishing Company

McLeod M (1997) 'Henri Lefebvre's Critique of Everyday Life: An Introduction', in Harris and Berke (eds) (1998) pp9–29

Marcuse H (1956) *Eros and Civilisation*, London, Routledge & Kegan Paul

Marcuse H (1968) 'Liberation from the Affluent Society', in Cooper (ed) (1968) pp175–192

Marcuse H (1969) *Essay on Liberation*, Harmondsworth, Penguin

Marcuse H (1972) *Negations*, Harmondsworth, Penguin

Marcuse H (1978) *The Aesthetic Dimension*, Boston (MA), Beacon Press

Massey D (1994) *Space, Place and Gender*, Cambridge, Polity Press

Matilsky B (1992) *Fragile Ecologies*, New York, Rizzoli

Matless D and Revill G (1995) 'A Solo Ecology: The Erratic Art of Andy Goldsworthy', *Ecumene*, vol 2, no 4, pp423–448

Meadowcroft J (1999) 'Planning for Sustainable Development: What Can Be Learned from the Critics?' in Kenny and Meadowcroft (eds) (1999) pp12–38)

Meller H E (ed) (1979) *The Ideal City*, Leicester, Leicester University Press

Meskimmon M (1997) *Engendering the City*, London, Scarlet Press

Metz H (1992) 'The Ark of the Broken Covenant', *Public Art Review*, vol 4, no 1, Summer/Fall, pp22–3

Mikellides B (ed) (1980) *Architecture for People*, London, Studio Vista

Miles M (1997a) *Art, Space & the City*, London, Routledge

Miles M (1997b) 'Another Hero? Public Art and the Gendered City', *Parallax*, no 5, September, pp125–135

Miles M (1998) 'A Game of Appearance: Public Art and Urban Development – complicity or sustainability?' in Hall and Hubbard (eds) (1998) pp203–224.

Mitchell W J T (1992) *Art and the Public Sphere*, Chicago, University of Chicago Press

Mozingo L (1989) 'Women and Downtown Open Spaces', *Place*, vol 6, no 1, Fall, pp38–47

Murphy A (1998) 'Let's Play House . . .' *The Observer*, 22 February, colour magazine pp12–16

Myerscough J (1989) *The Economic Importance of the Arts in Britain*, London, Policy Studies Institute

Naess A (1989) *Ecology, Community and Lifestyle*, trans. D Rothenberg, Cambridge, Cambridge University Press

National Health Service Executive (NHSE) (1993) *Environments for Quality Care*, London, HMSO

National Health Service Executive (NHSE) (1994) *Environments for Quality Care: Health Buildings in the Community*, London, HMSO

Nijkamp P and Perrels A (1994) *Sustainable Cities in Europe*, London, Earthscan

Nochlin L (1967) 'The Invention of the Avant-Garde: France 1830–80', in Hess and Ashbery (eds) (1967) pp1–24

Owens C (1983) 'The Discourse of Others: Feminists and Postmodernism' in Foster (ed) (1983) pp57–82

Paetzold H (1998a) 'The City as Labyrinth: Walter Benjamin and beyond' in Paetzold (1998b) pp14–27

Paetzold H (ed) (1998b) *Issues in Contemporary Culture and Aesthetics*, no 7, April 1998, Maastricht, Jan van Eyck Aka

Papanek V (1984) *Design for the Real World*, London, Thames & Hudson

Papanek V (1995) *The Green Imperative: Ecology and Ethics in Design and Architecture*, London, Thames & Hudson

Parker A and Neal A (1995) Hajj *Paintings: Folk Art of the Great Pilgrimage*, Washington (DC), Smithsonian

Pearson D (1994) *Earth to Spirit: In Search of Natural Architecture*, London, Gaia Books

Peattie L (1998) 'Convivial Cities', in Douglass and Friedmann (eds) (1988) pp247–253

Pendleton-Jullian A (1996) *The Road That Is Not a Road: and the Open City, Ritoque, Chile*, Cambridge (MA), MIT

Phillips P (1988) 'Out of Order: the Public Art Machine', *Artforum*, December, pp93–96

Pointon M (ed) (1994) *Art Apart*, Manchester, Manchester University Press

Pollock G (1988) *Vision and Difference*, London, Routledge

Pomian K (1990) *Collectors and Curiosities*, Cambridge, Polity Press

Potter M and A (1984) *Everything is Possible – Our Sudan Years*, London, Alan Sutton

Prigann H (n.d.) *Circle of Remembrance*, Berlin, Verlag Dirk Nishen [exhibition catalogue, text in German and English]

Ray M-A (1997) 'Gecekondu' in Harris and Berke (eds) (1997) pp153–165

Rees, W E (1999) 'Achieving Sustainability: Reform or Transformation' in Satterthwaite (ed) (1999) pp22–52 (reprinted from *Journal of Planning Literature*, vol 9, no 4, pp343–361)

Rendell J (1998) 'Doing It, (Un)Doing It, (Over)Doing It Yourself; Rhetorics of Architectural Abuse, in Hill (ed) (1998), pp229–246.

Robbins E (1996) 'Thinking space/seeing space: Thamesmead revisited', *Urban Design International*, vol 1, no 3, pp283–291

Roberts M (1991) *Living in a Man-Made World*, London, Routledge

Roelofs J (1999) 'Building and Designing with Nature: Urban Design', in Satterthwaite (ed) (1999), pp234–50

Rojas J T (1993) 'The Enacted Environment of East Los Angeles', *Places*, vol 8, Spring, pp42–53

Rose G (1992) *Broken Middle*, Oxford, Blackwell

Rosler M (1991) 'Fragments of a Metropolitan Viewpoint' in Wallis (ed) (1991) pp15–44

Rosler M (1994) 'Place, Position, Power, Politics', in Becker (ed) (1994) pp55–76

Rossi A [1966] (1982) *The Architecture of the City*, Cambridge (MA), MIT

Sandercock L (1998a) *Towards Cosmopolis*, Chichester, Wiley

Sandercock L (1998b) 'The Death of Modernist Planning: Radical Praxis for a Postmodern Age' in Douglass and Friedmann (eds) (1998) pp163–184

Sandercock L (ed) (1998c) *Making the Invisible Visible: A Multicultural Planning History*, Berkeley (CA), University of California Press

Sasaki K-i (1998) *Aesthetics on non-Western Principles. Version 0.5*, Maastricht, Jan Van Eyck Akademie

Sassen S (1991) *The Global City*, Princeton (NJ), Princeton University Press

Sassen S (1994) *Cities in a World Economy*, London, Pine Forge Press
Satterthwaite D (ed) (1999) *The Earthscan Reader in Sustainable Cities*, London, Earthscan
Savage M and Warde A (1993) *Urban Sociology, Capitalism and Modernity*, London, Macmillan
Savitch H V (1988) *Post-Industrial Cities*, Princeton (NJ), Princeton University Press
Scarman (Lord) (1981) 'The Brixton Disorders 10–12 April 1981', London, HMSO
Schneider E A (1985) 'Ndebele Mural Art', *African Arts*, vol XVIII no 3, pp60–66 and 100
Schwartz W and Schwartz D (1998) *Living Lightly – Travels in Post-consumer Society*, Charlbury, Jon Carpenter
Scott Brown D (1990) 'The Rise and Fall of Community Architecture', *Architectural Design*, Profile 83 'Urban Concepts', vol 60, no 1/2, pp30–49
Seabrook J (1993) *Victims of Development: Resistance and Alternatives*, London, Verso
Seabrook J (1996) *In the Cities of the South*, London, Verso
Selwood S (1995) *The Benefits of Public Art*, London, Policy Studies Institute
Sennett R (1990) *The Conscience of the Eye*, New York, Norton
Sennett R (1994) *Flesh and Stone*, London, Faber & Faber
Sennett R [1970] (1996) *The Uses of Disorder*, London, Faber & Faber
Shields R (1999) *Lefebvre, Love and Struggle*, London, Routledge
Shirer W L (1981) *Ghandi – A Memoir*, London, Abacus
Sibley D (1995) *Geographies of Exclusion*, London, Routledge
Simmel G [1903] (1997) 'The Metropolis and Mental Life' in Frisby and Featherstone (eds) (1997) pp174–185
Simmel G, [1907] (1990) *The Philosophy of Money*, London, Routledge
Simony C, Brodt J and Pryor K (eds) (1998) *Ample Opportunity: A Community Dialogue*, Pittsburgh (PA), Studio for Creative Inquiry, Carnegie Mellon University
Skinner R J and Rodell M J (eds) (1983) *People, Poverty and Shelter*, London, Methuen
Smith G (ed) (1986) *Walter Benjamin – Moscow Diary*, trans. R Sieburth, Cambridge (MA), Harvard University Press
Smith M P (1980) *The City and Social Theory*, Oxford, Blackwell
Smith M P and Feagin J R (eds) (1987) *The Capitalist City: Global Restructuring and Community Politics*, Oxford, Blackwell
Smith N (1996) *The New Urban Frontier* London, Routledge
Soja W (1989) *Post-modern Geographies: The Reassertion of Space in Critical Social Theory*, London, Verso
Soja W (1996) *Thirdspace: Journeys to Los Angeles and Other Real-Imagined Places*, Oxford, Blackwell
Sonfist A (ed) (1983) *Art in the Land*, New York, Dutton
Sorkin M (ed) (1992) *Variations on a Theme Park: The New American City and the End of Public Space*, New York, Hill & Wang
Stacey M [1960] (1970) *Tradition and Change: A Study of Banbury*, Oxford, Oxford University Press
Steele J (1988) *Hassan Fathy*, Architectural Monograph 13, London, Academy Editions
Steele J (1997) *An Architecture for People: The Complete Works of Hassan Fathy*, London, Thames & Hudson
Stewart S (1987) 'Ceci Tuera Cela: Graffiti as Crime and Art' in Fekete (ed) (1987) pp167–174
Taylor L (ed) (1990) *Housing: Symbol, Structure, Site*, New York, Cooper-Hewitt Museum
Ter Heide H and Wijnbelt D (1996) 'To Know and to Make: the Link between Research and Urban Design', *Journal of Urban Design*, vol 1, no 1, February, pp75–90
Tester K (ed) (1994) *The Flâneur*, London, Routledge
Till J (1998) 'Architecture of the Impure Community', in Hill (ed) (1998) pp61–76

Toulmin S (1990) *Cosmopolis*, Chicago (IL), University of Chicago Press

Towers G (1995) *Building Democracy: Community Architecture in the Inner Cities*, London, University College of London Press

Turner J F C (1976) *Housing By People*, London, Marion Boyars

Turner J F C and Fichter R (eds) (1972) *Freedom to Build: Dweller Control of the Housing Process*, London, Collier-Macmillan

Turner R K (1988) *Sustainable Environmental Management*, London, Belhaven

Vale B and Vale R (1991) *Green Architecture: Design for a Sustainable Future*, London, Thames & Hudson

Venturi R (1966) *Complexity and Contradiction in Architecture*, New York, Museum of Modern Art

Wall D (1999) *Earth First! and the Anti-Roads Movement*, London, Routledge

Wallis B (ed) (1991) *If You Lived Here*, Seattle (WA), Bay Press

Warner M (1987) *Monuments and Maidens – The Allegory of Female Form*, London, Picador

Wates N and Knevitt C (1987) *Community Architecture: How People Are Creating Their Own Environment*, London, Penguin

WCED (World Commission on Environment and Development) (1987) *Our Common Future*, Oxford, Oxford University Press

Welsch W (1997) *Undoing Aesthetics*, London, Sage

Wenzel M (1972) *House Decoration in Nubia*, London, Duckworth

Westwood S and Williams J (1997) *Imagining Cities – Scripts, Signs, Memory*, London, Routledge

Whyte W H (1980) *The Social Life of Small Urban Spaces*, Washington (DC), Conservation Foundation

Whyte W H (1988) *City – Rediscovering the Center*, New York, Doubleday

Wigglesworth S and Till J (eds) (1998) 'The Everyday and Architecture', *Architectural Design*, profile 134, July-August

Wilson E (1991) *The Sphinx in the City*, Berkeley (CA), University of California Press

Wirth L (1938) 'Urbanism as a Way of Life', *American Journal of Sociology*, vol XLIV, no 1 1–24

Wolff J (1989) 'The Invisible *Flâneuse*: Women and the Literature of Modernity', in Benjamin A (ed) (1989) pp141–156

Woods L (1993) *War and Architecture/Rat I Arhitektura*, New York, Princeton Architectural Press, Pamphlet Architecture 15

Woods L (1995) 'Everyday War' in Lang (ed) (1995) pp46–53

Young J E (1992) 'The Counter-Monument: Memory Against Itself in Germany Today', in Mitchell (ed) (1992) pp49–78

Zukin S (1987) 'Gentrification, Culture and Capital in the Urban Core', *American Review of Sociology*, vol 13, pp129–147

Zukin S [1982] (1989) *Loft Living: Culture and Capital in Urban Change*, New Brunswick (NJ), Rutgers University Press

Zukin S (1995) *The Cultures of Cities*, Oxford, Blackwell

Zukin S (1996) 'Space and Symbols in an Age of Decline' in King (1996) pp43–59

List of Illustrations

Acknowledgements

This book has taken shape over the past three years. I would like to thank Tristan Palmer, first at Routledge then at Wiley (and now at Athlone Press) for his encouragement in developing the original proposal; and Maggie Toy at Wiley for her help in arriving at a final synopsis, and patience in accepting various extensions of the timescale for delivery. Many conversations, with dwellers (in New Gourna, and Almere, for two contrasting examples) as well as professionals, have informed the book, as have the responses of students during seminars at the University of Portsmouth, Chelsea College of Art and Design, and Oxford Brookes University. Some of its material was used in conference papers for the Design History Society, the Association of Art Historians, the Tate Gallery in Liverpool, and the Cities at the Millennium Conference at the RIBA, and in workshops in Rotterdam and Barcelona for the European League of Institutes of Art; questions and comments from these fora provided useful aids to revision. Of particular help in refining the book's critical frameworks have been discussions with Iain Borden, Michael Corris, Tim Hall, Nabeel Hamdi, Richard Hayward, Valerie Holman, David Reason, Antoni Remesar, Jane Rendell, Marion Roberts, Joost Smiers and Heike Strelow. Artists have been generous with their time, particularly Tim Collins, Reiko Goto, Bob Bingham and Carolyn Speranza of the Studio for Creative Inquiry at Carnegie Mellon University in Pittsburgh, Peter Dunn and Loraine Leeson of The Art of Change, and James Marriott and Jane Trowell of Platform. Financial support for a visit to Egypt was received from Chelsea College of Art and Design, and for a visit to Amsterdam from Oxford Brookes University; part of the writing took place during a period of unpaid leave from Oxford Brookes University.

Permission to reproduce images is gratefully acknowledged from: Steve Parish Cards; Chris Donaghue; Sofia Fotinos; Van Greaves; the Salmon Studio; Harold Higgs; Scancolour; Hedgerow Publishing Ltd; J B Jeffers Ltd; The Art of Change; Common Ground; and Nabeel Hamdi. Every effort has been made to contact the owners of rights, and apologies are given for any omission (which, if notified, the publisher will endeavour to correct at the earliest opportunity).

Index

Notes are indicated by page number reference followed by the number of the note in brackets – eg 99(*4n*)

Index compiled by Anne McCarthy